Pick of PUNCH

Pick of PUNCH

Edited by David Thomas

'89

A PUNCH BOOK
Published in association with GRAFTON BOOKS

"I'm afraid he still hasn't quite mastered the new technology."

Grafton Books
A Division of the Collins Publishing Group
8 Grafton Street, London W1X 3LA

Published by Grafton Books 1989

Copyright © Punch Publications 1989

A CIP catalogue record for this book is available from the British Library

ISBN 0-246-13583-2

Designed by Chris J. Bailey and Lisa Goldsworthy

Printed in Great Britain by
William Collins Sons Ltd, Westerhill, Glasgow

All rights reserved. No part of this publication may be reproduced, stored in a retrieval system, or transmitted in any form or by any means, electronic, mechanical, photocopying, recording or otherwise, without the prior permission of the publisher.

CONTENTS

"I wish you were on strike – the neighbours are beginning to think you don't have a proper job."

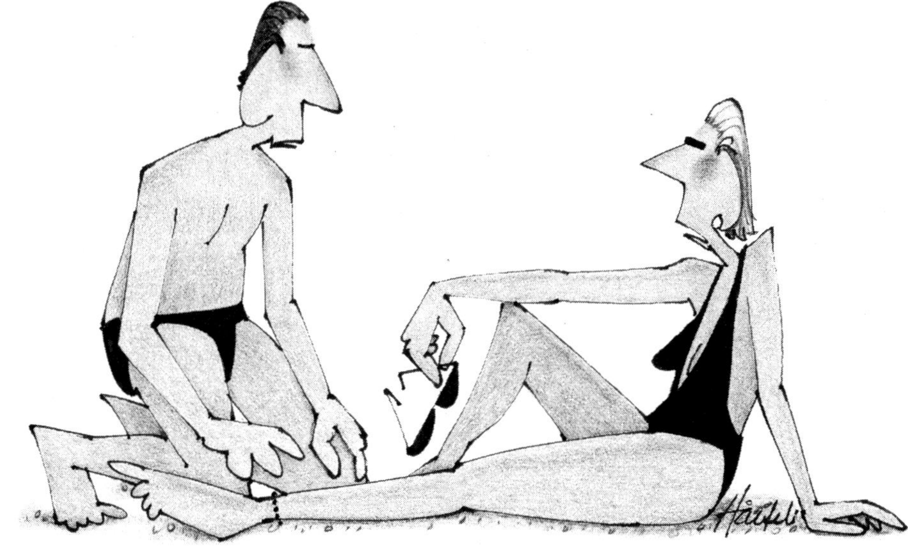

"I had you under my skin, Carlos, but now I'm peeling."

▶

"That reminds me – the strap broke on ours. I must get it repaired."

"I thought we might as well get rid of a few

CONTENTS

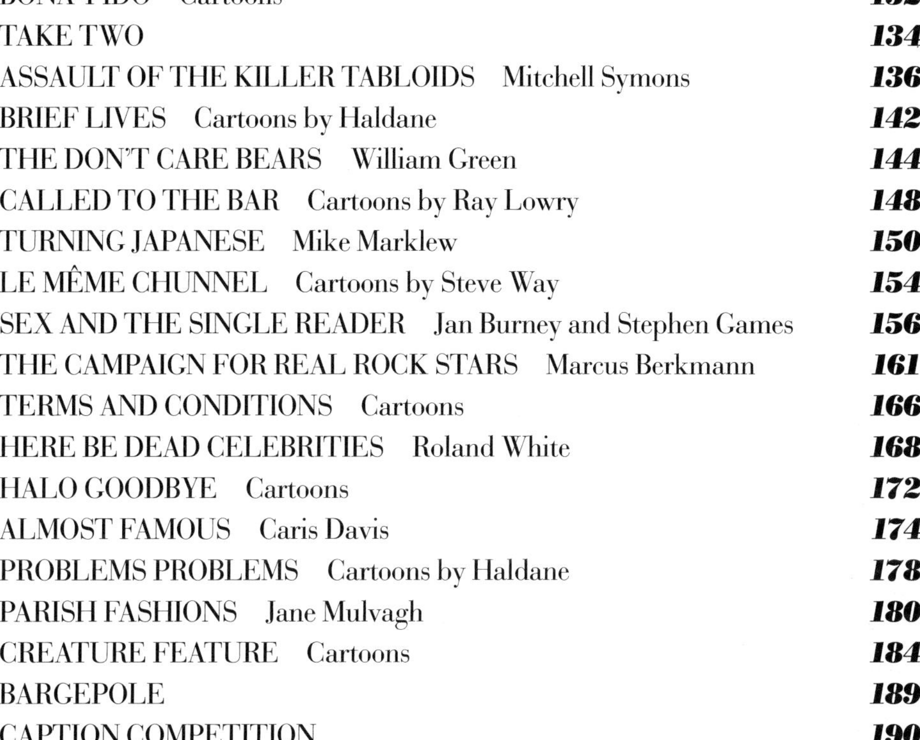

head lice while we're here."

"He's an accountant."

First published in 1963

Everything and the girl

"Research assistant, dearie?"

First published in 1989

I am in love with Pamella Bordes. How do I love her? Let me count the ways.

In the first place, she is, to judge from the photographs – and Mr Punch is one of the few journalists in London not to have met her in person – quite remarkably beautiful. In the second, she inspired the *News of the World* to one of its classic feats of sleazy journalism. Gone, it seems, are the days of paying some silly scrubber to spill the beans about her dangerous liaisons. Now we are returning to the classic years of yore, when an innocent hack, confronted by a pouting vice-girl, made his excuses and left. The moment at which the *NoW* described how its man turned down an allegedly naked Pamella was one of the high points of modern journalism. What principles! What self-denial!

But the third reason for my love is by far the most significant. It really has nothing to do with Pam (I think we all know her well enough by now to call her that, don't you?). It has to do with the men with whom she has been associated. Two in particular have caught my eye; Colin Moynihan MP, and Andrew Neil, the editor of *The Sunday Times*. Here are two men who, in their different ways, embody the most loathsome aspects of modern Britain. Any woman who can cause them the embarrassment generated by the lovely Miss Bordes has got to be all right by me.

Now, let's get one thing absolutely clear. There is not one jot, tittle or scintilla of evidence to suggest that even if the allegations against Miss Bordes are true, which she disputes, Mr Neil was in any way aware of her extra-curricular activities. Nor has it ever been suggested that there was any physical or emotional relationship between Mr Moynihan and the controversial Commons research assistant.

But can one not imagine the delight that the half-pint-sized Sports Minister must have felt at being photographed in the company of such a dazzling companion when they attended a ball together? And is it not delicious now to contemplate his embarrassment at the revelations that surround her?

I can scarce contain my joy at the little tyke's come-uppance. He has devoted the past year or more to diminishing my freedom of movement and association through his half-baked Football Membership Card scheme. The fans don't want it. The clubs don't want it. Most people who think about the erosion of personal liberties don't want it. Even the police don't want it.

At a time when violence in football grounds is under better control in Britain than almost any other European country; when the most striking image on the terraces is that of thousands of jolly inflatable haddocks and bananas, Mr Moynihan is hell-bent on introducing a scheme whose effects will be to discourage occasional supporters (such as Mr Punch), cause chaos and frustration at the turnstiles and push troublemakers away from grounds and into town centres.

So why pursue the matter? Because She wants it. And confronted with the presence of his mistress – Mrs Thatcher that is, not Pamella Bordes, who isn't his mistress, of course – our noble Sports Minister reminds one of nothing so much as a yapping little lap-dog. He yelps his squeaky threats at all the bigger boys secure in the knowledge that as long as he stays in mummy's arms no harm can come to him.

Any schoolboy knows his type. He's the little lad who was ribbed by all the other boys and now is hell-bent on revenge. He seems to pay no heed to fact or principle. One might think him the very worst form of New Tory. If it wasn't for Andrew Neil…

Let us be fair; there can be no denying that Neil is, at the very least, an extremely effective editor. Whatever one may think of his paper's attitudes, he has made it into the unmatched leader in its market-place. Its upmarket competitors look paltry by comparison. *The Observer*, in particular, seems whingeing and totally ineffectual. If Rupert Murdoch was the Lenin of the Wapping Revolution, then Neil was his Trotsky and now he is extending that revolution to the airways.

Yet there remains something deeply unlovable about the man. Is it his wiry hair? Is it his mottled skin? Is it, perhaps, his unabashed self-righteousness?

One cannot but think of his personal and professional campaign against the makers of the infamous *Death on the Rock* documentary. On the evening of the publication of the Windlesham Report Neil appeared on television with Roger Bolton, the programme's editor. Adopting a tone of high moral superiority, Neil affected to ignore the findings of the report – which vindicated the programme – whilst refusing to acknowledge any suggestion that his own journalists might have been less than happy with the way *The Sunday Times* had handled the story.

It may be that Neil genuinely felt that his paper had done a more honest job of reporting, although there were those who would question that. And he may have had sincere feelings of doubt over the independence of Lord Windlesham, irrespective of the slur such feelings caused to the reputation of a man of scrupulous and unchallenged integrity.

But might Neil's opinions not be connected in some tiny way to his position at Sky Television? And was there not the possibility of a conflict of interest between his responsibility as the editor of a quality paper to present a fair account of events, and his responsibility as a senior executive of a new television organisation to do his utmost to undermine the competition? Could it not just be that we are faced here with a case of rampant hypocrisy?

It is not for Mr Punch to say. But the thought that Pamella Bordes, having dated Andrew Neil, might then cut holes in his clothes, send him noxious packages through the post, and finally be caught up in a messy scandal in the *News of the World* is one that fills my twisted heart with glee.

Go get 'em Pammy! I'm right behind you all the way… ■

"Just look at him . . . he doesn't even do his own huffing and puffing any more."

The CLIVE COLLINS collection

CLIVE COLLINS

"Which wine would you suggest to go with an enormous expense account?"

Hating in vain

Mrs T and sympathy don't mix. JULIA LANGDON on our respectful dislike of the PM

It is an interesting phenomenon that opinion poll findings on the public's view of Mrs Thatcher very much reflect the political opinion of her as well. The fact that people respect the Prime Minister, but dislike her personally, has been recorded by the polls ever since they started asking questions about her. The figures now show that two-thirds of the country dislikes the Prime Minister but very nearly as many people respect her. That probably represents a similar proportion holding the same views in the House of Commons – although it perhaps underestimates her unpopularity.

Even her own ministers don't like her. For years now I've been asking them, in private, if they do and the only person who has ever said "Yes" without equivocation was Norman Tebbitt. And that was before the rows over the running of the last election and his somewhat controversial memoirs. Most of them pause and clear their throats and say: "Well, er ... hurrumph ... a difficult question..." Some of them blush and say that 'like' isn't exactly the word that springs to mind. The most honest told me recently: "I'm frightened of her."

It is probably best summed up in the extraordinary interview 'Willie' Whitelaw gave Brian Walden (in order to make *The Sunday Times* serialisation of his otherwise forgettable memoirs a little more interesting). No, he hadn't liked her, said Willie, and despite their close political relationship they would never meet socially, avoided going to the same parties and certainly, most certainly, never visited each other's homes. It was rather clumsily put, but it was obviously the truth. If I were Mrs Thatcher, I think I would have been a bit offended.

But then you can't afford to take offence when you're Prime Minister, particularly when you're dishing it out all the time to others. Anyway, she doesn't have time for that sort of triviality. "You had a hell of a day," one of her colleagues said to her in genuine sympathy the other day. The Prime Minister hasn't even got time for sympathy. "Every day is a hell of a day," she replied crisply.

Mrs Thatcher has never worried about her apparent lack of friends or propensity for making enemies

And that probably is why politicians don't like her. Supermag the Superwoman appears untouched by the human frailties which affect the rest of us, not least the touch of time. If anything, she looks better these days than she did a decade ago when she was still dressing in the styles of the Sixties and hadn't learned how to use make-up. The point is best made, though, by the fact that the few occasions when she has demonstrated intense personal emotion – when Mark was lost in the desert, when she wept in a TV interview for her father's lost Aldermanic seat, when we became a grandmother – are recalled because such an event is so rare. The comparison with someone like Willie, who reveals his humanity at every turn, whose eyes no doubt well with tears at the very thought of the film *Bambi*, let alone at the latest atrocity in Northern Ireland or the Lebanon, could not be more marked.

It is very difficult to spend five minutes in politics without making enemies and politicians have to learn not to worry about this early on in their careers. The most helpful advice in this area was that reportedly once proferred by some wise old bird of an MP to an earnest young newcomer. "Never worry about making enemies in this place, lad," he said. "Just remember that every time you make one enemy in the House of Commons you immediately make 649 friends." Mrs Thatcher has undoubtedly taken note of this advice and has never worried about her apparent lack of friends or propensity for making enemies. She couldn't afford to do so, of course, which is one reason why her dominance of the political scene has been so complete – and remains so despite her unpopularity. The only issue of any ongoing political interest in the last few years has been when she will retire and who will replace her.

Yet even so, it must still be rather galling for Mrs Thatcher that so many of her former so-called colleagues are crawling out of the woodwork in the House of Lords – and after she's been good enough to send them there, too! And make ladies of their wives! – to share their doubts about her policies and style, and their personal distaste for her. She must be even more infuriated by the attacks coming from the likes of Sir John Nott, the former Defence Secretary, who went into the City on the strength of his Government reputation and who is now reputed to be earning £400,000 per annum – and getting his own back. You would have thought that he, at least, would have had the decency to keep his trap shut.

Some enemies, of course, are only too obvious and the sniping from their direction is always to be expected. John Biffen, for example, who has always demonstrated an alarming independence of mind – and has never been afraid to speak it, either in Government (which was why he lost his job) or out of it. Mr Biffen is a little too subtle for Mrs Thatcher normally, but even she cannot have missed the point when he told his friends that he planned to spend her ten-year anniversary "among another persecuted minority" in Turkish-occupied Cyprus. If one had not learned to behave so well, it would be enough to make one want to spit. ■

"They're share applications for gold, frankincense and myrrh."

Home News · Page 3
Comment · Page 21
Arts · Page 7
25p
Tuesday
May 5
1989
The Sun

Heil fellow, well met!

GILLESPIE on the early sporting career of Adolf Hitler

Here in Troon, the festivities to commemorate Adolf Hitler's centenary are still in full swing – though we were all a bit disappointed that none of the television documentaries made any reference to the many happy summers the *Führer* spent as a lad on the Clyde Coast. It may interest readers to learn that, before the Great War, the Hitlers invariably spent their holidays in Troon, where they had a small, well-appointed cottage ('Dun Röhmin') not far from the sea front. What brought them to the West of Scotland was, of course, the golf, a sport to which young Adolf was passionately addicted.

His fascination with the game was partly political: "The questions of the day," I remember him saying, "will not be decided by speeches and majority decisions... but by blood and a three iron." But there was also an element of romance involved. For it was on the links at Old Troon that Hitler met his first and only sweetheart: junior ladies champion Eva Broon.

I will never forget how, in that idyllic summer of 1913, the two of them entered the mixed doubles. All went well until the final fairway when Adolf, to his mortification, sliced the ball wildly. For what seemed like eternity, Eva was silent. But finally she found her voice. "Never mind, Wulfie," she said (to the locals, he was always just 'Oor Wulfie'), "I always had a feeling the two of us would come to grief in a bunker." Troon folk date Hitler's insane craving for world domination from that moment.

While we are on the subject, I notice that our dear Prime Minister is also doing her bit to honour Hitler's memory. It appears that she has given her Transport Secretary the task of constructing "eight-lane super motorways between Britain's leading industrial centres", in response to "growing anxiety... about clogged motorways" (*The Sunday Times*). The more intellectually supine among you may see in this little more than an emergency measure to keep the lid on unemployment when Mr Lawson's interest rate rises finally begin to take effect. But I am not fooled. These are *autobahns, liebe Volksgenossen*, and every hideous mile will be a monument to their deranged Austrian inventor.

Like Hitler, Mrs Thatcher has an *autobahn* fixation. Her ultimate goal, I firmly believe, is to turn the entire country into one vast spaghetti junction, with no more than a few rusting rails and fenced-off footpaths to remind us that there were once other ways of getting about the place. Unlike Hitler, Mrs Thatcher prefers to get the Japanese in to build the actual cars: but the principle is essentially the same.

This may seem an eccentric viewpoint. But how else are we to account for the Government's systematic denigration of every other available mode of transport? If you attempt to get anywhere today on foot or by bicycle, you risk being killed in one of the car chases our policemen delight in; if you try to take a tube in the capital, you experience tortures hitherto reserved for the fish in John West's factories.

If you attempt to get anywhere today on foot or by bicycle, you risk being killed in one of the car chases our policemen delight in

But have you any idea of the fearful atrocities currently being perpetrated on our trains? By way of an example, I feel obliged to cite a report in last week's *Daily Mail*, concerning a British Rail ticket inspector who ran amok on a train to Bristol after a passenger asked to buy a ticket from him. The man apparently began ranting (not railing, if you don't mind) at the poor woman, snatched her passport from her and promptly landed one on an American tourist who ventured to intervene on her behalf.

The only thing which astonished me about the story was that the *Mail* back bench should have judged it newsworthy. In my experience, such altercations are a more or less routine occurrence on British trains. In fact, the only aspect of the story I have not encountered on numerous occasions is the bit about the passport. To my knowledge, passports are not at present required for trips to Bristol – though it is possible that someone naïve enough to try and buy a ticket aboard a train might think they are.

It may strike some of you motorists as slightly odd that the sale of tickets aboard trains should be prohibited by British Rail, particularly in view of the fact that it takes on average half-an-hour to procure one in a station. But that petty rule pales into insignificance alongside some of the other bizarre regulations which have recently been introduced by BR. Nowadays, for instance, when the guard makes his customary 'passenger announcement' prior to the departure of a train, the hapless passenger enters the realm of Franz Kafka: "*Passengers are reminded that ordinary Bluesaver return tickets, special standard class Awayday tickets, peak-time Capitalcard round-trip, green tickets, blue tickets, tickets bearing the letter 'e' and all other apparently valid tickets are not, I repeat not, valid for this service.*"

The upshot of all this is that, in order to get from A to B, most of us now elect to go by car; and the upshot of this is that most of us now spend an average of one day a week sitting in twenty-mile tailbacks somewhere between A and B. So desperate has the situation become that advertisements have started appearing in journals like *The Economist* for (I am not making it up) "VTOL aircraft... designed to revolutionise personal transportation. Our M200X takes off and lands vertically ... cruises at 322 mph ... and fits in a single car garage". Behold the *reduction ad absurdum* of Mrs Thatcher's maniacal individualism: she and a few others zipping overhead in flying saucers, while the rest of us sit fulminating in a jam stretching from Wessex to Wick.

I cannot believe that I am alone in regarding railways as this country's single greatest contribution to world civilisation. Why then do I find myself watching impotently as the woman who professes to believe in Victorian values systematically scraps the iron legacy of Stephenson and Brunel? Making the trains run on time was an achievement associated with dictatorships like Hitler's. But I ask you: what good is a dictator who stops them running altogether? ■

HEINZ
COUNTRY LAMB WITH CARROTS
SHARDS OF GLASS WITH CARROTS
DRAWING PINS WITH CARROTS
CAUSTIC SODA WITH CARROTS
WARHOL

No rest for the wicket

FRANK KEATING on the opening of the cricket season and the close of play for some

I see that George Bush greeted the first highspot of his Presidency the other day with due solemnity. "Go, get 'em, guys!" he exhorted the favourite pitchers and sluggers on the flag-flying, drum-bashing, tiddly-om-pom opening day of their new baseball season.

England does things differently. At Lord's this Saturday morning, just a couple of seconds after Ned Sherrin has gushed out his cheery byes on Radio 4's *Loose Ends*, a long-johned, thermal-vested, crouching umpire at the Nursery End will mutter "Play!" – and the cricket season will be under way again in front of a smattering of hardy, huddled souls, each with a packet of soggy sandwich-spread sarnies in their Pacamac pockets. Mrs Thatcher will not be remotely aware of the fact, let alone be up there in the Ladies' Stand shrilling "Go, get 'em, Botham, m'boy!"

It would be unthinkable for Bush to miss the first pitch. Since 1910, baseball's opening day has been attended by 13 Presidents on 62 occasions. More often than not, the Senior Citizen has wound himself up and fired down the first ball himself. Harding, Truman and Kennedy never missed one opening day. Roosevelt attended seven, come want, war or wheelchair. Coolidge was dragged to four by his Gracie, who loved the game and its guys. Ike was right in there. When Carter said he had more important things to attend to one particular April, the American nation reacted rather like the crowd scene in a Bateman cartoon and you knew then, for sure, that the Peanut hadn't the slightest chance of being re-elected. No way Nixon or Reagan (who both did radio commentaries on the game as young men) ever missed out on opening day – and even President Ford cashed in on the *kudos*, in spite of winging down a wide when he strung the first onion of April at Houston in 1976.

With Thatcher's affection for interminable, droning slabs of statistics, you'd have thought she might have had some glimmer of regard for cricket. The game remains obsessed with stats and, to many, the swot Bill Frindall is as much an heroic figure in the legend as Grace, Gower or Gavaskar. The copperplate clerk, Frindall, is

England's best batting by far came the day after the alleged "orgy"

chief mathematician of *Wisden*, out again to greet the new season in all its regal, primrose glory. Every spring's certain best-seller is, this time, slimmer than last – a mere 1,264 pages to 1988's 1,296.

Perhaps because all last year's sex has been censored. For instance, in the new almanack's hefty report of the first Test match against the West Indies at Nottingham last June, there is not so much as a comma which mentions that England's best batting by far of the whole series came the day after the alleged "orgy" by leading members of the team in their Leicestershire hotel. The night of Cap'n Gatt's birthday drink with a barmaid was followed by England's resplendent total of 301 for three wickets. Thereafter in the series, England's wimpish all-out totals were 165, 307, 135, 93, 201, 138, 205 and 202.

The coincidence is striking, but warrants not a footnote in *Wisden's* report. Again, the Yanks do it differently. For instance, their last-season's stats show how the Boston Redsoxer, Wade Boggs – who is being sued for $12 million in a "palimoney" case by his ex-mistress, Margo Adams – averaged 0.341 (hits per time at bat) when Margo was watching, and only 0.221 when his wife, Mrs Boggs, was. Now that's what I call stats.

The paradox of *Wisden* is that for the real, honest to goodness, flesh and blood of cricket, you always have to turn to the Obits. This year is well up to standard. Between the reasonably well-known names whom God, in His wisdom, clean bowled last year – the likes of Hugh Bartlett, Tom Burtt, Cliff Gladwin, Gordon Garlick, Cliff Roach and Reg Sinfield – there are touching little end-of-innings entries for such as:

"COPE, Sidney Alfred, at Gravesend, aged 81, made a single appearance for Kent in 1924; a left-arm fast bowler, but failed to make an impression with one wicket for 27 runs in seven overs. Later given a trial by Warwickshire, whose authorities unfortunately pronounced him to be temperamentally unsuited to a cricket career."

What a curse to carry to the grave for 64 years; alas, poor Sid. Another did at least manage to nudge – once – those same hard-hearted Edgbaston selectors, namely:

"SHUCKBURGH, Sir Charles Gerald Stewkley, aged 77; a right-handed batsman considered good enough to fill a place in Warwickshire's side in a Championship match against Nottinghamshire in 1930 in spite of an unsuccessful Freshman's match at Oxford that summer. Kilner and Staples between them arranged for the young sprig of nobility to be allowed to get off the mark; but when the chance came he was too petrified to move from the crease to respond to this act of courtesy. Whether he went through similar anguish before making his one catch has not been recorded".

Even *Wisden's* meticulous *Errata* can compound a cricketer's gloom. The new edition states, "In the 1988 Almanack, there was an obituary notice for J. W. Brook. We regret this should not have appeared, and any distress caused is sincerely regretted". Mr Brook will doubtless be pleased that reports of his death had been somewhat exaggerated last year – but not that everyone (like me) has rushed to last year's Obits to see what sort of send off the bible had given him. Simple and to the point:

"Great local reputation as a batsman but, appearing in one match for Yorkshire in 1923, failed to score in his only innings".

Ahh! And he lives on to tell the tale. Even baseball ain't as heartless as that. ■

GRANDPAPA? 'WISDEN' HAS APOLOGISED! YOU'RE NOT DEAD!
GERALD J. GUNGEBUCKET
INNINGS OPENED
1901
INNINGS CLOSED
1988
TOLD YOU SO!

How we all laughed as Emma
performance. She sat down and
ran his playful fingers through her
pouring us all glasses of sparkling

The Punch Imaginary Interview

KENNETH BRANAGH & EMMA THOMPSON

[f]inished her [K]enneth lovingly [h]air before [L]emon Barley

As the saying goes, the bigger they are, the nicer they are. And who, these days, is bigger than Emma Thompson? Of course, Robbie Coltrane is bigger in a merely physical sense. But no one, surely, is bigger in heart or soul than this charming young star of the British stage and screen.

I had arranged to meet her, along with Kenneth Branagh, her co-star on-stage and off, in the Green Room of the London Coliseum. There this sparkling young couple were rehearsing their starring roles in the Renaissance Theatre Company's forthcoming Royal Command Performance of John Osborne's *Look Back In Anger*.

Butterflies were fluttering about my stomach at the prospect, nay ▶

"We're thinking of doing a musical film version of *The Magic Roundabout*. Kennykins is just perfect for Zebedee"

the thought of meeting such an illustrious duo. But Emma, with all the natural grace of the genuine star, had thought of that possibility and had therefore prepared a delightful greeting.

As I walked through the door, she switched on a tape-recorder, which played the jazzy Dave Brubeck theme tune from her recent TV series. And then, as she had done at the beginning of her show, she did a little dance – a private performance that said, in movement rather than words, "Come in. You're welcome here. We don't mind that you're not famous."

How we all laughed as Emma finished her performance. She sat down and Kenneth lovingly ran his playful fingers through her hair before pouring us all glasses of sparkling Lemon Barley drink. His theatre company, Renaissance, is well-named, for Branagh is a man of many parts; an actor, director, author and the proprietor of Kenneth's Coiffure, a trendy salon in Selly Oak. As for Emma ... what can one say?

"Well, Emma," I said, "Let's start with your one-woman television show. Many critics claimed that it wasn't funny. How do you feel about that?"

Her delightfully-chiselled nostrils flared briefly, then she spoke: "Funny? I always think it's frightfully banal when people expect comedy to be funny. Certainly we never thought about being funny when we were at Cambridge. Were you at Cambridge?"

Indeed I was, I replied, but only at an unfashionable college.

"Oh dear," said the delicious young thespian before adding, considerately, "Still, never mind, Kenny wasn't at Cambridge at all, were you, chickadee?"

"Oh, fie on you," quipped the brilliant young Shakespearian.

As the two lovers cuddled on the Green Room sofa, I asked them about the choice of play for their royal performance. *Look Back In Anger* seemed a surprising title for them; what did they have to be angry about?

Emma was the first to reply. "I discovered the other day that someone had taken the last black Le Creuset casserole dish from the stock at The General Trading Company, which means that we can't have it on our wedding list. That made me pretty angry, I can tell you."

"I wouldn't say you were angry exactly, darling," said her husband-to-be. "A little cross, certainly, but never angry."

Surely, I interjected, surely the whole point about Osborne's classic play was that it was infused with rage. It was more than angry. It was furious. How could two such happy, talented, wealthy people convey the essential loathing and contempt at the heart of the work?

"Because we're actors, of course," replied Emma, dismissively. "We simply pretend to be angry. It's not difficult, you know."

"Now, now, dear," said her partner, soothingly. "This gentleman is only doing his job."

"Thank you, Sir Kenneth," I gasped, astounded by the strength of feeling that lay behind Miss Thompson's divine countenance. "Tell me," I continued, "you have already established a reputation as the finest theatrical couple since Olivier and Vivien Leigh, perhaps even since Eric Sykes and Hattie Jacques ... do you have any plans for future collaborations?"

"Actually," said Branagh, "I was rather hoping that after dinner tonight we might..."

"He meant plays, cretin," rasped his bride.

"Right. Absolutely. Yes, well we definitely have a few theatrical plans. I've always thought of myself as a sort of young Tolstoy-esque type of figure. I'm really tremendously keen to do a production of *War and Peace*. I'll direct it, of course, and I thought that I might even play Pierre Besukhov, too."

"I can't wait to be Natasha," said Emma.

"Of course," continued the man in her life, "I think I'll do Andrei, as well. And Napoleon if there's time."

This was fascinating. And Lord and Lady Branagh were happy to reveal still more of their plans. Emma continued: "We're thinking of doing a musical film version of *The Magic Roundabout*. I've always felt like a natural Florence. And Kennykins is just perfect for the part of Zebedee."

"Dougall, too, I thought. And maybe even Dylan, the rabbit. It really all depends on my schedule," he agreed.

If the project goes ahead, it will do so under the aegis of the film studio that the Branaghs will soon be setting up. It was the obvious question, but I had to ask it; did he feel that he might be trying to do too much?

"Good Lord, no," said the man they are calling the successor to Ralphie and Johnnie and Co. "I think actors appreciate it when things are being run by someone just like them. They don't want to be told what to do by directors and producers. They would much rather be told what to do by me."

At that moment I noticed a piece of paper, lying on the ground between the Prince and Princess of contemporary drama. I could just make out some sort of design – a shield on which were drawn the letters K and E, entwined in gold upon a field of ermine. Below the shield was a scroll, but the writing on it was indecipherable. What, I wondered, was this?

"Oh," laughed Emma, "it's frightfully silly, really. We just thought that, what with the Birthday Honours List coming up any day now, it might be sensible to have a coat of arms drawn up. You know, just in case. Of course, any award or recognition always comes as the most utterly delightful surprise, but I always say it's better to be safe than sorry."

The writing on the scroll still intrigued me. Without wishing to appear indiscreet, I asked Her Highness what it might say.

"It's our new motto. We wanted something that expressed our profound devotion and commitment to drama in this country, but we didn't want to seem ... how can I say? ... well, pretentious, if you know what I mean. So we didn't go for any of the obvious Shakespeare lines like, 'All the world's a stage,' or, 'The play's the thing'. We were very much looking for something a bit more contemporary."

What, therefore, had they chosen in the end?

"Oh, simple ... 'Darling, you were wonderful'. We really felt that summed up everything about the theatrical life. Don't you agree?"

Oh, goodness, how I agreed. Dear, dear Ken. Lovely, lovely Emma ... how could I impose upon their valuable time for a single moment longer? I salaamed before this magnificent, semi-divine couple, then stepped backwards to the door, my eyes fixed meekly on the carpet. Truly, I felt, I was privileged to have been granted such a blessed audience. Oh yes, indeed – how very, very privileged ... ■

DAVID THOMAS

CAR BOOT SALE
CAR BOOT SALE HERE
CAR BOOT SALE
CAR BOOT SALE HERE
CAR BOOT SALE
CAR BOOT SALE HERE
CAR BOOT SALE
CAR BOOT SALE HERE
CAR BOOT SALE
CAR BOOT SALE HERE
CAR BOOT SALE
CAR BOOT SALE HERE
CAR BOOT SALE
CAR BOOT SALE HERE
McLACHLAN

B'STARD: THE LAW

INSIGHT

● As Alan B'Stard, Tory MP for Haltemprice, lies wounded in hospital, startling evidence has come to light of his astonishing attempt to influence the contents of the Budget, due on 14th March. People who like to put "-gate" on to the ends of words to make them sound like conspiracies are already calling it B'Stardgate. Except for the ones who are calling it Budgetgate. And a few who insist on Lawsongate.

LAURENCE MARKS and MAURICE GRAN, creators of *The New Statesman*, the TV documentary series that has followed B'Stard throughout his parliamentary career, have investigated Thingummygate for this exclusive Hindsight report. These are their startling conclusions.

Evidence has come to light of a disturbing secret correspondence between The Right Hon Nigel Lawson, the Chancellor of the Exchequer, and Alan B'Stard, the self-styled "Rising Star of the New Right". These letters were found in a black plastic bin-liner, at a central London cemetery recently sold by Westminster Council for five pence to a company called "B'Stard Stiff Disposal PLC". They were discovered by a Mrs Hilda Prosser, when she visited the cemetery to place fresh spring flowers on the grave of her late husband, Ralph.

Confronted by a sign on the locked cemetery gates, saying "Closed for Redevelopment, Keep Out On Pain of Death", the plucky mourner clambered over the wall, only to discover that her husband's grave, and hundreds of others, had been bulldozed into a gruesome mound. In searching this horrendous hillock for her husband's remains, she stumbled over this disturbing correspondence.

Mrs Prosser immediately took these letters to the *Daily Mail*, the newspaper she has faithfully read every day for nearly sixty years. The editor of that famous organ recognised at once that these letters should be published in the public interest, and therefore refused to do so. Mrs Prosser then passed the letters on to this week's editor of *Punch*. We publish them as a warning to the nation.

The first letter was sent from an organisation called GLOBAL RESEARCH for EDUCATIONAL AND ECONOMIC DEVELOPMENT, or GREED; founder and director of research, Alan Beresford B'Stard, MP. It was addressed to The Right Honourable Nigel Lawson, Chancellor of the Exchequer, 11 Downing Street, London SW1, and dated 20th February, 1989.

The letter read as follows:

Dear Right-On Nige,

Well, it's that time of year again, so here are GREED's proposals for this year's budget. You'll see that we've reflected the need to maintain economic activity without fuelling the inflationary spiral, through a range of startlingly innovative ideas. Don't flinch, I know that Her Next Door will love 'em!

Best Wishes,

Alan

PS. Please find invoice enclosed for £50,000.

Enclosed with the letter was a four-page document, which we are able to print in full.

BUDGET DAY 1989 – SOME NEW APPROACHES

1. INCOME TAX Reverse the

ON CONNECTION

"progressive element". Double the lower rate and halve the upper rate. Thus the rich will keep a far higher proportion of their income, as is only right.

Conversely, lower wage earners will find their take home pay greatly reduced, and so will have an incentive to work harder to earn enough to live on. This will act as a major incentive to enterprise.

2. TAX ON UNEARNED INCOME It is patently absurd that in a capitalist society income from investments should attract any tax at all! Abolish all such penalties.

3. CORPORATION TAX See above. Abolish it.

4. CAPITAL TRANSFER TAX Likewise.

5. MORTGAGE TAX RELIEF This should START at £50,000, and have no ceiling. (Unlike the houses concerned, hopefully.) This would ▶

ILLUSTRATION BY RICHARDSON

encourage rich people to buy stately homes, and so help protect the nation's heritage. If the Government is serious about encouraging wealth creators, then there should also be tax relief on second homes (and third, fourth and fifth homes).

6. VAT We should acknowledge that Britain is far better at manufacturing luxury goods than everyday consumer necessities. Therefore, VAT should be abolished on all UK-made luxuries: cars costing over £40,000, Savile Row Suits, Jermyn Street shoes and shirts, hand-made shotguns, very old malt whisky, etc. The shortfall should be made up by imposing VAT on food and children's clothes. People still have to buy these, regardless of tax. And VAT on books should be increased to 100%; there are far too many radical books being written and read today, and those of us who are trying to export for Britain, for example by selling much British-made armaments to Iran, are not helped by the rabid, anti-Islamic outpourings of so-called prize-winning novelists.

7. ALCOHOL Obviously, alcohol abuse is a major problem. Drink driving causes terrible anguish, particularly to innocent people who leave their Bentleys outside expensive restaurants, only to have drunken reps in polyester suits, and nasty souped-up Ford Escorts, run into them in an inebriated haze. Therefore, duty on beer, lager, cheap wine, cider and brand-name spirits should be trebled. However, fine single malt whisky, Napoleon brandy and any wine costing more than £250 a case should be duty-free. The people who enjoy these superior beverages pose no threat to life or safety – we – rather they – all have chauffeurs, or ministerial cars.

8. TOBACCO Duty should be raised to punitive levels on cigarettes, cheap so-called cigars with silly names like Manikin, Tom Thumb and Hamlet, and pipe tobacco, as an aid to the nation's health. Havana cigars should be exempt of duty. They're good for you.

9. OLD AGE PENSIONS Abolish them. The world is becoming over-crowded, and we must do our bit for population control. After all, hypothermia is only nature's way of saying you should have invested prudently in your youth. As a bonus, statistics show that most old people living on state hand-outs vote Labour.

10. UNEMPLOYMENT BENEFIT AND SOCIAL SECURITY Abolish these socialistic crutches! How can a free labour market flourish if we subsidise people not to work? If the going rate for, say, a farm labourer is ten pounds a week (personally, I never pay more than £7.50, if I can help it), how can the state justify paying the same man the huge sum of thirty pounds a week to stay at home?

11. NEW SOURCES OF INCOME It really is time that this Government abandoned its hypocritical opposition to certain market sectors. Entrepreneurs, operating in the most hostile environments, have proved there is a demand for drugs and pornography. Moderate taxes – we shouldn't aim to kill the golden goose – could generate billions of pounds of extra income for the Exchequer, income that could reduce the top rate of income tax to, well, nothing!

NB. In presenting your budget, I suggest you mention booze, fags and mortgage tax relief early on. Listeners and viewers will then switch off, and you can slip the controversial

ON OUR OTHER 3,649 PAGES

stuff in without the Ordinaires noticing.

Lawson waited for two days before replying to this extraordinary document. When he finally did so, his dismissal of B'Stard's ideas appeared to be total. His letter, dated 23rd February and written on 11 Downing Street notepaper, was short and to the point.

Dear B'Stard,

Thank you for your letter, and your amusingly original advice. I'm sure it was as well meant as it was unsolicited. However, in what must be a year of economic prudence and consolidation, I hardly think your proposals merit serious attention. And your invoice merits no attention at all.

Cordially,

N.L.

If this letter was intended to be a dismissal of B'Stard's ideas, it failed totally. On 25th February, the rampant Member for Haltemprice wrote once more to the Chancellor of the Exchequer. As before, the letter was written on GREED notepaper.

Dear R.O.N.,

"Unsolicited"? "Hardly merit serious attention"? Dear oh dear, the old memory isn't what it was, is it? Surely you can't have forgotten the pleasant afternoon we spent with the brandy decanter at your club – Pratt's, isn't it? – just after you'd been promoted to Chancellor. Give me some radical suggestions, Alan, you said, help me make a splash. And that's what I did. Privatise everything, I told you, even Coal. And I showed you how you could con Scargill into calling a National Strike, beat him, close down all the unprofitable pits ... Of course, you said Her Next Door'll never wear it. But She did, didn't She? Because She knew that GREED has its finger on the popular pulse. (After all, wasn't it GREED who told Her, back in '81, when the SDP were leading in the polls, that the only way to ensure winning the next General Election was to find some Third World country to declare war on?)

So unless you want the transcripts of the tape of our 1983 meeting to be sent to The Guardian *– and I assure you* my *tape recorder never malfunctions – please honour the attached invoice for £55,000, being my standard fee plus 10% surcharge for late payment.*

Yours,

Alan

This letter seems to have provoked a fundamental change of heart on the part of Mr Lawson. His reply to B'Stard was written from The Old Rectory, Stoney Stanton, Leics, and possessed a much more friendly tone-of-voice.

My Dear Alan,

Was it really as long ago as 1983 that we had that delightful lunch at Pratt's? Good Lord, how time flies. I've mulled over your interesting ideas with a certain blonde lady, and as this is going to be my last budget before I accept the editorship of the Financial Times *(which I will immediately have printed on pale blue paper), I've decided to incorporate certain of your proposals into my speech. I cannot pay your invoice out of public funds at this time. However, if you pass the attached list of companies on to your stockbroker, you should be able to realise considerably more than a lousy 55k.*

Best wishes,

Nigel

There remains some confusion as to the whereabouts of the "attached list of companies" referred to by the Chancellor in his letter and Mr B'Stard is still too idle to make any statement to the press.

We tried to contact Mrs Prosser, but her butler informs us that she is at present cruising the Caribbean on her new two million pound yacht, and is not expected to return to Britain in this financial year. ■

PROFILE

Alan Beresford B'Stard has a typical New-Tory pedigree. Born in a council house in Halesowen, in 1956, he attended state schools until the age of fourteen. Then his thrifty parents managed to send him to Fiskes, a minor public school, from where he won a place at Brownose College, Oxford, to read Economics. His stunning and unexpected A-Level results might have been linked to his father's work at a security printers where the examination papers were produced.

At Brownose B'Stard quickly rose to prominence as Chairman of the Federation of Conservative Students, and contemporaries fondly remember the torchlight parades and book burnings he instituted. B'Stard was still at Oxford when he made his first million through the activities of such companies as Elite Discreet Escorts and Pasha Massage Parlours. He also became a highly paid lobbyist for the South African arms importer, The Omnivore Group.

Graduating weeks after Margaret Thatcher's first General Election victory, B'Stard took the 1980s by storm. Utterly without scruple – he lists his recreations in *Who's Who* as "Making money, dining in expensive restaurants at other people's expense, grinding the faces of the poor, and droit de seigneur" – he rapidly amassed a huge fortune. Then in 1985 he married Sarah Gidleigh Park, only daughter of North Yorkshire Landowner, and ex-Oswald Mosley bodyguard, Roland Gidleigh Park, OBE. Soon afterwards, B'Stard was selected to stand for the safe seat of Haltemprice at the 1987 General Election. His new father-in-law happened to be Chairman of the constituency Conservative Party.

B'Stard's rabid electioneering style threatened to turn Haltemprice into a Tory/Alliance marginal, until a fortuitous freak motor accident, involving the Labour and Alliance candidates, removed these two opponents from the running three days before polling.

Returned with the largest majority in the Commons (26,737) B'Stard quickly made his mark by piloting through the Police Firearms Act, 1987, as a result of which we are now used to the sight of armed Bobbies patrolling our streets. Never out of the headlines, B'Stard is tipped for a great political future. An un-named Tory minister told us, "B'Stard will inevitably achieve Cabinet rank – if he's spared." ■

Naked in the Dust

KIM BASINGER

Hollywood's sultriest screen queen has just bought an entire town. TONY GLOVER was there

Kimberly felt bored. As the world-famous actress and model stared at her latest paycheck, a mere $5 million, she idly wondered what she could buy. Houses were boring, she had at least ten of those. The hotels she had bought last year were no fun either. You could always stay in a hotel whether you owned it or not. Same with the 100 miles of beach she owned; anybody could lie on a beach. How about buying some people? Well, God knows she owned enough of those already.

Looking in the mirror at the loose, luxuriant blonde waterfall of hair flowing over her tawny skin, she parted her wet lips a fraction to reveal a perfect set of teeth. A sigh escaped the pneumatic lips as the truth dawned on her. Of course, it was staring her in the face all the time. She was still a country girl at heart.

What she needed was an escape from the false lifestyle which surrounded her. Her mouth formed the world-famous bruised pout as she pictured her return to small-town life. She envisaged a slow camera shot of cornfields. A figure was running through the long yellow corn. It was a beautiful girl. Herself, naturally.

As she ran, her worn cotton dress tore and was pulled away from her pulsating body and her breath came in hoarse gasps as she began to slow down. Behind her ran her tall, dark, virile pursuer. She turned to face him. Her face was a mask of sensual vulnerability. "What do you want of me?" she whispered as he forced her down on to the warm, soft earth.

Yes, that was what she needed, a return to the simple country pleasures. She knew the answer. Her long, elegant fingers curled around the telephone as she called her agent.

"Larry, find me a lawyer. I wanna buy me a town," she drawled in a voice that made Larry's mouth go dry.

Later the same day…

Most of Bernie Finglestein's clients were major corporations or rich elderly widows. Acting for Kimberly had had a cataclysmic effect on Bernie's bio-rhythms. He spent most of his day in his private office waiting for Kimberly to call and slavering over pictures of her in the fashion magazines. How did she manage to look like that? It was as if a platoon of marines had spent all afternoon…

His face flushed as the telephone in the centre of his big mahogany desk rang. It was her. Jesus, that voice. So Southern, so husky. Oh, why in God's name didn't they have video phones yet. His hand shook as he poured himself a generous measure of Jack Daniels. As the whisky burned his throat he imagined Kimberly sprawled across his big old desk, her sultry voice begging him to…

"Hello, are you still there?" he heard her ask. My God, he hadn't taken in a word of whatever she had been saying.

"Kimberly, baby, honey, I was just examining your, er, file. What was it you wanted to know?" "Exactly what you've been up to," she drawled. "Have you managed to find me a likely town yet? Because if you haven't, I'll have to try and find myself another lawyer, *honey lamb*."

"I've found just the place," Bernie lied.

"Great, where is it?"

"You'll love it," he stalled, frantically staring around the room for inspiration. His eyes locked on to the label of the Jack Daniels bottle.

"Lynchburgh, Tennessee," he blurted.

"Whaaat?" shrieked the voice at the other end of the line. Shit, he had blown it.

"How did you know? Why that's in my home county," purred Kimberly.

"I knew you'd be pleased, I wanted to surprise you," improvised Bernie.

"Do I actually own it yet?" asked Kimberly.

"Not quite, Kimberly, I just have to tie up a few loose legal ends."

"Okay, well, I suppose you can have a few more days. We're still filming *Naked in the Dust*. What's that noise, Bernie? It sounds as though someone's trying to strangle you."

A week later Kimberly woke up filled with the excitement she always felt when she had a new toy. Today she was going to catch a plane and then drive down to her town. *Her town*. The words had such a majestic ring to them.

"What do you want from me?" she whispered as he forced her down on to the soft, warm earth

Today she would dress like a queen, a queen of the South. She padded across the three-inch white pile carpet to her wardrobe and selected a demure strip of ripped chamois leather which she wrapped around her trembling lithe body.

That day began quietly enough in Lynchburgh's town square. No one and nothing moved in the noonday heat. Even the mangy old mut who usually scrounged scraps from the good ol' boys in Al's bar only had the energy to lie in the shade of one of the trees at the foot of the white courthouse steps.

In the old days LBJ himself had sat on those very courthouse steps and shared a meal of spicy chicken wings with the town's good ol' boys. Some of the white-suited old men sitting in Lee's barbershop still remembered it as they looked out across the square at the fine white courthouse building.

The younger fellas didn't spend so much time in the barbershop. They preferred to sink a few cold ones and sprawl out on the veranda at the front of Al's bar and poolhall. But this morning's calm was deceptive. All week an ugly rumour had been circulating round the town . Some rich New York attorney called Finglestein had been buying up all their outstanding mortgages through the local bank.

Ever since the rumours started some of the boys had made a habit of bringing their firearms into town. What they'd like to do with this New York lawyer man… they'd been talking about it all week. And it wasn't a marshmallow and weenie roast. But for the townspeople of Lynchburgh, events were about to take a direction all their own.

A screech of brakes announced the arrival of something which looked as if it had just beamed down from another planet. A cloud of dust settled to reveal a long pink Caddy. Blackened windows prevented the townsfolk from seeing who was inside. Not a dog flea stirred as the driver's door slowly opened.

A long, tanned and exquisitely female leg slid on to the hot earth and stretched five perfectly-formed toes in the dust. The square fell silent as Kimberly showed herself – the only sound, the thud of jaws hitting the dusty sidewalks. She ran her hands over her ripped clothing and gave a breathless shudder as she surveyed her new domain. Only one thought occupied the minds of the men whose eyes were riveted on the beautiful but abused and dishevelled young white woman: "Who dared defile this paragon of Southern womanhood, the lucky bastard?"

It was at this moment that Kimberly's black chauffeur "Blues" got out of the driver's seat. All the way down he had let Kimberly persuade him that his fear of the Deep South was irrational paranoia, the result of too great a fondness for what he liked to call "nose candy" or "cute toot". Although she hadn't been home since she was thirteen she assured him the South had changed.

Sheriff "Bull" Gowry stared speechless, wondering how he was going to be able to get this big Yankee nigger into the jailhouse before the good people of Lynchburgh strung him up on one of the old courthouse trees.

"Bull" slowly advanced towards the tall black man, his hand on the pearl butt of his .45. But before he could reach him Kimberly spoke: "Why, Sheriff Gowry, how kind of you to arrange this reception and take the trouble to come and meet us in person. As your new boss I shall take the opportunity to give you your first paycheck."

The sheriff opened the envelope and swallowed hard when he saw the amount written on the cheque. It was more than he had managed to save in twenty years of regular police work. Whatever fears "Bull" had about the safety of Miss Kimberly's conspicuous employee were temporarily allayed by her announcement that the town was to be used as the set for her new big movie *Naked in the Dust II*. A casting director and technicians would shortly be arriving and anyone who wanted work as an extra at $250 per day should form a line by the casting coach which was pulling into the square.

Casting director Gene Pucepiece was soon drooling in ecstasy over the never-ending stream of eager, bigoted redneck faces appearing at his window and by evening the refreshments coach was handing out cold beer and burgers to anyone and everyone. But even as Kimberly and "Blues" were complimenting Sheriff Gowry on his nice clean town they could not help noticing some figures in pointed white hoods quietly moving around on the edge of the square. Strange, the studio coach with the costumes was still two hours away… ■

running gags

There is nothing the British enjoy more than mass participation events, particularly those which offer the chance to witness ritual humiliation under the guise of a Good Cause. An outlet for this national perversion has been absent from the social calendar since the demise of *Jeux Sans Frontières*. However, ADT, a company with little more than an appalling advertising campaign to its credit, plans to fill the void with the New, Improved London Marathon, appearing in a street near you sooner than you'd like. As a veteran with a personal best time of 5hr 50min 07secs, JUANITA LOFTHOUSE presents a timely survival guide for this year's also-rans

Puffed out

SPONSOR'S ADVICE:
ARRIVE EARLY AND ENJOY THE PRE-RACE ATMOSPHERE.

OUR EXPERT RECOMMENDS:
It is possible to have too much of a good thing. Under favourable climatic conditions, the atmospheric levels of liniment in Greenwich Park reach 70 per cent, and since it's hard to run with scorched alveoli, plan to arrive no more than one hour in advance. Change before you go, or prepare to cast off more than your inhibitions in the watchful company of 70 complete strangers on a Red Rover Bus. Joining the 30-yard queue at the last chemical toilet for five miles is optional, as is the ability to whistle the theme from *Chariots Of Fire* whilst using them.

PROVIDE US WITH ANY INTERESTING INFORMATION ABOUT YOURSELF WHICH COULD BE USED IN THE BBC COVERAGE OF THE EVENT.

This is a personal decision. Max Ehrmann's *Desiderata* insists that even the dull and ignorant have their story to tell; unfortunately Desmond Lynam uses this tract as the mainstay of his interviewing technique. Unless you are an explorer who has circumnavigated the world three times in a Tupperware container, or are attempting the course in an iron lung, you are unlikely to attract very much attention. Only dress as a French maid if being chased across Tower Bridge by Bob Wilson with a stiffy strikes you as a life-enhancing experience.

LUBRICATE ALL MOVING PARTS WITH VASELINE.

Serious athletes smear enough around the armpits and thighs to prevent chafing. Fun Runners use enough for a two-way Channel swim-crossing in November. Sexual deviants have so much fun at this stage that they immediately withdraw from the race, and retire in pairs to the nearest chemical toilet.

WARM UP THOROUGHLY BEFORE THE RACE BEGINS.

This is the most hazardous part of the Fun Runner's day. Whilst it may be tempting to join in with the veterans as they perform "The Strutting Cusp", "The Ripsaw" and "The Teplitz Pretzel", if you have been unable to touch your toes since Denise Nolan's first confession, it is unlikely that they will have got any closer to your head in the interim. May I emphasise the inadvisability of performing an advanced Callanetics routine whilst dressed as Humpty Dumpty or the Hofmeister bear; some moving parts don't.

WRITE ANY PERTINENT MEDICAL INFORMATION ON THE REVERSE OF YOUR RUNNING NUMBER.

Simply tattoo "I am a Fun Runner" on your forehead, and the medics will realise that you smoke at least twenty a day and have blocked arteries. Avoid St John's Ambulance-persons working for their "Sporting Injuries" badge, since it is

La chasse

impossible to complete the course after being put in traction. Jogger's Nipple may be avoided by the strategic placement of Elastoplast. Jogger's Penis, always a sore point, may be avoided by not dressing up as the aforementioned French maid on Tower Bridge.

TRY NOT TO IMPEDE THE PROGRESS OF SERIOUS ATHLETES.

The Serious Athlete is male, fortyish, overweight, and is not competing against you. Easily identified by the sweatbands on his

t-t-timing

ankles, his race is against middle age, and he knows he cannot win. Other telltale signs are the "Athlete at C&A" tracksuit, the Argos Digital Pedometer and the Nike Fluorescent Bum Bag containing his personalised Cell Net telephone. The latter accessory allows the serious athlete to score at least ten Brown Nose points with Sir, using phrases like "I'll have to get back to you with that when I've finished this Marathon". Do not become perplexed if he elbows your guts at the start muttering "Bloody amateurs" whilst he studies the split times Biroed onto his forearm; you will pass him at the five mile mark, he'll be wearing an oxygen mask, trying desperately hard to ring Sir to explain how his old rugger wound has let him down again. Why these people don't choose to die in the relative privacy of a squash court is more mysterious than the contents of Joanna Southcott's box (which were unknown even to fellow members of her cricket club).

DO NOT SPIT OVER YOUR SHOULDER.

Successful gobbing is an advanced technique, demanding accurate tongue control and precise judgment of wind speed to induce a dispersive aerosol effect. For the inexperienced athlete, spitting straight ahead is no more than a particularly unpleasant way of getting your own back, literally. ►

Pressure points

DRAWINGS: JAMES SILLAVAN

DO NOT ALTER COURSE SUDDENLY WHEN OVERTAKING WHEELCHAIRS.

It is best not to attempt to overtake wheelchair competitors. I failed several times last year, and believe me, there is nothing worse than a smug face freewheeling past you with a "Paraplegics Do It Sitting Down" sticker on his back bumper. Changing course to avoid collisions is encouraged; changing course to the more scenic Paris Marathon may lead to disqualification from both events.

DRINK PLENTY OF WATER.

Cruising at a steady five mph, 90 per cent of your fluid intake takes the shortest route possible to your bladder. After eighteen miles you will be walking with all the elasticated grace of Virgil Tracy, and assuming you have the strength to mount the steps of a Portaloo, if you do sit down, you will be unable to stand up afterwards. Moderate intake is advised unless you wish to finish the race in the squatting position, or intend competing in a fully-functional spacesuit.

Resist the high-tech allure of isotonic salt drinks. These potions are concocted to replace the vital metabolites lost in perspiration, i.e. they contain all the constituents of sweat; real ale enthusiasts may prefer to drink straight from a passing armpit. Under no circumstance drink water from the reusable sponges provided en route; it is so disconcerting to witness somebody using one to remove excess crotch Vaseline a little further down the road.

ENJOY THE PRESENCE OF CELEBRITIES.

1) Jimmy Saville finishes the course in around four hours, 2) Eighty per cent of the competitors finish at least one minute before him; the two facts are related. Wherever possible, run behind Eric Morley, since a) it is possible to slipstream in the trail of excess Brylcreem, and b) the view is preferable.

ENJOY THE CROWDS.

Most of the route is lined with the type of person who attends traffic accidents with a Thermos flask and an Instamatic, but they also serve who only stand and mock. Enjoy the limitless hospitality of East Ferry Road, where pork, beef or lamb sandwiches are offered by every householder, and cups of tea are yours for the asking. Contrast this with the total absence of human life as you turn the corner into Yuppieland; Bernice will be too busy trying to get through to the "Next 24-hour Designer Insemination Service", whilst Adrian spends his Sundays working out (what to do with £100K per annum).

FINISHING THE MARATHON.

If you want to, rest assured you will. Even if Ingrid Christiannsen is half-way back to Norway by the time you cross the finishing line, there are no recriminations for the Fun Runner, since the distinction between finishing 22,004th and 22,005th is minute. Do not arrange to meet your family at the alphabetically arranged Reunion Area in Jubilee Gardens, as you will probably not be able to remember your own name for a few hours. Head straight for McDonald's; you'll be so hungry that even the suspicious green bits will taste like Ambrosia. Do not attempt to consume ADT's commemorative security camera, as it has even less nutritional value than a Mars Bar. Do not plan activities requiring legs for at least three days afterwards, and as your ankles swell with pride, you can bask in the knowledge that you now have a personal experience to recount at parties which will beat the couple who've done their own conveyancing hands down. You really have to be there to appreciate it. ■

Survival of the fittest

"... meanwhile, here's one I made earlier."

Good afternoon, sir.... I wonder if you would mind answering a few questions for our survey?....
....on the possibility of the main Opposition parties forming one party to oppose the Tories in the Election Who do you see as Leader of this single Party?
Grrr!
If there was a General Election tomorrow, he or she would have to take on the formidable Mrs Thatcher in a straight fight. Neil Kinnock for instance?
Snarl..
Kinnock? Bloody useless!!..... Thatcher would bloody murder him!
Ashdown against Thatcher?...
Ashdown!?!... Bloody useless!! Thatcher by bloody miles!!
What about Owen to face Thatcher?
Owen!?!... Bloody useless!! Thatcher would slaughter him and anyone else of that bloody pathetic bunch!!
So, according to you, sir, the Opposition has no-one of sufficient stature worthy of leadership and if they put up a wall-eyed, retarded chimp with a wooden leg, that couldn't do worse against Mrs Thatcher!
The chimp, by a landslide.
McLACHLAN

"No, he hasn't always had money. How did you guess?"

ILLUSTRATION BY ALAN MORRISON

HOW TO BE CLINT

Can you speak with your teeth clenched together? Can you shoot four men with three bullets? Can you kill a man just by talking to him? Of course you can't. You're not Clint. But you could be. Just follow MITCHELL SYMONS's step-by-step guide

A man is lying on the pavement. He is injured having been shot whilst trying to rob a bank. He is eyeing his sawn-off shotgun and deliberating whether to reach for it. A taller man says, "Uh uh." The injured man looks at him. The taller man points a gun at the injured man and, in a deliberate voice, delivers the most famous soliloquy outside the works of Shakespeare.

"I know what you're thinking. Did he fire six shots or only five? Well, to tell you the truth, in all this excitement, I've kinda lost track myself. But being this is a .44 Magnum, the most powerful handgun in the world and would blow your head clean off, you've got to ask yourself one question: do I feel lucky? Well, do you, punk?"

The soliloquiser is, of course, Clint. It's true, he's playing a part (Inspector Harry Callahan) in a movie (*Dirty Harry*) but to millions of people, whatever the name of the character or the film, he is still Clint. Say it, say "Clint" and as you do so, you'll notice your eyes narrowing and your teeth clenching. Clint is a Clint: Clint is the ultimate Clint. It is indeed fortunate (for him and us) that he was not christened Jeremy or Andrew for it just wouldn't work. When Clint says, "Go on, punk, make my day," the punk had better reach for a dictionary of last words; if a Jeremy were to say the same thing, the punk would also die – laughing.

Clint's latest movie – his 43rd (45th, if you include *Breezy* and *Bird* which he directed) and his fifth in the role of Harry Callahan – is entitled *The Dead Pool* and opens on 14 April. To mark this latest film, *Punch* is proud to offer the first analysis of Clint... the killer.

Because that's what Clint's good at. Killing. Forget the fact that Clint Eastwood is a first-rate actor (not to mention a skilful director, hailed by the *auteur*-obsessed French as a genius), Clint is a killer. Forget the fact that Clint Eastwood very often plays a self-deprecating character who's often a loser (*Bronco Billy, Honkytonk Man* and *The Beguiled*), Clint is a total winner. Forget the fact that he sometimes plays a "liberally minded man intent on upholding the letter as well as the spirit of the law" (*Tightrope, Pale Rider* and even *Magnum Force*), Clint is a fascist. Forget the lighthearted roles (*Any Which Way You Can, The Witches, Every Which Way But Loose, City Heat, Paint Your Wagon* and *Kelly's Heroes*), Clint is menacing.

For everyone who cares – that's to say, anyone who matters – Clint is a killer.

Clint Eastwood, however, is not the same person as Clint. Clint Eastwood is an actor pushing 59 years of age. Clint Eastwood is the son of an accountant. Clint Eastwood is careful about his diet. Clint Eastwood enjoys music and has a fine baritone voice. Clint Eastwood is a non-smoker who gets nauseous when a script compels him to smoke a cigar. Clint Eastwood is a husband and a father. When Clint Eastwood became Mayor of Carmel, his first act was not to run the bad men out of town but to open an ice-cream bar. Clint Eastwood makes President Bush look like a he-man. Clint Eastwood is, for want of a better word, a wimp.

But Clint kills.

After bit-parts in ten, largely forgettable movies (although he did get to appear with Ginger Rogers, George Sanders and Donald O'Connor) and 217 (count them) episodes of *Rawhide* in the role of the all-American cowhand, Rowdy Yates, he at last became a star in Sergio Leone's *A Fistful of Dollars* as The Man With No Name (if you watch the movie, you'll see that it's actually entitled *Fistful of Dollars*: one can only surmise that Leone's budget for titles didn't stretch to indefinite articles). It was also the first film in which Clint killed gratuitously. Clint rides into town. Three men fire shots at his mule (without killing it). Clint learns that they work for the enemy of the man from whom he wishes to seek employment. Clint decides to kill them in order to ingratiate himself with his putative employer.

Consequently, Clint approaches the men – pausing only to tell the undertaker to prepare three coffins – and says: "You see, I understand you men were just playing around but the mule doesn't." He asks them to apologise. They laugh. "I don't think it's nice you laughing. See, my mule don't like people laughing. Gets the crazy idea you're laughing at him. Now, if you'll apologise like I know you're going to, I might convince him that you really didn't mean it." Clint draws on his cigar and then draws his gun and kills four men (although he never actually fired in the direction of the one on the left). Clint goes over to the undertaker and says: "My mistake, four coffins."

This incident at the beginning of the film set the tone for the whole movie and, indeed, all the spaghetti westerns. *For A Few Dollars More, The Good, The Bad and The Ugly* (both for Leone), *Hang 'Em High* (which nowadays looks more like a traditional rather than

A BUNCH OF RIGHT CLINTS

As if to prove the point that there's a little Dirty Harry in every man or woman, Mr Punch is proud to present this unique photo-montage of celebrity Clints, each of whom has been armed with The Most Powerful Handgun In The World. But remember, children, don't try the same game at home. It wouldn't make mummy's day.

Sureshot cover girl Muriel Gray

Martyn Lewis: "Go ahead – read my news."

Dirty Harold... Macmillan

Killer vet Peter Davison

spaghetti western) and *High Plains Drifter* (directed by Clint himself) all featured Clint as The Man With No Name, Few Scruples and even Fewer Words.

You see, Clint doesn't like talking. As far as Clint's concerned, actions speak louder than dialogue. He pared his dialogue to a minimum in all his spaghetti westerns and he's not exactly "gassy" in his other roles. A typical example was *Where Eagles Dare*. When he was given the script, he noticed that he had an enormous amount of dialogue. So he told the director, "Burton has a magnificent voice: let him do the talking, I'll do the killing."

GREAT CLINT DIALOGUE

Dirty Harry: *The Mayor tells Clint that his policy is "no trouble".*
Clint: "Well, when an adult man is chasing a female with intent to commit rape, I shoot the bastard. That's my policy."
Mayor: "Indecent? How did you establish that?"
Clint: "When a naked man is chasing a woman through an alley with a butcher's knife and a hard-on, I figure he isn't out collecting for the Red Cross."

The Enforcer: *The Police Captain reproaches Clint for using violence towards criminals.*
Clint: "What do you want me to do, yell trick or treat at 'em?"
This goes down badly with the Captain who tells Clint he's transferring him to Personnel.
Clint: "To Personnel? That's for assholes."
Police Captain: "I was in Personnel for ten years."
Clint: "Yup."

The Outlaw Josey Wales: *A bounty-hunter confronts Clint in a bar. He tells Clint he's a bounty-hunter.*
Clint (who's always wanted to start up a careers information service): "Why's that?"
Bounty-hunter: "I got to make a living."
Clint: "Dying ain't much way of making a living."

Magnum Force: *Beautiful girl:* "What does a girl have to do to go to bed with you?"
Clint: "Try knocking on the door."

Sudden Impact: *A case is thrown out because Clint used illegal search methods. The defendant (who was of course guilty) calls him "a fool".*
Clint: "Listen, punk, to me you're nothing but dog-shit, you understand? Now a lot of things can happen to dog-shit. It can be scraped up with a shovel off the ground, it can dry up and blow away in the wind or it can be stepped on and squashed."

Sudden Impact: *Four black guys hold up Clint's favourite coffee bar. Clint tells them to put down their guns and adds:* "We're not going to let you just walk out of here."
A punk asks – without much respect – who "we" is.
Clint: "Smith and Wesson and me."

ACTION REPLAYS

The Good, The Bad and The Ugly: *Clint kills a baddie who is positioned on top of a roof. The sun is in Clint's eyes and the angle is 70°.*

High Plains Drifter: *Clint is sitting in a barber's* ▶

Deadeye Dick Baker

Fearless Frank Longford – porn to be wild

Paul Daniels: "You'll like this, not a lot . . . punk."

► *chair with shaving-foam on his face. Three men burst in. Clint kills them all (although the angles were impossible).*

Sudden Impact: *The chief psycho is unreachable and yet Clint says, "Come on, make my day," and shoots him (again from an impossible angle). The psycho crashes through the roof and ends up impaled on a fairground horse.*

Where Eagles Dare: *Clint kills half the Wehrmacht (the other half is killed by Richard Burton and Mary Ure). What makes this highly implausible is the fact that we never see him reload his machine-gun.*

For A Few Dollars More: *Bounty-hunter Clint kills three men who try to stop him apprehending a fugitive (he then kills the fugitive). Not only are the angles impressive but he doesn't seem to use enough bullets.*

CLINT'S IDIOSYNCRASIES IN WESTERNS

Clint always goes to sleep fully dressed (including cigar).

Clint doesn't like a one-to-one gunfight – the odds are too good – he prefers one-to-three.

Clint kills the worst baddies very slowly indeed.

Clint prefers guns to rifles.

Clint always manages to have a three-day stubble growth.

Clint's opponent(s) always goes for his gun first and always ends up dying.

Clint is an Arsenal supporter (we know this because in The Good, The Bad and The Ugly *he kills two men and says to a third man, "You're Spurs," and then kills him. It is, of course, entirely possible that he meant to say: "Your Spurs?").*

Clint wears the sort of coat you wore to Jethro Tull concerts in the early 1970s.

Clint detests monopolistic practices.

CLINT'S IDIOSYNCRASIES AS DIRTY HARRY

Clint is not *into feminism. He regards equal opportunities as just being "stylish".*

Clint is not interested in bureaucracy. He describes a personnel board as "an encounter group".

Clint always wears suits.

Clint usually wears shades.

Clint doesn't approve of the justice's decisions in Supreme Court v. Miranda *(the one which gave crooks rights).*

Clint takes his position (though not himself) seriously. When told "It's a whole new ball game," Clint replies, "Funny, I never thought of it as a game."

CLINT'S LEXICON

"That possibility does exist" (yes).

"You can count on it" (yes).

"What do they call you?" (What's your name?)

"Who might you be?" (What's your name?)

"A maggot who sells dirty pictures" (pornographer).

"Can" (lavatory).

"I reckon not" (no).

TEN THINGS *NOT* TO DO IF YOU *DON'T* WANT TO BE KILLED BY CLINT

1. Be cruel to kids.
2. Be cruel to animals.
3. Stand in his way.
4. Be found not guilty of a crime you committed.
5. Attempt to lynch him for a crime he hasn't committed.
6. Ask him to sign a petition outlawing heterosexism.
7. Tell him that the hotel's fully booked.
8. Call him "pig shit".
9. Bull-whip him.
10. Tell Clint that you've got rights.

DIRTY HARRY – A ONE-MAN CRIME WAVE

What is this sickening tide of violence washing over Britain and corrupting our nation's youth? Why, what else but Clint's series of Dirty Harry movies, the main contributors to the £1 billion he has earned for his studio Warner Brothers. Here, for the first time in British journalism, Punch *presents a film-by-film analysis of the rising crime-rate represented by these films, particularly the cool-blooded killings carried out by Harry himself.*

1. *Dirty Harry* (1971)

Clint confines himself to shootings, stabbings and beatings-up. The final death-toll (all shot) consists of:

4 punks
1 psycho
Total: 5

For definitions of terms, see below.

2. *Magnum Force* (1973)

This film represents a quantum jump in the number and variety of Clint's victims, plus a broader range of methods used to dispose of them. One man is shot through the partition at the back of an airliner's passenger cabin. Another is beaten-up and thrown into a river (he counts as dead; if Clint knocks you out, you *stay* out). And Hal Holbrook, playing a corrupt police captain, is bombed to death in his car. The tally reads:

2 hijackers
2 hoods
2 punks
1 senior corrupt police officer
4 junior corrupt police officers
Total: 11

3. *The Enforcer* (1976)

For the third in the series the death-count dropped somewhat, perhaps in deference to the sensibilities of Harry's new female partner, played by future *Cagney and Lacey* star Tyne Daley. And to satisfy the demands of her feminist principles, the killings – all shootings – were shared out. Clint got six, Tyne got three. Body-bags, please, for:

3 punks
2 revolutionaries
1 psycho
3 Daley victims
Total: 9

4. *Sudden Impact* (1983)

Now we're talking. This is by far and away Harry's most brutal film, notable for the entirely non-racist way in which he refuses to discriminate between black hoodlums and white ones when it comes to finding targets for his big .44. This film also contains a scene in which Harry kills a gangland boss *just by talking to him.* Confronted by our hero whilst celebrating his daughter's wedding, the baddie in question is so overcome by their little chat that he has a heart-attack there and then.

Conversational coronaries apart, Clint's technique in *Sudden Impact* is relatively straightforward, even if some of the angles at which he shoots anyone who happens to wander into his field of fire would be enough to boggle Pythagoras. In this case, the close-of-play score is:

3 black punks
3 white hoods
1 gangland boss
3 punks in a car
1 additional hood
2 punks on foot
1 psycho

5. *The Dead Pool* (1989)

Alarmed, perhaps, by the success of recent campaigns against film and television violence, Clint Eastwood – the human being, that is, rather than the icon – has said that he wants this fifth outing for Dirty Harry to reflect on the man's whacky sense of humour, rather than his compulsive, nay pathological, streak of violence. Detailed perusal of the script notes (we have, as yet, been unable to catch the film itself) suggests that the death-toll may be as low as one. We find this to be a scarcely credible prospect, but the film's less-than-record-breaking performance at the American box office may suggest that it lacks the violence needed to sate the blood-lust of the slavering beast that is the American film-going public.

Total: ?

Definition of Terms

PUNKS are freelance crooks who wear jeans. They have no right to live.
HOODS are crooks employed by gangland bosses (qv). They wear suits, but are equally lacking in the old right-to-life department.
PSYCHOS are sicko, pervy, commie punks who have even less claim to existence than the common-or-garden variety.
GANGLAND BOSSES employ hoods (qv) and can usually avoid justice thanks to the pinko-liberal system of justice that puts their rights ahead of the need to keep evil off the streets (which is why Harry has to keep it off the streets ...permanently).
CORRUPT POLICE OFFICERS are a disgrace to their badge (which Harry, incidentally, refers to as "a seven-point suppository") and should therefore be shot, blown up or thrown in the nearest river.
HIJACKERS are punks who think they can travel for free. No chance.

Scenes of the crimes

If you happen to be in the San Francisco area and you want to avoid places likely to be chosen by Dirty Harry as good spots for a shoot-out, stay clear of:

Coffee bars
Airports (and aeroplanes)
Liquor stores
Cement works
Old battleships
Hotels (and motels)
Roads, and
Fairgrounds

HAEFELI'S

Mid-lifestyle

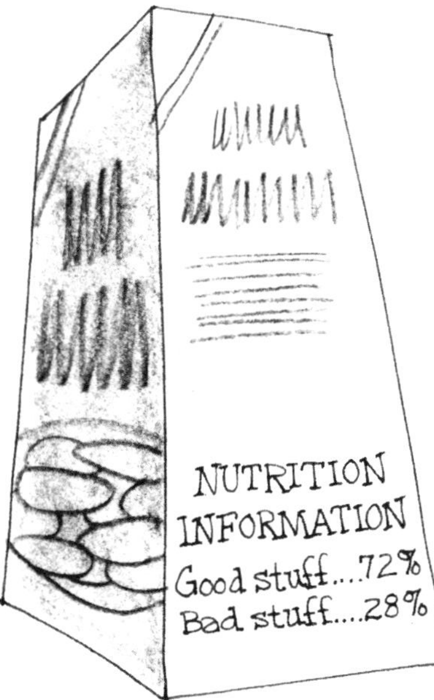

"We're not going to usher in the New Year. We're saving ourselves for the turn of the century."

"I met him at the health club. I had no idea he was like this in street clothes."

"Clarissa wishes she had the shoulders for a shoulder-bag."

crises

"I want a phone that looks like a phone."

"You are not an absolute failure – you're a relative failure."

"I don't want a rug that's more interesting than I am."

THE ROCK BABES A-Z

Where oh where are they now, those curvy young ones? They were the Rock Babes, the golden girls whose honeyed looks inspired the silver voices of the platinum age of pop. Now they could be standing next to you at the supermarket. Or potty-training their brat in Welwyn Garden City. Twenty years on they could look like a million dollars – or smell like the inside of your liver. Now, thanks to years of exclusive, painstaking research by famed rock archivist and internationally-respected rock historian **CARIS DAVIS***, Punch reveals all . . .*

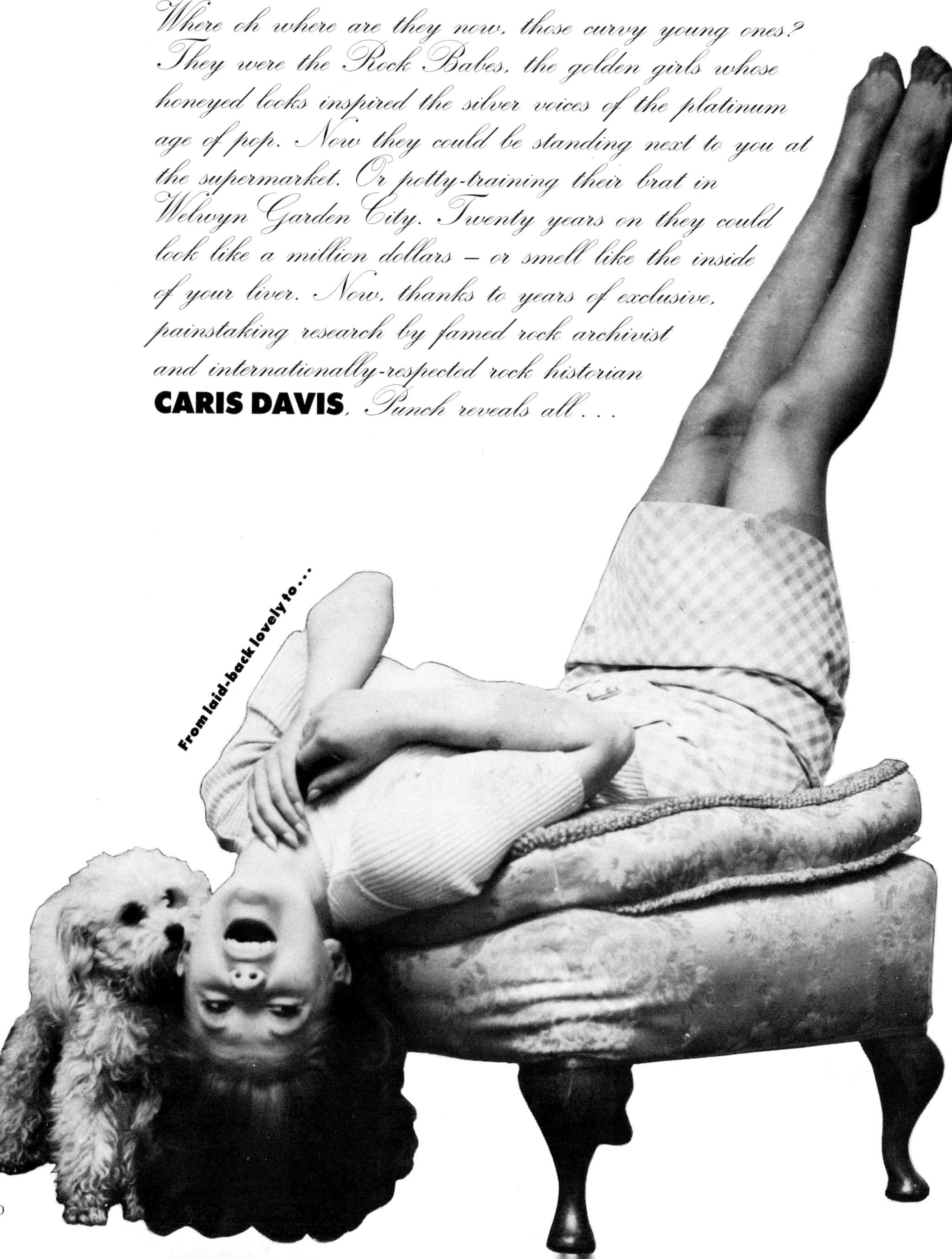

From laid-back lovely to . . .

Help me Fonda

ALISON
(Elvis Costello album track)
Alison O'Dwyer was a spotty girl in the social security office where Declan McManus (aka Elvis Costello) used to sign on. "Alison my aim is true" was a remark he was alleged to have made after she refused to hand over a giro in May, 1974. In a major career move, she transferred to British Telecom's internal fraud squad in 1982, relocated to Milton Keynes and had a baby – which she christened Elvis, after her lifetime hero. Elvis Aaron O'Dwyer: bloody stupid name for a little girl, isn't it?

AMAZING GRACE
(The Royal Scots Dragoon Guards, 1972)
Grace really was amazing. Very few people have the ability to perform acupuncture on goldfish while reciting pages 428-627 of the London *Yellow Pages* verbatim. As advertised last week on the back page of *The Stage*.

ANGIE
(Rolling Stones, 1973)
"Oh maaaaaan it was such a draaaaag when Keith split 'cos he like took the house keys with him, yer know? And I haven't been able to get back inside since '72, right?"

BEN
(Michael Jackson, 1972)
It's a little known fact that Ben was in fact a girl – Benjamina, Berry Gordy's house-plant waterer. Sadly, she was run over by a steam-roller one dark night in Detroit in 1983.

BETTY DAVIS EYES
(Kim Carnes, 1981)
Contact lenses actually.

LONG TALL SALLY
(Little Richard, 1957) and

BRIDGET THE MIDGET
(Ray Stevens, 1971)
In fact these two are one and the same person (Mrs S. B. Wignall, of Bournville, Birmingham BN21 XHP). Both singers suffer from chronic astigmatism.

BILLY JEAN
(Michael Jackson album track)
"Next time I'm gonna use them dang birth control pills," bouncy Billy Jean, a go-go dancer in Trenton, NJ told the *National Enquirer* last year. "That boy shifted 12 million units of Bad and what do I see in child support? Not a cent. Two Christmases ago I got a signed photo of Bubbles. I kept it in Michael Junior's room until some crack dealer torched my apartment last year."

BOBBY'S GIRL
(Susan Maughan, 1962)
The identity of Bobby's girl has attracted as much learned debate as the identity of Shakespeare's dark lady. On the one hand Robin Denselow insists that she is Miriam Piggiwinkle, an Ipswich housewife. But in an authoritative new tome *B.G. Now It Can Be Told*, David Hepworth cites conclusive proof from the Bobby Darin archives that in fact Bobby's Girl was none other than Sharon Smith, briefly a check-out chick during the long, lukewarm-with-the-possibility-of-light-showers Summer Of '61 at the Woolworth's pick'n'mix counter in Britain's very own Rock City: Slough.

CAROLINE
(Status Quo, 1973)
A pseudonym for Frances Morrell, the well-known libertarian, minder of her own business, totally unbossy freethinker and hey dude, I mean like good-time girl.

CATERINA
(Perry Como, 1973)
Caterina is the alter ego of Yoko Ono, for whom Perry Como has nurtured a lifelong fascination. Ms Ono is currently a full-time stupendously rich mother-earthing-person who lives in New York and founded the influential new age group Lentils for Peace. She was once married to a man called John Lennon.

Cheeky check-out chick

Now married – fur better, fur worse

▶

CHRISTINE
(Siouxsie and the Banshees, 1980)
In July 1976, *Just 17*'s problem page ran a missive that read: "Help, I am a terminally ugly zit-faced tottie who'll do anything to get attention and make a quick buck. What do you advise? Slaggy Sue, Bromley." Agony aunt Christine Windsor came back, quick as a flash with: "Change your name to Madonna and screw every man you meet for the next ten years." She was immediately fired for being "too futuristic".

CLAIRE
(Paul and Barry Ryan, 1967)
Claire presents the astrology segment on the Sky Lifestyle channel.

CLEMENTINE
(Bobby Darin, 1967)
Clementine introduces the cowboy boots section on Sky Lifestyle channel.

COLETTE
(Billy Fury, 1960)
Colette presents the Derek Bough Gin and Tonic segment on the Sky Lifestyle channel.

DIANE
(Bachelors, 1964)
Diane is anchor-girl on the Batchelor's soup half-hour on the Sky Lifestyle channel. Her husband is a shrub.

Oh, those lacy Sunday afternoons

Go-Go getter, now on Sky TV

DONNA
(Richie Valens, 1959)
Donna Tickinara, the 6' 4" amazon who inspired the eponymous tweeter-busting high-harmony anthem from hell, was working as a go-go dancer when the song was written: a fact curiously omitted from the movie biog of Valens' life. Shortly after her triumph, the muse reappeared as a dogcatcher on the Nixon ticket in the small Tennessee town of Ukelayle (pop. 278).

ELENORE
(Turtles, 1968)
Went up the hill (with Jack) to fetch a pale of water, Jack fell down and broke his crown (E9, dental fans) and now she goes out with some guy from LA. Or am I mixing her up with someone else?

ELEANOR RIGBY
(Beatles, 1966)
Eleanor Rigby was a matron at St John's Boarding School for wayward boys 'n' girlies, c. 1967. She left the country to take up a similar position in the United Arab Emirates in the early Seventies. A person of the same name created a public disturbance in Walthamstow High Street in 1983 and was confined to Broadmoor at Her Majesty's pleasure.

EMMA
(Hot Chocolate, 1974)
Emma is actually the stable-lad's name for Gainsay, Errol Brown's racehorse. Banged a blue-spot on it last time out and, for all I know, it could still be running.

ENOLA GAY
(OMD 1980)
A four-year-old ankle-biter that OMD met on their Apocalypse Wow tour of Japan, 1986. A child dies, a star is born – and Don McCullin is there to take the photograph.

GAYE
(Clifford T. Ward, 1973)
Gaye Somerville is a very nice girl who works in the Theydon Bois High Street branch of Tie Rack. "I don't want to talk about it," she says. "I've put that part of my life behind me now."

GEORGIE GIRL
(The Seekers, 1967)
"You're always window shopping but never stopping to buy," burbled the fresh-faced Ozzie warblers at the acme of the Swinging Sixties. Twenty years later, it was rather a different story when American Express agents caught up with Georgina Crokablabba in Darwin, Northern Territory. Meryl Streep has expressed interest in playing her in the movie.

GLORIA
(Laura Branigan, King, Patti Smith, U2 album tracks)
Gloria was the ultimate super-groupie – examine those backstage pix carefully and there she is: helping Branigan complete the *Country Life* crossword behind the scenes at the Hammersmith Odeon, changing Smith's lightbulbs at the Portobello Hotel, fixing King's teeth at the Iris Murdoch home for resting rockers – and adjusting Bono's intimate apparel on a rock in Donnegal. Rumoured to be none other than Monotony Maker's Steve Sutherland in drag.

JEAN GENIE
(David Bowie, 1972)
Jean Genie is actually a pseudonym for David Bowie during his 'interesting' period: the only person who 'understood' the 'controversial artiste' at that 'time'.

JENNIFER ECCLES
(Hollies, 1968)
The fat, flatulent granny who runs Old Baldies Pie'n Liquor Store, North Road, SE26. The boys only wrote the song to repay an extensive bill they'd run up while waiting to become rich.

KITTY
(Cat Stevens, 1967)
A financial PR in Iran. Have you ever tried financial PRing in a yashmak?

LAYLA
(Derek and the Dominoes album track)
Patti Boyd. Crikey, everybody knows that.

MARY OF THE FOURTH FORM
(Boomtown Rats, 1977)
Became Paula of the sixth form.

MANDY
(Barry Manilow album track)
Mandy LaFox, *Playboy*'s Miss July 1975, is reliably reported to be the real reason for Barry Manilow's now total celibacy. Behind his perfumed quiff and almost plausible imitation of Liberace – heartbreak. After their romance finally floundered in 1981, Mandy ran the Hot LaFox talk show on KSMUT radio, which was taken over by Oral Roberts last year. Mandy now breeds snails near Düsseldorf.

MONY MONY

(Tommy James, Billy Idol and Amazulu, 1968-1987)

Litigation is still still pending following Miss Mony Mony Martindale's lawyers' £678 billion claim that Billy Idol, Tommy James and Amazulu's "merciless harassment" of their client lead to "irreparable career damage, irreversible downward social mobility and shunning by right right-thinking members of society and disrespect among her peer group resulting in consequent consequent emotional distress under 82 heads, listed herewith c'mon yeah yeah yeah" following the loss of her job as a cleaner in the WEA canteen.

ROXANNE

(The Police, 1979)

Once she realised it was no longer necessary to turn on the red light, she switched to stickers that say Call 555-7667 and ask for Rowena.

ROSIE

(Joan Armatrading, 1978)

Now a scrumptious newsreader and television personality not working for the Sky Lifestyle channel.

RUBY

(Kenny Rogers, 1969)

She did take her love to town and her old man blew her away with an Uzi when she got back.

SARA

(Fleetwood Mac, 1979)

Sara Cruzadio writes, in green ink no less, from The Lyndsey Buckinghamshire Rehab Clinic, Marin County, CA: "Hi dudes and pet rocks and citizens of Planet Earth! I'm currently re-evaluating my life potential as a channeller! Just for the record I'd like to say I'd rather Fleetwood Mac than Applejack or eat Big Mac! Is that a wrap? Can I have some money now? Excellent."

SHERRY

(Four Seasons, 1962)

She's that crazy woman sitting next to you on the tube, the subway, the metro, the last non-smoking seat on the midnight flight to Georgia. Her breath smells foul and she says disturbing, peculiar things.

SYLVIA

(Focus, 1973)

Another clog-wearing, chocolate-munching, lace-curtain-peeping, dope-smoking, bicycle-riding, addle-brained, muesli-breathed, emotionally-overwrought burgeress in the urban bio-mess called Amsterdam.

SYLVIA'S MOTHER

(Dr Hook, 1972)

As above, but with stretchmarks.

TWINKLE

(Terry, 1964)

Gone to that great big Harley factory in the sky.

VERONICA

(Elvis Costello, 1989)

Elvis Costello's gran – more displaced rock star guilt.

Chains of love

Missing slink

How can I sell my hous
Is it possible to divorc
I've been burgled. How d
smack his teeth in
What's the best way to hot
I want to take up dog
Is there a decent mas
What's the access
Express computer
How can I sto
ozone layer
We're drifting apart
process
I am an alcoholic and

what's your

Every Sunday, you shamble round to the newsagent to buy *The Sunday Times*. Does this make you a sophisticate? No. It makes you a victim. What is more, it makes you a *guilty* victim. You are very unhappy. Things trouble you. *The Sunday Times* knows what these things are, and what to do about them.

It is no good sitting there thinking you are happy. That will not do at all. As you stride down the road to the newsagent's, you may be thinking: *What a nice day! Listen to the birds! No work until tomorrow! When I get back I shall have a hot bath, then I shall talk to my wife until lunch-time. Then I'll do a few odd jobs. It is good to be alive*! But you are mistaken.

Underneath yesterday's shirt, your heart is labouring horribly against a glutinous tide of cholesterol. You are not breathing easily enough, you are balding and the hair that remains is riddled with scurf, you are coming down with a cold and your constipation is making your piles worse. Indigestion is eating you up, you are still biting your nails, you smell and your breath is bad. You are failing to cope with the seven year itch, but you can't have an affair because you are unsuccessful with women and anyway Aids is a worldwide danger. There's always incest, rape and other forms of sexual abuse, but you would still have to overcome premature ejaculation. The best thing would be to dress up in women's clothes (a mainly male quirk) and abuse yourself in the privacy of your room but that, too, is fraught with dangers, mostly to do with losing your reserves of zinc.

You can forget chatting with your wife, as well. Your marriage is a minefield. You are failing to balance work and home, you are not coping with jealousy, you lack self-confidence and your energy level is low. You are unable to make friends and you cannot share. You have failed to ▶

without my wife knowing?
one's children?
track down the bastard and

wire a Porsche?
fighting. How do I go about it?
sage parlour in Wallasey?
code for the American

people talking about the

How can I accelerate the

don't give a damn.

problem?

MICHAEL BYWATER dials W for worry and seeks the answers to all his neuroses in *The Sunday Times Guide Lines*

STAGES IN MITOTIC DIVISION

1. Prophase

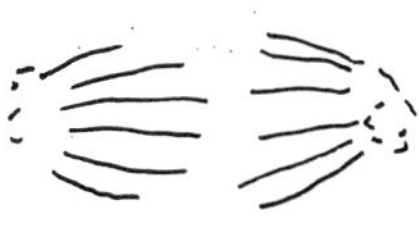

2. Anaphase

3. Metaphase

4. Analysis

5. Court Order

6. Visitation

Krimstein

improve your memory and half the time you cannot recall your wife's name; no wonder you are crippled with shyness. Before long it will be personal injury, separation, divorce and maintenance, rows about children's custody, trouble with the neighbours, credit blacklists, drink-driving and Powers of Arrest.

How lucky you are to have *The Sunday Times* to help, to understand, to counsel, sympathise and (let us be frank) to apportion blame. For all this is your fault. You have failed to get to grips with your life. The light shed upon the extent of your pathological delinquency has hitherto been sporadic. Once a week, you have been forced to confront your guilt about cancer, heart disease and impotence. Each Sunday, you are thrust, wriggling, into the foaming nexus of late twentieth-century morality with its searing challenges. Sometimes they are almost negligible: are you risking premature senility from your aluminium coffee pot? Sometimes, they are, quite literally, global: you are screwing up the entire planet; what are you going to do about it?

In Maoist China, anguished self-criticism was a monthly event in the village hall. Here, things are better; thanks to modern communications technology and boundless greed, you can lacerate your conscience *at any hour of the day or night.* No need to wait for Sunday; you can participate any time you find yourself near a telephone with *The Sunday Times Guide Lines* booklet to hand. *Two hundred and ninety five things to worry about*, available at the touch of a button and a pound or so a time, insinuated directly into your innocent ear, often *in the very voice of medical correspondent Neville Hodgkinson himself.* Truly an offer you cannot refuse. You would not be able to live with the guilt, the self-loathing, the shame, the dishonour, the disgust, *the smell*, God damn it, if you did.

Now, let's dial those numbers and find out exactly what* The Sunday Times Guide Lines *have to say about…

Female sexual response

We were excited to see what Neville has to say about this. "None, in my experience" would have been the answer most ethically consistent with his own position on the matter, but instead he makes it all seem just as unattractive as it really is: a measles-like rash which will disappear at orgasm (E.T.A. 1992, on average); involuntary twitching; screaming, lip-biting, moaning. This all sounds a bit like wishful thinking, but we come back to ground-level: "Often there is no arousal at all… this may happen in most long-term relationships. No woman can possibly remain aroused by the same man for years on end." Years? Months, more like. Well, that's that then. Back to the stamp collection.

★★★★★★★★★★★★

Masturbation – a cautionary note

They changed the number on this one; a frightfully brisk female voice like an American Express "customer service" woman told us, "To hear the Guide Line tape on Masturbation, please call 0898-555 623." It was rather exciting, actually, like being directed to a nasty cathouse or a Patpong Road vegetable cabaret. The tape itself was all about zinc. Galvanising stuff. Lack of zinc makes you go blind, mad, spotty and sterile. Constant, er, masturbation can lead to heart attacks. In a lifetime of this, you could lose enough zinc to galvanise a shed. It "can become a kind of drug in much the same way as" – all together now – "alcohol and cigarettes". In the long-term it can lead to "a build-up of stress in the system". (What system? How?) It is not satisfying for long. The less you do it, the less you will want to.
In time the frustration simply vanishes. Definitely something that a mature adult should grow out of. Nothing about hairy palms, but otherwise, come back Lord Baden-Powell, your hour has come round again.

★★★★★★★★★★★★

Gaining self-confidence

Number unobtainable on our first try. It took several hours to pluck up enough courage to have another go. But it was worth it. Original, helpful, searingly un-clichéd advice: "A lack of self-confidence can manifest itself in many different ways," said the Woolwich Girl at the other end. "Have you ever taken a dislike to someone rude and abrasive?" Yes. Oh yes. Also wimps, train-spotters, people who sing bits of Wagner at us in the car, fat entrepreneurs inappropriately dressed in Workers for Freedom bolero jackets, pimps in Ferraris, teetotal non-

smoking vegetarians and members of the Commission for Racial Equality. This is good! This is our meat! Why compete with people who brag?" Yes! Quite! Shut up and listen! "Once you have decided on your most important fault, put it out of your mind. Being as relaxed as possible is important. Try not to rush things. Look at your good points. Maybe you are particularly knowledgeable about one subject in particular." Yes! Computers! Hey everybody, come over here and listen to me!

How to improve your memory

Not an unusual problem. Turning up late for a job interview. Keeping a diary. Making a list. Practise at home. Memorise facts. Forgetting someone's name can be embarrassing. Something else, too... What was it? Mind's a blank. Sorry. Completely gone. Ah well.

★★★★★★★★★★★★

"Yes, by God, my mind is made up! I'm going to grow a beard and wear a Greek fisherman's cap. People respect you when you do things like that."

★★★★★★★★★★★★

Making relationships work

"You're the girl who can get away with the gold lamé cocktail dress with shoulder-pads wider than Sue-Ellen's... making offers no hot-blooded male could resist. You really work at your sexual performance!" A narrow view of relationships, but not without appeal; alas, it appears that we were connected to a horoscope for sex-club artistes born under Leo; redialling produced more startlingly illuminating pabulum, for example: "No two relationships are the same... it takes hard work to maintain a good partnership... discussing everything is

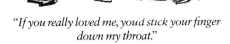

"If you really loved me, you'd stick your finger down my throat."

very important... keeping the lines of communication open... try to get away for a weekend together... are you sure your partner isn't nursing a grudge against you?" No, and who wouldn't frankly?

WHO IS NEVILLE HODGKINSON?

Neville Hodgkinson has neat crinkly hair, a neat crinkly forehead, neat modern glasses and a crinkly, modern voice. He is Worrying Correspondent of *The Sunday Times*. It is the most Serious newspaper of our horribly Serious age, but even it is not Serious enough to be open about having a Worrying Correspondent, so they call Neville the "Medical" correspondent. Life, for Neville, is a dangerous thing and he wants you to realise that, and stop having fun, drugs, money, whisky, deviant sex and package holidays. Neville has been a Worrying Correspondent for twelve years. He is married to Liz Hodgkinson, another Worrying Correspondent. They do not have sex, on purpose. She wrote a book about not having sex. He then wrote an article about how it was all his idea as well. She has now written a book about how marriage is an awful, nonsensical thing. Neville has not yet written his article, but he will.

Neville eats vegetables and does Raja Yoga. This means that the real core of his self, the "I" within, is essentially spiritual, a soul, rather than a brain or body. He is no longer either a beggar or a beast, and is hardly ever a victim of irritability or fear, although his work for the Serious Times abundantly generates both emotions in his readers.

TWENTY THINGS NEVILLE HODGKINSON WORRIES ABOUT AND THAT HE WANTS *SUNDAY TIMES* READERS TO WORRY ABOUT, TOO:

1. A holiday ("Can damage your health")
2. Alcohol ("Threat to babies")
3. Anorexia nervosa ("A family problem")
4. Anti-impotence drugs ("Safety warning")
5. Arthritis drugs ("Cripple, not cure")
6. Brain implants ("Doubts linger")
7. Cars ("Mad drivers in fast lane")
8. Condom failure ("Leads to abortion rise")
9. Contaminated food ("Kills 200 a year")
10. Dog poo ("Park danger to children from parasite that can blind")
11. Heart attacks ("All mother's fault")
12. Low-calorie diets ("Dangerous")
13. Miracle sight operations ("Unsafe")
14. Hospital equipment ("Can kill, not cure")
15. Organ sales ("Puts ethics in the dock")
16. Russian nerve gas ("Used in Angola")
17. Swimming pool parasites ("Pose threats to swimmers")
18. Videos ("Inspire violent urge for nasty side of life")
19. Yuppie flu ("All in the mind, say doctors")
20. Yuppie flu ("Doctors finally prove shirkers really are sick")

SEX AND VEGETABLES IN THE NEVILLE/LIZ LIAISON – A DOZEN FACTS IN THEIR OWN WORDS, AS THE HODGKINSONS TELL US MORE ABOUT THEIR PRIVATE LIFE THAN WE REALLY WISH TO KNOW:

1. Right from the start, negative aspects to the sex drive were apparent to Neville.
2. His perceived need for sex meant that he was becoming increasingly dependent on another person (See *Masturbation: A Cautionary Note*)
3. He found himself, in 1981, in the position either of a beggar or a rapist. Dynamics of this kind started to eat away at his happiness.
4. Neville interpreted Liz's increasing uninterest in sex as a rejection of himself.
5. It took him two to three years before he felt that he was for the most part no longer liable to be troubled by the familiar pattern of sexual arousal.
6. Liz thinks that romance is a bit like eating a Mr Whippy ice cream, but she is not against people forming loving relationships.
7. They had to avoid 'cues' that could set a programme in motion against his will, and that included close physical contact with each other.
8. He finds the emotional economy that celibacy has contributed to his life compensates for the lower energy-input of the strict vegetarian diet that is vital for the maintenance of a celibate life.
9. As he sees it, they are running away from contributing further to the greed, possessiveness, misunderstandings, violence and grief which afflict our society and for which he believes wrong attitudes, expectations and actions in regard to sex are a root cause.
10. Mr E. N. Heaton of East Grinstead wrote and advised Neville to "Get in a dolly bird *au pair* and let Liz listen to *The Archers*". Neville did not take this advice.
11. Liz invited a journalist from *Today* to meet her in Cranks health food restaurant.
12. The more she thought about marriage, the more she realised what nonsense it is.

▶

Turning your home into income

Nobody home when we rang.

****

Getting a good night's sleep

Another encounter with the wonderful Neville Hodgkinson, the Cassandra of Wapping. Continuing exposure to Hawksmoor's brooding church of St George in the East seems to have exerted a malign influence upon Neville, perhaps explaining his use, in speech, of the antique "long 's'". To stay healthy and happy, says Neville, "we all need a good night's ſleep . . . deep ſleep where your body repairs itself and builds bones". We should supply ourselves with a "firm clean mattress – no squishy featherbeds and absolutely no messy, er, ſtains – and have a hot milky drink, which contains tryptophan". Tryptophan makes the brain produce serotonin which makes us go to sleep. Fish contain tryptophan, too. Who will be first to the market with a fish-flavoured milky drink? Breathe deeply. Say "Calm in, stress out" with each breath. Do not be surprised when your bedmate rejects your advances. Lying next to a fishy, milky, deep-breathing mutterer exerts a depressive effect upon the libido of even the most dedicated eroticist.

****

Getting rid of bad breath

Smokers almost always have bad breath, says Neville. You should ask a relative or close friend to tell you candidly. On a fast, bad breath is caused by the rapid elimination of toxins from the body. Who the hell goes on fasts? Sunday Times *readers, of course. They also go easy on mucus-forming foods and are aware that teetotal, non-smoking vegetarians don't get bad breath even first thing in the morning. Now who does that remind us of?*

****

The menopause – both sexes

This means no more monthly periods, says Neville. The worst symptoms can be avoided by embarking on a vegetarian diet. Women often come into their own after the menopause. Their own what? Neville doesn't say. Nor does he mention men. The both sexes bit is either an oversight or a marketing ploy. Clever.

****

Getting ahead at work

Are you bright, reassuring and professional? Stuck in a rut? Prepare the ground. Take an interest in the way the company is run. Suggest new ways of working. Follow this advice and you will last about three weeks.

****

Making friends

This message mentions (a) amateur dramatics, (b) evening classes and (c) making an effort to meet other parents. Nothing more need be said.

****

How to be a success with men

"Seeing men as a race apart is a mistake. Being successful with men means treating them as individuals." Nonsense. Men are collectivist aliens and only interested in one thing. Give it to them with no fuss and no conversation and you can't go wrong.

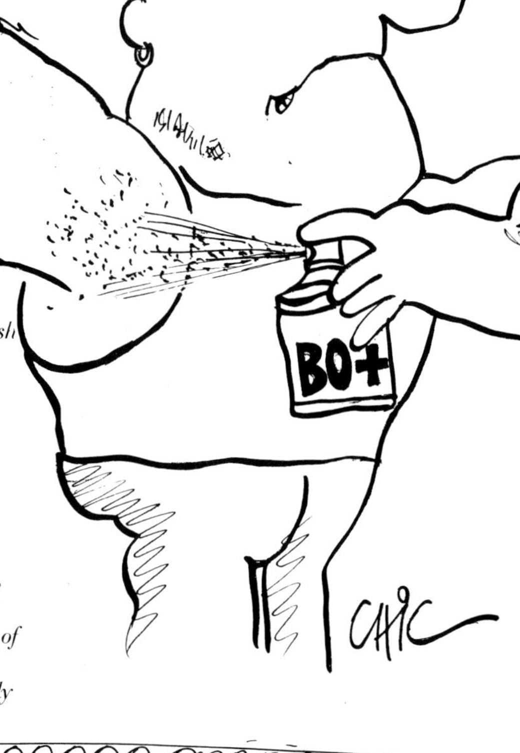

****

How to be a success with women

"Money and glamour aren't enough. Honesty is the best policy. Try reversing the roles [see "Transvestitism: a mainly male quirk"]. Relax and try not to rush things. Try not to be disheartened if you are rejected." There. All you need to know, you collectivist sodding aliens.

****

The Civil Service: keeping government going

Attempt 1: Engaged. Attempt 2: Number out of service. Attempt 3: Skiing in Switzerland. Attempt 4: No reply. This message was clearly designed by someone who knew his subject.

"We like him to get plenty of exercise."

Punch Lines – helping you to help yourself

Are you worried about the cost of your mortgage, or your child's school progress? Do you have a health problem? Would you like to know more about it before you see a doctor?

For God's sake stop whining. Life is a mess. Learn to live with it, or shut up. You are only worried because you are a neurotic, ill-informed conformist with a mind like a damp biscuit. Forget what people think about you. Stop worrying about your family and friends; they're just a pack of leeches and it's time they stood on their own feet. From now on, all you have to worry about is getting caught. Punch Lines offer you non-factual, anecdotal and often rather brutal reinforcements of all those prejudices you've been ashamed of for far too long. They tell you what YOU want to hear. Keep this directory handy. Next time some boring, serious person in Timberland shoes asks you what you are doing about the environment, roll it up and poke it up his nose.

PERSONAL FINANCE

Jason "The Knife" Tyson, Finance Editor of *Punch*, has been in personal finance all his working life, and has just completed an extended field-trip on the Isle of Wight. He is well known in finance and security circles for his innovative, free-ranging approach.

- You and that bastard, your bank manager 0897-333 100
- Turning family silver into hard cash 0897-333 101
- Trading in partly-used bearer securities 0897-333 102
- The Black Economy – everyone's at it, eh? 0897-333 103
- Complaining without words 0897-333 104

MEDICAL AND SEXUAL

Willy McHuge, our Medical and Sexual Adviser, is a GP on the Scottish island of Yech. A six foot two alcoholic with legs like tree-trunks and a head like a log, Will McHuge disnae hauld with any of this new fangled nonsense. A good bellyful of meat and spuds washed down with Monster's Choice twice a day is all you need to keep fit. That, and a virgin once a week. What was guid enough for the Da is surely guid enough for him.

- Venereal disease – serves ye right 0897-333 106
- Cancer – dinna worry about it 0897-333 107
- Problem teenagers – a clip roond the ear 0897-333 108
- Dandruff – ach for Christ's sake, mon 0897-333 109
- Alcoholism – a wee dram never hurt a soul 0897-333 110
- Masturbation – ye'll gang blind 0897-333 111
- Female sexual response – nae sich thing 0897-333 112
- Incest – worst in summer 0897-333 113
- Incest – och, sorry, thought ye said "insects" 0897-333 114
- Transvestitism – get oot of ma surgery, poof 0897-333 115
- Smoking – the Da smoked 100 a day all his life 0897-333 116

LIFE ADVICE

- Telling people where to get off 0897-333 117
- Stealing a whole bunch of stuff 0897-333 118
- Getting away with murder 0897-333 119
- The seven year itch – buggering off 0897-333 120
- Spending what you haven't got 0897-333 121
- Bribery and shouting 0897 333 122

LAW

- Where they can stick their summonses 0897-333 123
- Where they can stick their maintenance orders 0897-333 124
- Where they can stick their warrants 0897-333 125
- Lawyers? Dullards in their fathers' suits 0897-333 126
- Where they can stick their fathers' suits 0897-333 127

EDUCATION

- School's just for cissies 0897-333 128
- I never went to university and look at me now 0897-333 129

THE ENVIRONMENT

- Pollution – it's not your fault 0897-333 130
- Acid rain – no problem, really 0897-333 132
- The ozone layer – nothing you can do about it 0897-333 133

"I'm afraid cook was in one of her moods today."

"In my opinion, what lies at the root of all your problems is that you inhabit a fantasy world."

"Bless him, he has such an endearing honesty."

"Taxi for . . . It looks like a Mr and Mrs Rhinoceros."

"This is going to be bloody awkward – they've never used a defensive strategy before."

"The channel tunnel should ease the housing problem."

"Mr McGregor's got a Flymo!"

MAN and BEAST

Punch's cartoonists escape from the human zoo

"Oh my God! It's the wife!"

Unsolicited Masterpieces

Every morning a team of lavishly uniformed flunkeys place a groaning pile of manuscripts on to a priceless silver salver. They deliver it to the Editor's throne-room, there to await the scrutiny of Mr Punch's most trusted advisors and companions. These manuscripts, sent in by Mr P.'s devoted followers the whole world over, have traditionally been given scant attention before being callously disposed of. But no more. For now MARCUS BERKMANN has been entrusted with the task of selecting the finest examples of our readers' work for this unique showcase presentation, dedicated to the memory of the Unknown Contributor

"I-I-I-I-I-like you very much" – not a typical sentence from the massive piles of unsolicited manuscripts received daily in the *Punch* offices, but certainly one containing the requisite number of personal pronouns.

"It was my particular misfortune earlier this week to find myself on what I believe they call a commuter train."

So starts Andy Robinson's piece on "Commuting: an experiment", which, like many, is based on personal experience. Most people write of what they know, and what they know best is what they did about five minutes ago. So they write it, and they send it in. But is it funny? Is it well written? Is it original? And please, please, is it something other than an incredibly bad poem?

Punch, with its legendary reputation as a purveyor of jokes, japes, chuckles and chortles to the gentry, attracts a pretty bizarre range of contribution. Incredibly bad poems, for instance, are rarely if ever published in the magazine, but that does not stop incredibly bad poets sending them in by the skipload.

Then again, an extraordinary number of people write in and say how tremendously interesting their lives are, and would we like a regular column? It can be hard to know how to answer this, although "No" is generally the favoured option.

Personal experience, for sure, rarely travels well. Indian gentlemen writing about the vagaries of the subcontinental civil service, expat ladies describing the gripping vicissitudes of expat life (i.e. nothing to do but lots to drink) and pieces called "How I became a window cleaner" have much to overcome. But this does not discourage everyone. Vida Herbison, for instance, cheerfully discusses her piles at some length in "Even The Romans Suffered from Them":

"I didn't discover my piles in the jungle, I discovered them at the end of the war, sitting on a cold, hard ambulance seat. I was so young and unsophisticated that I couldn't even imagine why that part of my anatomy suddenly throbbed and itched as if I'd been stung by an army of ants." After further stomach-churning detail of the sort that a Channel 4 continuity announcer would describe as "explicit", she continues, "The word 'piles', I later discovered, is derived from *pila* – the Latin for ball. Roman ladies held small amber balls in their hands to keep them cool." When she enters the nursing home ("How well worth it is to sacrifice a bottle of gin a week for private health insurance"), her nurse warns her, "Don't worry if you can't feel your bottom when you wake up." Apparently Napoleon too suffered the condition. "Could that really be why he lost the Battle of Waterloo?"

Whatever you write about, though, you must maximise your chances of success, and that has to start with the covering letter. Here are some recent examples.

"As a regular subscriber to Punch I have noticed the appalling dearth of interesting and witty articles of late." (S. Hildebrand)

"In our household, *Punch* was always something that remained in its Cellophane wrapper collecting dust until it was relegated to the downstairs loo. The articles remained unread except in cases of chronic constipation." (Justin Ratcliffe)

"Please find enclosed the typescript of a short piece submitted for publication in *Punch* – I do realise it would have been more topical last year." (Geoff Norman)

Sometimes, it's impossible to stop despair creeping in, as in Ted Phillips's one-line letter:

"I know you will return this to me if you don't think it's funny."

Nothing, though, can even hope to rival the raw, spine-tingling horror of Alan R. Cooper's initial sales pitch:

"Please find enclosed a short article for your consideration which should strike a chord with a great many company car drivers."

Occasionally, aspiring contributors include a curriculum vitae:

"Collections of his writings are:
THE GENTLE ART OF CAMOUFLAGE
Prosepoems, 21pp., Fetish Books, 1980
THE STEEP DESCENT TO PARADISE
Stories, letters and articles, 30pp., Appliance Books, 1981" and so forth, even including critical comment as well:

"'Keith Dersley can pull off some very witty and amusing pieces when he wants to, and the amazing thing is... he makes it look as easy as pie.' Chuck Connor, *In Defiance Of Medical Opinion*."

His story, "Nor Iron Bars Knox Road", is no less bizarre. Short stories make up a large proportion of Punch's unsolicited stuff, even though the magazine does not publish them. They range from leaden political satires, through cosy episodes of rustic life to literary parody, a form that has afflicted even the most talented of writers down the ages – as readers of David Lodge's novels will testify. G. H. Frampton's Sherlock Holmes parody, "The Toothbrush Mystery", isn't too accurate, but it has some good jokes:

"Sometimes I get a bit fed up with Holmes and his deductions. Even when Mrs Hudson came in with our meal he couldn't resist showing off.

"'Ah! Mrs Hudson,' he exclaimed, rubbing his hands. 'Beans on toast, splendid. However I notice that you had to cook the baked beans twice and that your cooker exploded.'

"'Oh go on, Mr Holmes,' laughed Mrs Hudson, 'how could you possibly know all that?'

"'Firstly,' said Holmes, 'I heard the explosion. Secondly, your dress is scorched all down one side and thirdly, you have baked beans all over your hair.'"

Back in the realms of non-fiction (which *Punch* actually does publish), Mark Cullen has contributed a number of unsolicited bits and bobs. Mr Cullen is cross. Very Cross. He fancies a regular column: "What Do You Do for A Living, Exactly? – our regular column of sneering at the slightly famous."

He also supplies us with his very own gossip column, "Nigel Earwax's Diary", "Lord Olivier's latest daughter Xerxes, 19, is doing incredibly well. Her performance as Haemorrhage in Chekhov's 'Testicle' at the Lyric has been acclaimed as 'astonishing'. Xerxes, who shares a Fulham flat with her boyfriend Piers Excess-Tippex, 23, is spending Christmas at home with her father, who calls her 'a massively talented actress' and greets allegations of nepotism with the simple message 'B****cks'... Sexy actress Lysette Anthony, 24, elegant, pert, stylish, gorgeous legs, curvaceous oh all right I fancy ▶

They range from leaden political satires, through cosy episodes of rustic life to literary parody, a form that has afflicted even the most talented of writers down the ages – as readers of David Lodge's novels will testify.

► her, went shopping on Wednesday. 'Just Safeways,' giggles the really quite edible young beauty, 'I bought some French mustard. I usually have Colmans, but I fancied a change'... Massively talented restaurateur, artist, furniture restorer, whatever he's up to. Viscount Linley had a shock last week when his mother Princess Margaret stubbed her cigarette out in his face. 'She thought it was an ashtray,' said a spokesman. Beautiful actress Lysette Anthony, 24, posted a letter yesterday. Multi-talented Lysette, star of BBC1's splendid *Three Up Two Down*, is also able to buy stamps when necessary. She mastered the art some years ago. The yummy gorgeous lovely absolutely delightful young nymphette."

Michael Collins is another who wants his own column, but unlike most of the others he's sometimes very funny. "Since escaping beaten but not stirred from a Camberwell comprehensive in the punk summer of '77, I have made many attempts at divorcing myself from that phase of my personal history. At one time it was suggested that I change my name to a nickname out of school hours. But somehow 'pixie-eared pansy' didn't have quite the right ring to it. As it happened, only one person ever called me that anyway: my father, when he came home early and caught me trying on my mother's 'stays'." He rails against "Steves". "Steves osmoregulate. They split into student Steves and form clubs where the password is 'member'. Initially, one of the most notable characteristics of a Steve is his speech impediment. He can get his tongue around absolutely anything except other boys' Christian names. Anthony becomes 'Tone', Michael becomes 'Mick', Terence 'Tel' and Nigel 'Bender'. I am not now and have never been a Mick. A Mick's conversation is peppered with references to 'away wins' and 'points on aggregate'. My intense dislike of competitive sport was just one of the many idiosyncrasies that separated me from the Steves. When they were pulling the legs off spiders, I was pulling the sponge off cup cakes."

Other writers have hobby horses to ride, and can be just as cross as Mark Cullen. Roy MacGregor-Hastie has it in for literary criticism ("quirky and corrupt"). "More dangerous during the first half of the century was the invasion of public life, including public intellectual life, by homosexuals. The literary homosexuals manufactured reputations and destroyed others as easily as their fellow Oxbridge graduates Burgess, Maclean, Blunt, Philby and the rest destroyed the credibility of the security services. The famous chef of one of my clubs, the Reform, noted that public schoolboys, on their way to Oxbridge or not, seemed to have their sensibilities blunted at both ends, by evil food and sodomy..." Moving on, he observes that, "a stranger sort of slime, the lower class boys who oozed into Oxford and Cambridge during and after the Second World War, has combined to beautify one of their number recently. Their choice, Philip Larkin, is puzzling. Their motive is perhaps clearer. They 'only just go to Oxford in time', as one of them put it to me. The decline of standards of undergraduate teaching at Oxford, not to speak of the damage done by homosexual spies and other traitors and perverts, has gone so far that only the father of a mediocre boy would send him there, hoping for a mediocre job in the Ministry of Agriculture and Fisheries."

This sort of thing is unlikely ever to appear in *Punch* (except that it just has done). But what else shouldn't you do if you're planning to write for the magazine? After many hours trawling through the scripts, here are my handy hints 'n' tips for the aspiring funster:

- No articles about the perils of motoring. Please. Pretty please.
- Nothing about What You Did On Your Holidays.
- No poems, please. "Funny" poetry is not funny.
- Do not fall for the temptation and write about how wonderful your computer is. Only Douglas Adams can ever get away with this, and there are those who'd say he can't.
- Rip-offs of other people's ideas (the Willie books, Loadsamoney, etc) are never as funny as they were the first time around.
- Look, please, don't send us any more poems. How many times do I have to say this?
- Simply inserting the word "bleeding" into a passage of demotic speech does not a joke make.
- If *Punch* has already published a piece or two about listeria and salmonella, it's unlikely to want another 6,453 on the same subject.
- No country diaries of simple rustic folk, thank you very much. And finally:
- Send us any more poems and we'll shoot off your kneecaps. *Comprende?* ■

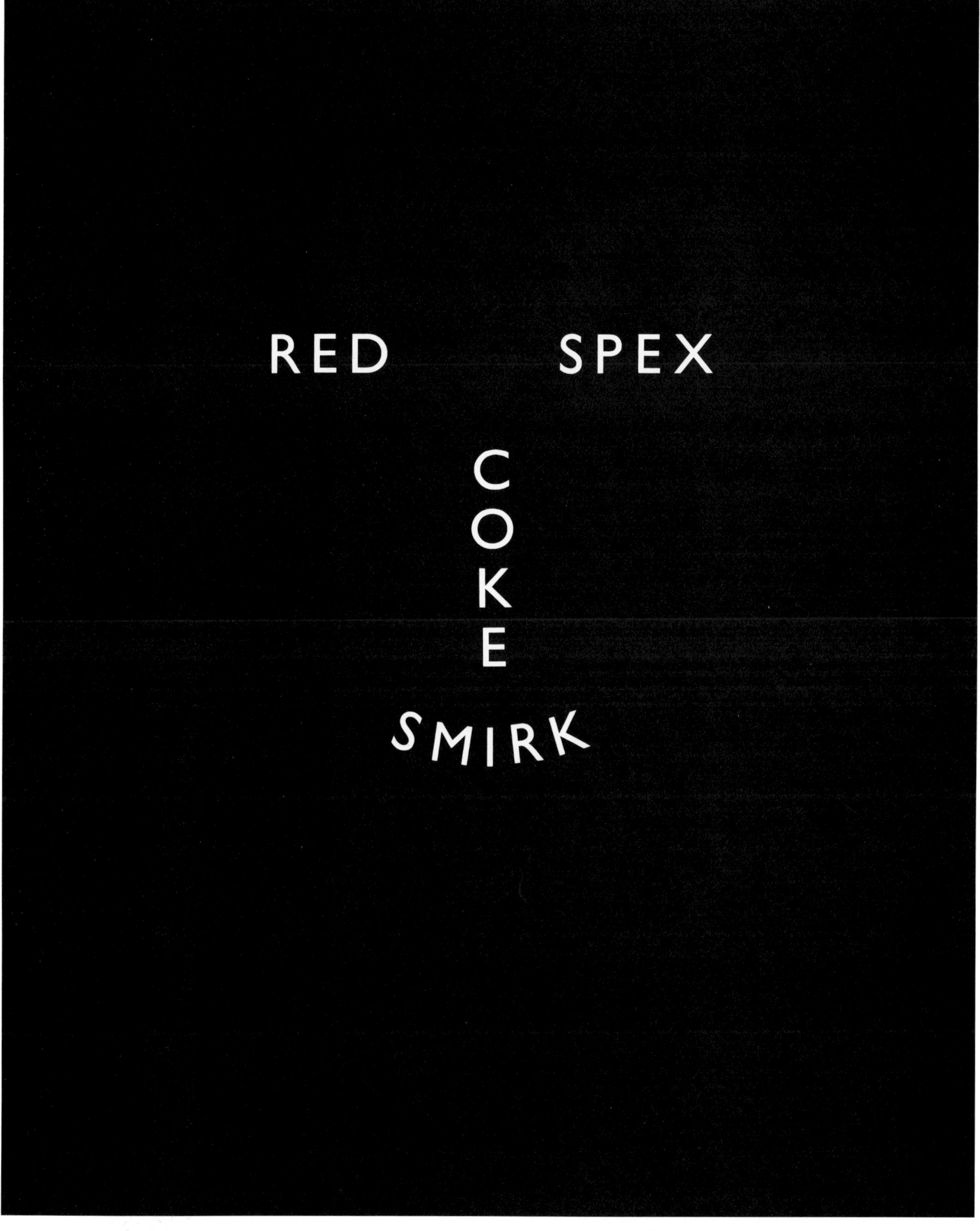

HOW TO RECOGNISE SOMEONE IN ADVERTISING

We all know how devastating the effects of ADS can be. But are you sure you could recognise someone in advertising, the people who give us ADS?

The fact is, people can work in advertising for years without any signs developing. During this time they may look perfectly normal.

But every day they are passing on ADS to more and more people. Thousands in this country are unaware that they have been infected with meaning-free ADS.

Obviously the more television you watch and magazines you read the more chance you have of being contaminated. But less contact with the media is only part of the answer. It also means using your brain. ADS are now a fact of life. And while infection may be impossible to recognise, fortunately it is possible to avoid.

soap

How the bubbles burst

Ends that were sorry but not spectacular: Brian Tilsley, Pam Ewing, Dirty Den, Andy O'Brien, Ena Sharples, Len Fairclough, Laura Gordon-Davi

Farewell then, Dirty Den of Walford; the latest soapland victim to bite the dust or – in his case – cop a good few pints of East End canal. Is Den, as we speak, en route to oblivion, toes-up and meandering towards that great lock-keeper in the sky? Who knows? All we do know is that around 20 million viewers – many of whom were still reeling from Brian Tilsley's untimely end in Coronation Street just the week before – tuned in for Den's demise, remote control in one hand, Kleenex in the other. It was to be a soap departure of epic, "A Nation Mourns" lines; Worthing to Wigan, not a dry eye in the lounge.

Only instead, as *The Sun* recalled – unrivalled critics as they are in the popular drama field – "it became the biggest let-down in TV history". To sum up the event in a nutshell: a gun appears from a bunch of daffs, the screen goes blank and a subsequent splash heralds hapless Den's dive towards the said canal. No blood, no body, none of those tear-jerking

Shoot them, burn them, stab them ... they keep coming back. Are soap stars the zombies of television? CAROL PRICE knows where the bodies are buried

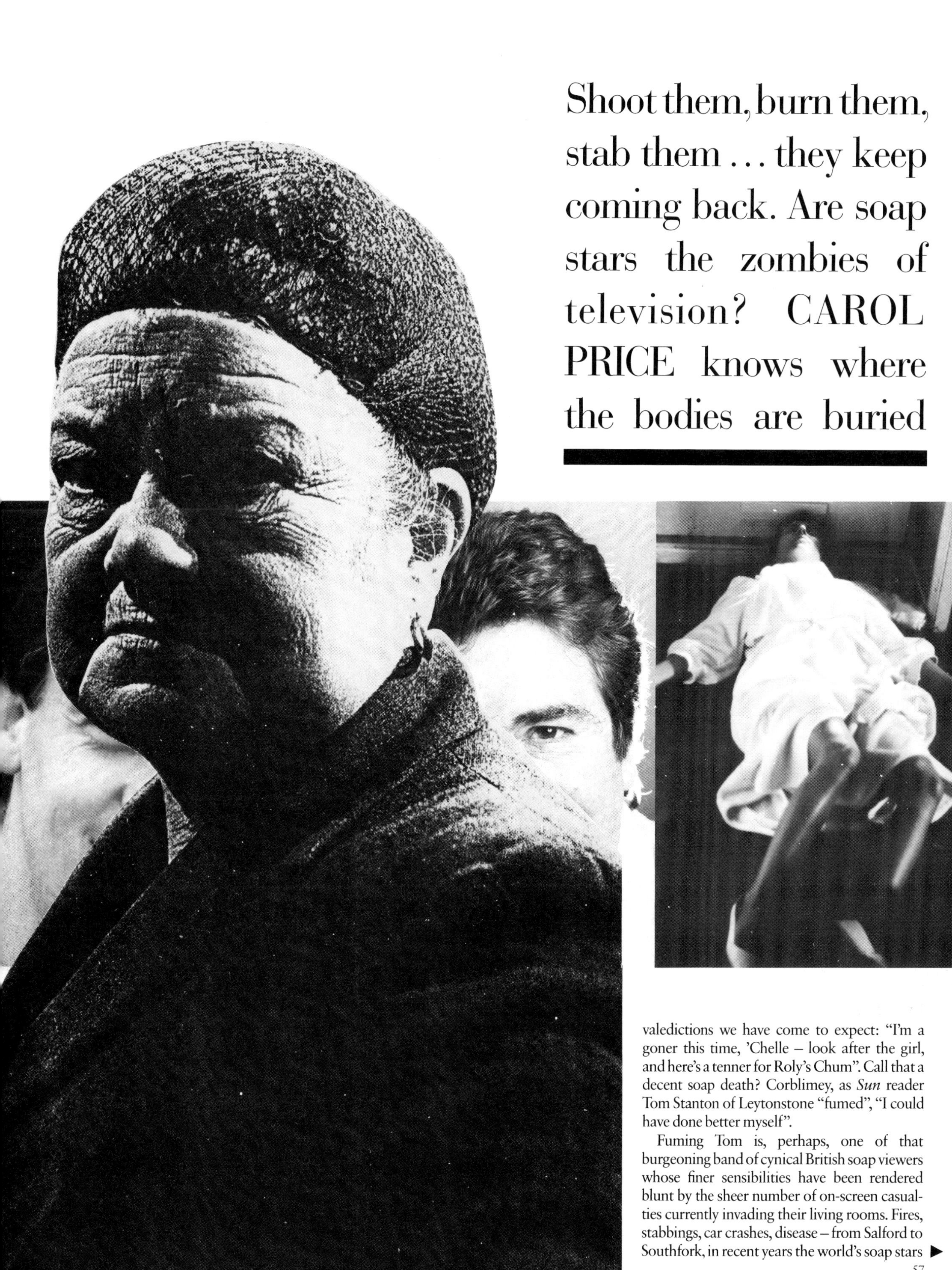

valedictions we have come to expect: "I'm a goner this time, 'Chelle – look after the girl, and here's a tenner for Roly's Chum". Call that a decent soap death? Corblimey, as *Sun* reader Tom Stanton of Leytonstone "fumed", "I could have done better myself".

Fuming Tom is, perhaps, one of that burgeoning band of cynical British soap viewers whose finer sensibilities have been rendered blunt by the sheer number of on-screen casualties currently invading their living rooms. Fires, stabbings, car crashes, disease – from Salford to Southfork, in recent years the world's soap stars ▶

have been dropping faster than you can say "Ena Sharples".

Naturally enough, in the wake of such global and persistent massacre, a chap begins to evince a certain compassion-fatigue. If these soap bods are going to keep exiting screen left with such tedious regularity, couldn't they at least put a bit of *spectacle* into it? – something a touch more exotic than the mundane clogs-popping he could hear down the pub any night.

Increasingly too, of course, the Fuming Toms of this world have come to suspect that most soap characters are pretty much indestructible anyway. Gone are the days when that lid on the coffin stayed down. What happens now? They die and then they come back.

Sometimes they come back looking pretty much as they did before – give or take the odd new hairdo that you would overlook after a year in the shower or long-term residence in an Amazonian sanatorium. And sometimes they appear to have been completely remodelled by master surgeons (eg Miss Ellie or Fallon Carrington) without their nearest and dearest suspecting a thing.

Such events take a credibility toll on viewers. JR gets shot yet again, and who cares? The man must have absorbed more bullets already than the average Paras' firing range. And who would still believe that Joan Collins' Alexis could die now even if she were chopped into chunks and padlocked in a strong box in the hold of a crashing space rocket?

To a great extent, soaps have become victims of their own success. They make their characters into "stars" – and when those stars move on to develop highly-publicised personalities distinct from their soap personas, the public whiffs a rather twee conspiracy of pretence. Why should they wring their emotions dry over the death of this week's soap victim when they know that in only a matter of days the departed will be popping back up – usually on *Wogan*'s settee to flog their panto season and diet book? Or, as in the case of Chris Quinten (Brian Tilsley), in the tabloid press: "I was *bored* with *Coronation Street*, *bored* with the life as a so-called celebrity ... Tomorrow: Why Julie Goodyear Called Me a Sex Pest".

Deaths, however, have to go on in the land of soap, character culling being an occupational hazard of the genre. Every year, a certain number must mysteriously disappear (as we have noted) and an additional percentage get definitively terminated – our chart shows the whole horrific scale of the recent pogrom. So, in these enlightened times, with a more aware and demanding audience, and a cast that will insist on endless cavalier to-ing and fro-ing about, let us have some sympathy for the TV scriptwriters whose job it is to play the grim reaper with any kind of plausible and spectacular effect. For years now, they've been stuck on a treadmill with the same quintet of old favourites; car crashes, stabbings, fire, shootings and, of course, unspecific illness.

They have flirted with the topical Aids. There was a time, for instance, when it seemed that soapland's best-known gays (Gordon in *Brookside* and Colin in *EastEnders*) could have been afflicted; all the signs were there – but then the writers seemingly got cold feet. It would have

TOP FIVE CHARACTERS FOR THE CHOP
Daphne (Neighbours). ***A disaster of a vehicular collision kind has been intimated for our Daphne, mother of Jamie, wife of Des. Chances are the emotional fall-out will inumbrate Ramsay Street for minutes, if not days.***
Colin (*Michael Cashman* – EastEnders). ***To date, our Col has merely got MS and disappeared. Does this sound like a man with a future?***
Donna (*Matilda Zeigler* – EastEnders). ***This morbid misfit, sunk as low in streetlife squalor as BBC scriptwriters' imaginations permit, has been looking on her way out for so long now we can only hope the end will be quick.***
Sue Ellen (*Linda Gray* – Dallas). ***Will it be the car smash, mystery illness or assassination squad of aggrieved Scotch manufacturers that claims Texas's most enduring lush this April? Some say it's in the lap of the Gods. Others say, if Linda gets a new contract of an alleged £45,000 a show she'll doubtless prove immortal.***
Alexis (*Joan Collins* – Dynasty). ***The rumours will keep persisting that Joanie's on her way out. Can it really be? The woman with the bulletproof Armanis and fire-resistant wigs? What soap scriptwriter has ever faced such a challenge? Something ultra-spectacular with nuclear warheads seems the only recourse.***

DOUBLE-TAKES
Characters who got surgically transmogrified – left a series in one guise and returned as baffling imposters:
***Miss Ellie, Jock Ewing* and – it looks likely – *Pammy Ewing* (Dallas)**
***Lucy Collins* and *Gordon Collins* (Brookside)**
***Steven Carrington* and *Fallon Carrington* (Dynasty). Not to be confused with *Krystle*, who – still more bewildering – played her own double**
***Lucy Robinson* (Neighbours)**
But we're not fooled are we; where are those missing bodies?

been a lengthy and unpleasant business. Perhaps they'll have better luck with a pioneering case of Bovine Spongiform Encephalopathy. Come to think of it, those meat pies Madge knocks out in Ramsay Street have often looked a bit crook to me.

Perhaps readers might like to offer their own suggestions with regard to interesting deaths, and the soap characters who might most be due them. Let us rally round, as it were, to get a Campaign for Realistic Deaths (if soaps must continue to have them so frequently) on the road; give a nudge to the apparent creative impasse. All we can hope for meanwhile is that neither Dirty Den, nor Brian Tilsley, will ever return to haunt our screens. The thought of "Brain Dead" Brian, having been stabbed to a pulp in a nightclub brawl, strutting back down The Street, rehashed like Frankenstein with – one of his car mechanic's spanners through the neck, for good effect – is likely to be more than I (and certainly any *Sun* reader) could stand.

DISAPPEARING ACTS

Characters who were the life and soul of the set-up one minute, and then suddenly vanished without trace.

From *EastEnders: Mags* (Kathryn Apanowicz) – missing since March '88; last seen driving a Honda vanload of vol-au-vents out of Albert Square.

***Lofty* (Tom Watt) – missing since April '88. A bitter man with dire domestic problems – not the least being his taste in wallpaper – and a skill for self-preservation on a par with an egg's. We must fear the worst.**

***Mary* (Linda Davidson) – missing since May '88. This punkette roared recklessly out of the Square on a Routemaster, with barely enough Maori warpaint to sustain her for the week.**

***Angie* (Anita Dobson) – missing since May '88. Supposedly sunning herself in foreign climes, but has forgotten how to operate a telephone.**

From *Brookside: Karen Grant* (Shelagh O'Hara) – scarcely been seen since going to university in 1986.

***Heather Haversham* (Amanda Burton) and *Doreen Corkhill* (Kath Fitzgerald) both did runners from The Close in November '87.**

***Shane Ramsay* (Peter O'Brien) and *Clive* the doctor (Geoff Paine) both apparently decided that when a man's got to do what a man's got to do, it doesn't include being a *Neighbour* any more.**

***Crossroads:* the entire acreage and population of a Midlands motel simply vanished overnight. This surely cannot happen often in the experience of the local police force. Very careless.**

The Carrington family butler *(Dynasty)* c. '84/85. Household discipline has since careered downhill. Anyone drained the ornamental pond yet?

VICTIM	RIP	CAUSE OF DEATH	DID THEY RETURN	OTHER POSSIBLE EXPLANATIONS FOR FATAL DEPARTURE
MEG RICHARDSON *(CROSSROADS)*	**1981**	Weirdly unexplained. Meg merely floated off to Australia on the QE2. Possible woman overboard on way back from 1983 (see right) visit.	Yes – for daughter Jill's wedding. Thereafter, never seen again.	Having been out of the series, actress Noel Gordon died in 1985. *Crossroads* itself finally died in 1988.
ENA SHARPLES *(CORONATION STREET)*	**1980**	Old age.	No.	Actress Violet Carson's retirement. She died in 1984.
LEN FAIRCLOUGH *(CORONATION STREET)*	**1983**	Motorway accident.	No.	Actor Peter Adamson never recovered from an incident involving young girls in a public swimming pool.
STAN OGDEN *(CORONATION STREET)*	**1984**	Heart attack.	No.	Actor Bernard Ewings had a heart attack in real life (five months after screen death).
JOCK EWING *(DALLAS)*	**1981**	Plane crash.	Yes – at first it seemed so. Then Jock II declared an imposter.	Actor Jim Davies died in real life.
BOBBY EWING *(DALLAS)*	**1985**	Murdered by jealous love rival Katherine Wentworth.	Yes – in 1986 it transpired that his wife Pam had dreamed it all.	Actor Patrick Duffy had a pressing engagement with another TV project.
PAM EWING *(DALLAS)*	**1987**	Almighty car crash.	Possibly – though as an imposter.	Actress Victoria Principal tired of role.
MARK GRAYSON *(DALLAS)*	**1986**	Odd one this. First had terminal illness then recovered to go down in a jungle plane crash.	Yes – seemingly indestructible. But not seen now for years.	Actor John Beck filming elsewhere.
ROSS DAVIDSON *(EASTENDERS)*	**1986**	Tragically run over trying to save a child.	No.	Actor Ross Davidson had panto commitments.
DAMON GRANT *(BROOKSIDE)*	**1987**	Stabbing by unknown assailants.	No.	Actor Simon O'Brien tired of role.
LAURA GORDON-DAVIES *(BROOKSIDE)*	**1987**	Electrocuted by a faulty light-switch.	No.	Actress Jane Cunliss rumoured to have fallen out with series management.
DEN WATTS *(EASTENDERS)*	**1988**	Shooting by The Mob.	No – but are we convinced he is truly dead?	Forthcoming new series for Leslie Grantham on TV.
BRIAN TILSLEY *(CORONATION STREET)*	**1988**	Stabbing by unknown assailants.	No.	Actor Chris Quinten "bored" – and planning to "start small" in Hollywood.

Space to let

British academics hope to organise private sector funding for the UK's first astronaut – clearly the first of many such hi-tech ventures. *Punch* is proud to bring you a leaked list of similar projects British industry has decided to sponsor. VERNON P. TEMPLEMAN counts down

☆ The Sun Probe

A question which has long intrigued men (especially those who drool a lot) is what effect weightlessness would have on Samantha Fox's bust. A number of theories have been proposed which would suggest effects as diverse as a three-million-mile shift in the Earth's orbital radius to a pair of black eyes from Ms Fox. A joint mission with the winner of *The Sun* Astrophysics Doctorate competition (complete in less than twelve words the sentence "I want to see Sammy in zero G-string because ...") will soar away from Cape Carnal on a three-day mission to put the Big Bang theory to the test. The mission will also attempt to retrieve the Sky Channel Astra satellite to see if there is any technical reason why all the presenters look like Keith Chegwin or Frank Bough. The climax of the mission will see our Sammy draw four numbers for Giotto Lotto.

☆ The Time Dilation Experiment

Ever since Albert Einstein's revolutionary papers on space-time curvature shocked the scientific establishment, physicists have attempted to prove his theories. The time dilation effect (for which you can be put into care in Cleveland) is one of the more intriguing predictions of his postulates. The Kookmerite Corporation, Britain's leading manufacturer of egg-timers, hopes to take advantage of the high velocities experienced during space flight to prove that time seems to pass more slowly in a moving frame of reference. In a tightly-controlled experiment, two boxes of eggs will be bought from the Lake Baikanour Tesco's. One box will be placed in a liquid nitrogen cryo-storage vault at mission control, while the second batch will be made into some rather nice sandwiches for a Soyuz mission. After 2,357 orbits the sandwiches will re-enter the Earth's atmosphere and an international team of Nobel Prize-winning temporal experts will compare the sell-by-dates.

☆ Stellar Noise Experiment

The Cool'n'Tastee ice-cream company has sponsored a series of experiments in which a one-gallon block of frozen sheep's milk yogurt will be fitted with the latest semi-quantum interference devices (SQUIDs) and placed in a geosynchronous orbit about the Earth. The SQUIDs are capable of detecting sonic emissions of less than one femtobel (equivalent to a beagle passing wind in New York, as heard by a deaf monk in Lichtenstein) and are particularly efficient under cool, raspberry-flavoured conditions. Ground-based listening stations will monitor GAL-LACTIC-1 transmissions, over a ten-day period, in the hope of detecting noise from the coolant source. This should determine, once and for all, whether "in space, no one can hear ewe's cream".

☆ The Search For Alien Civilisations

A recurring theme of modern research is the quest for evidence of intelligent alien life-forms. Over recent years certain near-space regions have been examined and ruled out (Mars, Venus and Reading, for example) but the vastness of space makes it statistically likely that alien civilisations do exist. The current state of space technology does not yet allow deep space to be explored and it is therefore argued that man should encourage aliens to visit the Earth. The Laura Ashley Group plans to sponsor an elegantly designed experiment to produce just such a "galactic invitation". In what is likely to be the largest soft-furnishing engineering project of all time, the Earth is to be wrapped in a 25-mile-wide strip of tastefully patterned chintz, encircling the planet at a height of 400 miles. The theory is that such a clear indication of the civilised and aesthetically advanced nature of the planet will have the aliens flocking here in their millions, hopefully just in time for the sales. Certain critical scientists, pointing out that the material strip will absorb a significant amount of the Sun's energy, argue that the whole scheme could mean curtains for the Earth.

☆ The Launch Dynamics Study

In the world of marketing and sales it is always vital to ensure any new product enters the market-place with maximum impact. Astro-advertising consultancy, Staarchi and Staarchi, intend to carry out a space-based campaign to demonstrate the effectiveness of high-level product launches. The company, extrapolating from the success of the Volkswagen advertisements of recent years, intend to open their Sinclair C6 campaign by dropping a vehicle from a height of 43,000 miles. Theoretical calculations suggest that the product will (at least in part) reach a large number of potential customers, results from recent Russian nuclear-powered satellites tending to back these predictions up. Such a venture does not come cheap, with a price tag of some £35m being suggested by some business analysts. But then again it has long been one of the fundamental tenets of marketing science that there is no such thing as a free launch. ■

Space...the Final parking place.. these are the voyages of ....

T. COLIN GLASSWAX AND THE LITTLE PEOPLE
PLEASE, NO, NO.... AAARGGH!

T. COLIN GLASSWAX FILLS IN FOR THE MAÎTRE D'
WALK THIS WAY, SIR.
Menu
I'LL STARVE BEFORE I'LL WALK THAT WAY.

T. COLIN GLASSWAX SAVES A MAN CHOKING ON A FISHBONE
YOU CAN RELAX NOW, SIR, I THINK I'VE GOT IT.

T. COLIN GLASSWAX ADDRESSES THE AESTHETICS OF URBAN LIFE
OFF THE STREETS! KEEP THE WALKWAYS CLEAR FOR THE DASHING AND DAPPER.

figure of FUN

CHARLES BARSOTTI multiplies

T. COLIN GLASSWAX STEALS FROM THE POOR TIPPERS TO GIVE TO THE COMPLEX-CARBOHYDRATE DEPRIVED

STUDENTS!...WORKERS!...
IT IS NOW TIME
FOR DEMOCRACY!...
WE MUST LOOK
TO THE WEST
FOR OUR EXAMPLE...
FOR INSTANCE...
MARGARET THATCHER'S
BRITAIN....
McLACHLAN

"God, what a dump!"

Lada

The Russian leader looked tanned and relaxed. He wore a shiny red Adidas tracksuit with Ray-Bans propped atop his head, a gold Lada badge slung on a chain around his neck. On his feet were a pair of high-top Nike basketball shoes

The Punch Imaginary Interview

MIKHAIL GORBACHEV

The President of the Soviet Union uses the Kremlin for official purposes, but his family home is the Gorbachev Mansion, a Hollywood-style pleasure palace on the outskirts of Moscow. There Mikhail Gorbachev – "Gorby" to friends, "Chev" to intimate associates – hangs out with his stunning wife Raisa, long-time Party pals and his retinue of beautiful assistants, the "Mikkimates".

The house is a stunning surprise amidst the dour landscape of the Soviet Union. Equipped with its own private cinema, heated swimming pool and what is claimed to be the largest Jacuzzi behind the Iron Curtain (a claim, incidentally, that is hotly disputed by Rumania's fun-loving President Ceaucescu), this is clearly the home of a man who knows how to live. A man, too, with a sense of humour. In the watered-silk-lined reception-area-cum-bar there hangs a sign, kept by the Gorbachevs as a souvenir of a recent visit to one of Russia's celebrated psychiatric institutions. "You don't have to be crazy to be imprisoned here," it reads, "but it helps."

Mr Gorbachev was late for our appointment. Finally, however, a scantily-clad usherette appeared and led me through to his magnificent drawing-room. The Russian leader looked tanned and relaxed. He wore a shiny red Adidas tracksuit with Ray-Bans propped atop his head, a gold Lada badge slung on a chain around his neck. On his feet were a pair of high-top Nike basketball shoes.

His face was somewhat flushed, a fact explained by his first remarks; "Jesus, look at the time. Hey, I'm really sorry, have I kept you waiting? I been working on my tan. Picked up some rays when I was over with Fidel in Havana, thought I oughtta keep it going. So, I'm on the friggin' sunbed all morning, right? Musta lost track of time. You know how it is."

Here was the first surprise. I had known that Gorbachev – though his public speeches are always in Russian – can speak perfect English. But I had not been prepared for the accent or the style of his conversation, both of which were blue-collar American.

A compliment seemed the best way of proceeding. "Mr President, you speak remarkable English. Can I ask you where you picked it up?"

"Sure you can, man, but that don't mean I'm gonna to give you an answer!" exclaimed the communist chief, roaring with laughter and slapping me on the thigh. He threw me a Budweiser and cracked open a can for himself. "Seriously, I'll tell you. It was my cousins, Josef and Ivan. They're on my mother's side. They emigrated to the States a few years back, set themselves up as the Karamazov Brothers Cab Co., out of Newark, New Jersey. What a shithole that is, let me tell you. Makes Stalingrad look like Monte Carlo.

"Anyway, I'd go over there, y'know, like drive a cab all summer, get to know the place a little. Saturday nights we'd take the tunnel route, drive into Manhattan for some action. Hell, those city girls are wild, I tell you. There isn't anything they won't do if you ask 'em right."

His revelations suddenly shed a whole new light on Gorbachev's passionate desire to bring Western-style freedoms to the Eastern bloc. ▶

► How, I ventured to ask, did he view the United States now that he was the leader of a rival superpower?

"How do I view it? Through the window of a limousine. Hell, it just ain't no fun any more. I mean, do you have any idea how boring it is to spend five hours in a meeting with George Bush? And his wife, what can I say? She looks like the back end of the battleship *Potemkin*.

"See, the problem is, I got power nowadays, but freedom? Forget it. In the old days me and Joe and Ivan, we could do what we wanted. Now it's official reception this, American Ballet that... what the hell do I want with ballet? It's the only thing we got too much of in Russia as it is. I'm up to my balls in ballet. Why can't they leave me alone and let me watch *The A-Team*. God, I love *The A-Team*. That big black guy with the chains... too much."

This was hardly the tone I had expected for a conversation with someone who is arguably the world's most powerful man. So I tried to shift tack towards a more political line of questioning. "Tell me, sir, what sort of impression did you get of Mrs Thatcher during your recent visit to Britain?"

"Maggie?" said the balding dictator, "I love her. Hell, she's a spitfire. But I like 'em like that. You should see Raisa when she gets going. Man, she puts on that French lingerie. Lace, garter belts, heavy shit like that. I call 'em her plastic panties 'cause she buys it all on American Express. But I gotta tell you, it's real hard currency. You know what I mean, right? Talk about athletic. She's the Moscow Dynamo.

"Hey, that reminds me," he continued. "What's the name of that chick you got over there in England these days? Pamella – am I right? Jeee-zus, that is one cool babe. Listen, tell me, man to man. You got her number? 'Cause I hear she digs men with power; politicians, royalty, all that capitalist shit. Well, let me tell you, if it's power she wants, I'm her man. Point her in my direction if you ever get the opportunity. Believe me, I'll make it worth your while."

In a desperate attempt to change the subject, I asked the man they call "Gorby" how he made it to the top. A theory had been put about (*Punch*, 14 April) that it had to do with his position as a Party official in the Black Sea holiday resorts. Bigwigs would come down from Moscow on holiday to be greeted by the young Gorbachev, complete with welcoming party and limousines. When they got back to the Kremlin, they remembered the eager young apparatchik and his career was made.

"Sure, it was kinda like that," agreed the Soviet supremo. "But I gotta tell you, it was more than limousines, you know what I'm saying here? We're talking broads, booze, a little blow maybe. Remember Nikita Kruschev? Man, that crazy sonuvabitch spent the entire Cuban missile crisis stoned out of his gourd on Afghan Black. 'Course, you can't get that shit any more. Not since we pulled outta Kabul.

"Thing is, see, I knew where all the skeletons were buried. They hadda keep promoting me justa keep me sweet. Take Leonid Brezhnev. What a sleazeball. I had to fix him up with wrestlers. Male wrestlers. He said they reminded him of his wife."

Gorbachev was clearly a man obsessed. Suddenly he got up from the table, took off his Lada pendant and the four chunky gold rings that had adorned his hands and walked across the room to where an exercise mat had been laid on the floor. He stretched out on his back and started doing sit-ups.

He called out from the far side of the giant chamber: "Listen, don't mind me. It's my doctors, they say I gotta stay fit. I tell them I get plenty of exercise already, but they say sex isn't as beneficial as some people try to make out. So I got this new routine, like, sit-ups, press-ups, squat-thrusts, bicep-curls. It's kinda based on how they train our boys in the Spetsnaz. And let me tell you, those boys really are in serious condition. You can keep your SAS – the Spetsnaz piss on 'em."

> **"God, I love *The A-Team*. That big black guy with the chains... too much"**

"Mr President," I shouted, "about your recent elections... were you at all bothered by the success of Boris Yeltsin?"

"Bothered?" he yelled back. "Hell, no. Boris is cool. Sure, we had a falling out. But it was strictly business, nothing personal. Raisa and me, we see him a lot. He comes over with his wife. The girls go off and talk about dresses, cooking, all that chicks' stuff. Me and Boris, we chug-a-lug some beers, watch a football game, take in a Swedish video maybe. I let him tape my Neil Diamond CDs. Really. It's great to have him back on the scene again."

Finally we seemed to be making constructive progress. This was an unmissable opportunity to introduce the subject of *perestroika*. Was it really going to work?

"Of course not," grunted Gorbachev as he pulled on a pair of 7.5 kg weights. "You gotta understand, it's like those lagers you got over in the West. They all taste exactly the same, right? You close your eyes, you could be drinking anything. But you got a million beer companies all want to sell you their Pils this, or Export that. Okay, so they put it all in different cans and then they advertise. They tell you this stuff comes from Australia, this is Canadian, the shit in the odd-shaped cans is Japanese. All the time it's coming out of the same factories.

"Well, it's just like that with *perestroika*. You gotta think of that and *glasnost* as new brands of communism. We put 'em in fancy new packaging. We've done a publicity job that Saatchi and Saatchi would die for. Now the whole world thinks they're getting something new. But I'm still in charge and the jerks out there on the street are still lining up for Lenin's tomb. You get my meaning?

"I mean sure, we mothballed a few tanks. But they were all falling apart anyway. The new stuff is all still sitting there on the East German border. What do you think I am, stupid?"

Obviously not. By now the interview was coming to an end. A pert blonde secretary was trying to bend down and whisper something in Gorbachev's ear, a task that was severely hampered by the tightness of her skirt and the height of her heels. The General Secretary, lying exhausted on the mat, was making no effort to meet her half-way.

Finally he got up, a broad grin filling that oh-so familiar face. He slapped the secretary's bottom proprietorially. "Meet Olga, my favourite cossack-artist, she brings a whole new meaning to shorthand technique. Anyway, I gotta go. They need me over at the Supreme Soviet. It's been a blast meeting you, see you around."

We shook hands and Gorbachev moved towards the doors. Just as he was leaving he turned and waved me over. As I jogged across the stateroom he said, "I nearly forgot. Can you do me a favour? When you get back home, could you send me a copy of *Neil Diamond Live At The Greek*? My one's all worn through." And with that, the leader of the communist world turned and made his exit. ■

DAVID THOMAS

IRON MIKE'S FAVE RAVES

Fave food:
Mini Kievs
Fave films:
Kremlins,
The Lada They Come
Fave songs:
Georgia On My Mind,
Wish Upon a Tsar
Fave clothes:
Commie des Garçons
Fave motto:
Rather cred than red
Fave author:
Joseph Comrade
Fave soap:
Imperial Leather
Fave TV:
The Galloping Gorby

"I suppose Jason is compensation for the Porsche we never had."

Cartoons by
HAWKER

HAWK EYE

"A good celebrity audience, but not a great one."

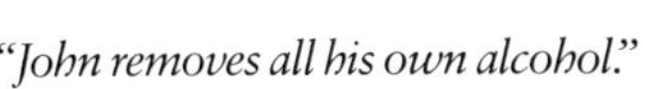

"John removes all his own alcohol."

TWISTED BY THE POOL

LOWRY GOES TO HOLLYWOOD

"The kidney-shaped swimming-pool cracked up about the same day as my kidneys."

"Apparently, it's an amazing, wonderful script. I've hired someone to read it for us."

"I think we all know each other – Harry and Don are working on the script together, Steven is directing for us, Bill and Louis are sound and lighting cameraman respectively, and Miss Dolores Von Tutu is here solely for my peace of mind."

"It says, 'The western is back'."

"I see the film as being aimed primarily at the children's market, but with a wink over their shoulder at the parents, a nudge in the ribs to the next generation up, a rock and roll sound-track for the teenagers and a proper ending with an obvious social message as a tip of the hat to the senior citizens and the moral majority."

"The script about the attack of the creeping aliens from beyond the planetary system that we felt would serve as a metaphor for the breakdown of the post-war consensus and the intellectual malaise of the day? They want you to rewrite it as a musical."

"Pathetic, isn't it? That's the new bratpack."

Lubbock

The Life and Times of the Great British Buffer by David Thomas

CALL MY BUFF

"Why oh why must the trendy educationalists once more tear down everything that makes Britain...

No, no, better not use why-oh-why. Did it for that piece last week; 'Why oh why must we destroy the beauty of the Book of Common Prayer?' Of course, trendy bishops rather than educationalists were the target that time, but it's still a bit too close for comfort. How about...

Was it G. K. Chesterton who wrote...

No, that's no good, either. ILEA was never one of Chesterton's major concerns. Oh, hell, there's nothing else for it...

There was a time when...

Yes, that's the ticket...

There was a time when any pupil in any school from Land's End to John O'Groats could happily recite 'The Rime of the Ancient Mariner', or

▶ chirrup his way through Gray's 'Elegy'. But now our children's heads are full of nothing more instructive than the mindless lyrics to the latest pop records.

And the latest decision by Thamesgrove Borough Council will only serve to make matters much, much worse.

For it seems that the embittered public-school rejects and polytechnic drop-outs who make up the militant clique that exerts ruthless power over the council's affairs have decided that…"

The Great British Buffer is composing his thoughts for the benefit of the *Daily Mail*. That new girl they've got running the features now – quite a sexy little tottie, he won't mind telling you – rang at half-past eleven. Apparently some damnfool council in Inner London, another bunch of bloody Trots no doubt, have banned English poetry from their school curriculum. They say it's all racist and sexist and has no relevance to the multicultural Britain of the Nineties. The *Mail* wants a thousand words, all good, strong, argumentative stuff, by 4.00 this afternoon. They'll pay £750.

Soon the Buffer is well under way. The keys on his word-processor – he swore he'd never get one, but he has to admit it's bloody useful; gave him something to write about in his column for *The Sunday Telegraph* the other week, too – the keys on his word-processor click-clack away beneath his nicotine-stained fingers and it seems like no time at all before 500 words have made their trenchant way into the memory-bank.

Time? Did somebody say time? Good Lord, it's half-past twelve already. Time for a quick half down at the Old Bull And Butter Mountain. Nothing like a tincture for putting a bit of life back into a tired brain. And doubtless the good, hearty yeomen around the saloon bar will have a few down-to-earth, common-sense remarks to make about all those sandal-wearing, bearded lefties that make London so unbearable these days. Not that there's ever been anything more poetic than "It Was On The Good Ship Venus" sung in the snuggery at The Bull. But that's the country for you. Good, red-blooded fellows to a man.

Was it G. K. Chesterton who wrote…?

Yes, actually it was. Good old G. K., trust him to come up with the poem that sums up the Great British Buffer's philosophy of life. Here it is, right here in the dog-eared collected poems that have given the GBB so much inspiration: "A Ballade of an Anti-Puritan". A nice touch that "e" on "Ballade", don't you think? Just the sort of literary embellishment that really adds to a fellow's Tingle Quotient. Well worth a couple of par's in the next book review, too, come to think of it.

On the way out of the front door, musing on the piece attacking Peter Bottomley's drink-driving campaign that he has to come up with for *The Spectator*, the Buffer fumbles his way through Chesterton's verses. He can't remember the first few lines exactly, some pretty sound stuff about the rubbish people talk about in the name of progress, but it's the last two-thirds of the thing that really drive the point home, viz:

I might have simply sat and snored,
I rose politely in the club
And said, "I feel a little bored,"
Will someone take me to the pub.

The new world's wisest did surround
Me; and it pains me to record
I did not think their news profound
Or their conclusions well-assured.
The simple life I can't afford
I want a mash and sausage, "scored" –
Will someone take me to the pub.

I know where men can still be found,
Anger and clamorous accord,
And virtues growing from the ground,
And fellowship of beer and board,
And song, that is a sturdy cord,
And hope, that is a hardy shrub,
And goodness, that is God's last word –
Will someone take me to the pub.

My word, they don't write 'em like that any more, eh? The Buffer ambles on, wondering whether Kingsley has put it into his latest anthology, "One Hundred Bloody Good Poems That Rhyme". If he hasn't, he might suggest it for "The High Life Book Of British Verse" (a little bit of culture for the tourists, lots of advertisements, another one of Bill Davis's cracking good ideas, that).

Heavy clouds hang over the Oxfordshire countryside as the Great British Buffer ambles towards the pub. The good, rich earth of England is thick with slumbering life, waiting only to burst forth into life at the first few rays of spring.

Pretty fine writing, don't you think? The Buffer used that sentence about the "good, rich earth" in a piece he did recently about moving to the country. Always good for an article or two, the country. Can't think why old Waterhouse insists on hanging around in Earl's Court. The country's the place – you just have to watch out for the neighbours, that's all. One feisty paragraph about the evils of egg subsidies and every damn farmer for miles around is collaring you at cocktail parties and spouting out the latest line from the National Farmers Union.

There's a bit of a nip in the air, so the GBB decides to warm up the old pipes by having a double whisky at the Bull. Must say, this saloon bar is everything you'd expect in a proper British pub; a good fire, low ceilings and walls decorated with regimental mementoes and Springbok rugby jerseys. Scruton, the proprietor, is a thoroughly sound chap, too, and his wife cooks a nice little dinner in the restaurant they've added in the last year or so.

Of course, the public bar's gone to blazes. They've put in a jukebox and some ghastly computer space game, but Scruton says the brewers are making the rents so high that he needs the extra money. Anyway, it keeps the yobbos happy and out of harm's way, so one will just have to grit one's teeth and try to live with it.

Not that one would for a moment consider abandoning the place. Habit of a lifetime, the lunchtime drink. And the evening one. That was what Fleet Street used to be like in the good old days, before it all moved to Godforsaken places in the middle of nowhere – however much one may admire Rupert Murdoch, which is very much indeed, he has absolutely no idea whatever about office location.

Of course, the papers are all filled with women now. Women and bloody nancy-boys. All they want to do is sit around clubs with silly names drinking fizzy water and eating fish. What's wrong with red wine and the roast beef of old England, eh? It's not what the Buffer would call proper journalism.

Particularly when a chap can learn so much in a pub. He can listen to the conversation of ordinary men. Feel the pulse of the nation. All these young things, with their trendy magazines and incomprehensible television programmes; they may think they know what's going on, but what do they know about the hopes and fears of ordinary, hard-working folk? The decent souls that make up the backbone of Britain, the silent majority – those are the people that the Buffer understands.

He chats to them at the Bull or after his many speaking engagements. He rides in their taxis. He reads the letters they send to him – green ink, capital letters – after each one of his forthright, perceptive features in the *Daily Mail*. Why do you think they call him "The Man Who Really Knows"? Because he does, that's why.

He knows there's nothing wrong with a proper British fried breakfast, whatever the self-appointed health-gurus might say. He knows that there was nothing wrong with British buildings either until the modern architects and the planners took over. He knows that a good, swift hiding is the quickest way of knocking some sense into a young man. He knows that sex and violence on television are responsible for this tide of filth that is swamping our nation in violence and crime.

Bring back the death penalty. Kick the lefties out of the BBC. And ITV. They're all a bunch of traitors. So a few paddies get shot by the SAS. So what? They had it coming to them.

And all those whingeing, over-paid arts pundits endlessly wanting more money off the long-suffering British taxpayer – Melvyn Mortimers, the Buffer calls them. Or did Paul Johnson call them that? Maybe he did. Sound fellow, Paul. Talks a lot of sense.

God bless Maggie.

Mine's a double Scotch.

Bu'ffer. *slang*. 1. A foolish fellow 1808. 2. A fellow: usu. slightly contemptuous 1749. "Here be a pair of buffers will bite as well as bark" – SCOTT.

(OED)

Declension of the verb "To Buff"

I buff
You buff
He is a bloody social worker
She is Mrs Thatcher

We work for the Daily Mail
You're on The Telegraph
They're a bunch of parasites

Where To Find The Buffers

1. *Journalism – absolutely stuffed with buffers, such as*

Paul Johnson
George Gale
Keith Waterhouse
Godfrey Smith
Alan Watkins
Peter Jenkins
Anthony Howard
Richard Ingrams
Geoffrey Wheatcroft
Peregrine Worsthorne

2. *Politics – bufferism, whilst completely absent from the present Cabinet, is definitely a creed that embraces all the parties, attracting such devotees as*

Lord Callaghan
Roy Hattersley
Lord Whitelaw
Lord Hailsham

Roy Hattersley: Northern attitudes, Southern income
Lord Hailsham: once Lord Chancellor, now bufferdom's keenest frogman

3. *The Arts – here we see not only traditional buffering, but also a new development: ageing, rich, leftish buffers who look lovingly back at the good old days of the Sixties, when they were young and Arts Council Grants grew on trees. People like*

John Mortimer
Sir Peter Hall
Melvyn Bragg
Harold Pinter
Colin Welland

4. *Old Cockneys – Fings ain't wot they useta be for*

Derek Jameson
Benny Green
Jimmy Greaves
(arguably football's only true buffer)

Buffers of the Future

Jonathan Meades – he loves his offal, his face is ruddy and he can't wait to ramble on about architecture – definitely one to watch.

Craig Brown – currently the greatest satirical scourge of the buffers via his "Wallace Arnold" column in The Spectator. *But looks like a buffer, has moved to deepest Suffolk and hates work which involves too much research – buffery awaits 'ere long.*

Robert Elms – do you remember the Eighties? Them were the days. Torn denims, minimal interiors, Spandau Ballet – they don't make bands like that any more. The first Post-Modern Buffer.

Auberon Waugh: too bilious to be a buffer

People Who Should Be Buffers, But Aren't

Auberon Waugh – would be a perfect buffer but for (a) his stylistic originality, and (b) his undisguised loathing for the common man.

Bernard Levin – capable of being suitably boring. But thinks too much and drinks too little.

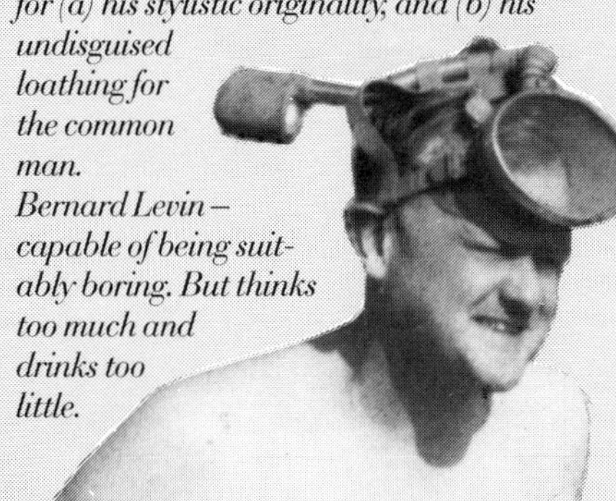

Young Melvyn: custodian of our nation's arts

Why Can't A Woman Buff Like A Man?

● *Women have traditionally not made good buffers. Even such professional ranters as Lynda Lee-Potter and Jean Rook put too much emotion into their work for bufferdom to stomach. All that calculated hysteria, it's, well, a bit too* female, *don't you know.*

● *But a new generation shows signs that buffering, like so many other professions, is now fully open to both sexes. Julie "Winston" Burchill, once a neo-Stalinist punk rebel, now a stupendously-paid* Mail on Sunday *columnist, can summon up a slab of controversial, hard-hitting, deliberately contrary prose on any subject under the sun.*

● *Our cover girl Muriel Gray paints on her clown-like make-up, screws up her face and sits there on the telly pontificating for a living. She is a fount of received opinion. You know that all her beliefs are firmly held, completely correct in a* Guardianesque *sort of way and charmingly predictable. Wee Muriel is a classic example of how – with Thatcherism as the revolutionary force in the land – conservative young people in the arts, keen to preserve (a) Britain's cultural heritage and (b) their own cushy numbers, have found a natural home for their buffery – on the left.*

Lord Callaghan: "Check my pacemaker, nurse. I'm about to wax indignant."

Great Moments In Buffer History

1. *Frank Giles discovers the Sony Walkman.* ▶

In the early 1980s, having stepped down as editor of The Sunday Times, *Frank Giles wrote a column for the paper. In one of these he announced – some two years or so after they had become a craze – that personal hi-fi's were an extraordinary boon and blessing. This established an important precedent, viz, the right of the buffer to discover, however eccentrically, the benefits of modern technology. See also…*

2. *Godfrey Smith discovers the lap-top computer.*
The amazing revelation that one might write, revise and despatch an article via a Tandy 200 computer measuring no more than 12" x 6" sustained hard-working country buffkin Godfrey Smith through an entire section of one of his recent columns. Nevertheless, it is by no means his greatest contribution to expanding the bounds of bufferdom. That was…

3. *Godfrey Smith discovers the Tingle Quotient.*
The Tingle Quotient was Godfrey's way of measuring the emotional effect of a piece of music, as evinced by the tingle it sent up the spine of the average listener. He invited his readers to send in examples of works with a high TQ factor, most of which turned out to be middlebrow popular classics like Albinoni's Adagio or Pachelbel's Canon. The ensuing correspondence kept Sunday Times *readers engrossed for weeks on end and gave Smith an unending source of material which occupied much of his column and required little or no effort to sustain. Truly the work of a master buffer.*

4. *Kingsley Amis and "Sod The Public".*
In October 1985 cantankerous Old Devil Kingsley Amis published his theory that all sorts of disreputable types – playwrights, interior designers, governments, shopkeepers, etc – had as their working slogan the words "Sod the public", although this might sometimes be varied to "Sod the audience" or "Sod the customer".

Three years later he updated his account to include, in alphabetical order: actors, advertising on television, the Arts Council, bookshops, buffet cars, club (how it will go down at the…), film directors, music in pubs, newsreaders, restaurants, television critics and the Writers' Guild. Perceptive readers will note that most people would find something to grouse about in at least fifty per cent of these cases – a fine average for any piece of bufferdom.

5. *The Conversion of St Paul the Pontificator.*
Once on the left of the Labour Party and a former editor of the New Statesman *(1965-70), Johnson switched sides following the decline of Harold Wilson and the rise of Margaret Thatcher. The tabasco-faced Mr Angry has subsequently become – via his articles on page six of the* Daily Mail *– Mrs Thatcher's staunchest supporter on Fleet Street.*

Johnson's most significant recent contribution to historical debate is the discovery that intellectuals – Rousseau, Sartre, Brecht, Marx, you name 'em – are all a bunch of hypocritical, thieving, mendacious lefties, many of whom have terrible problems associated with their penises.

In this, of course, he is absolutely correct.

Could You Be Godfrey Smith? A Well-Nigh Perfectly Jolly Punch Quiz

GODFREY SMITH

"The computer stood next to the hamster. On it, some children were composing a jolly tune. Their average age

out the best time and place for his attack to minimise casualties. He lost half as

many men as Haig did that day. Then I saw a girl use a program they had fed into

Note to candidates: All the questions (and their answers) below are taken from a genuine Godfrey Smith column in The Sunday Times, *printed in January 1989.*

Questions

1. *During the course of his column, did Godders enjoy…?*
(a) "a well-nigh perfect evening"
(b) "an enchanted evening"
(c) "an extremely jolly party"
(d) All of the above

2. *To whom did he refer as "the old crosspatch"?*
(a) Adolf Hitler
(b) W.C. Fields
(c) Edward Heath
(d) Princess Anne

Heath: who are you calling a crosspatch?

3. *Which of these women does* not *appear in Smith's column?*
(a) Moira Shearer
(b) Susan Hampshire
(c) Joyce Grenfell
(d) "A tarty woman"

4. *Which of these men* does *appear in the same column?*
(a) "the Greek impresario Eddie Kulukundis"
(b) "that genial old rascal Robert Maxwell"
(c) "the Celtic visionary Arthur Machen"
(d) "my old friend Keith Banks"
(e) All of the above

5. *Which of the following phrases is missing from the sentence, "The music was ravishing, ……..went down a treat and the church ended the evening £1,031 better off"?*
(a) "the luscious young Thai dancers"
(b) "Ludo Kennedy's customary eloquence"
(c) "the mulled claret"
(d) "mine host's fine local ales"

6. *Between which two towns did Smith encounter "some of the most magical country in England"?*
(a) Sheffield and York
(b) Woking and Weybridge
(c) Settle and Carlisle
(d) Oxford and Evesham

7. *What little-known fact will please "all those proponents of the theory that England is a village"?*
(a) Hugh Gaitskell was a cousin of P. G. Wodehouse
(b) A new society has been formed to protect old pub signs
(c) The art of blacksmithing is making a comeback
(d) Geoffrey Howe and Tony Benn both played cricket together at Winchester

Answers
SCORE 10 POINTS FOR ALL RIGHT ANSWERS

1. *(d) All of the above. It was a splendid week for Godders, although somewhat marred by the funeral of a local man who had worked for the aircraft company, Hawker's. "There was hardly a dry eye in the village," Smith mourned. There were, however, 25 lines in his column.*

2. *(c) Edward Heath. Had Smith attended a concert at which any of the other candidates was present (as was the case with Heath), possible descriptions might have been:*
"that amiably deranged dictator, Adolf Hitler"; "that crusty old joke-master, W. C. Fields"; or, "that splendidly forthright horsewoman Princess Anne".

3. *Joyce Grenfell. How long, we wonder, before the dear old girl will be back in Godders's column? Ideas for any good stories about her will be received with the customary bottle of champagne.*

4. *(a), (c) and (d). Score 10 for each correct guess, but subtract 10 for every wrong 'un.*

5. *(c) "the mulled claret". Ludovic's "customary effortless elegance" actually appeared in the preceding sentence to the one quoted. Thai girls are more often to be found in the writing of Auberon Waugh. The ale was a perfectly reasonable suggestion. It just happens to be wrong.*

6. *(b) Woking and Weybridge. That this patch of Surrey should win out over Yorkshire, Cumbria or the Cotswolds exemplifies the classic Buffer's essentially suburban concept of the English countryside. Paul Johnson, for example, who regularly waxes lyrical about his close ties to nature, lives in the wilds of Iver, Bucks – ooh-arr,* very rustic, *m'lord.*

7. *(a) Gaitskell was a cousin of P. G. Wodehouse. This does not illustrate that England is a village. It actually illustrates that the Buffer's England is a saloon bar conversation occurring somewhere within a 50-mile radius of London. Smith asked readers to send in examples of other village-style whacky relationships. This could be the Tingle Quotient all over again.*

Anyone scoring 60 or above should send completed answer forms to: Godfrey Smith, "Can I Have Your Job, Please?" Competition, The Sunday Times, *Pennington Street, The Highway, London E1 9XW.* ■

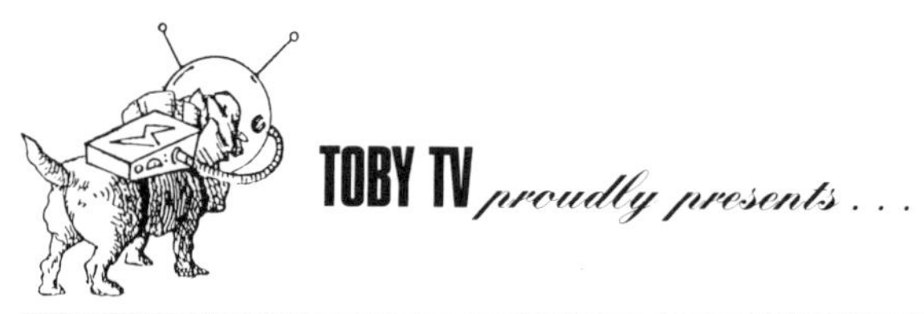

Murdoch.

What a concept, eh?

Murdoch is omnipresent, omniscient and omnipotent.

Next to Murdoch, Tyson's a cissy and Thatcher's the babe coyly fondling the Cadbury's flake. One minute this maverick media maven is taking on the corrupt wiseguys and surly, burly bully-boy unionists overmanning *The New York Post* – and **winning**. The next he's calling Kelvin MacKenzie at home about Elt the J – and *both* the king o' smut and the queen of camp are **grovelling**.

Before you can say Donald Trump's got a boil on his rump, the Dirty Digger's dynamically driving through downtown Tokyo to convince baffled Jap caps of leisure industries to reach for the SKY. Japan Inc? They're **buying**.

Somewhere in between Rupe took over Collins publishing and fired off a memo to the leader writer of *The Australian* telling him – in no uncertain anatomical terms – to lay off his old mate Bob Hawke.

What **everyone** wants to know is how he does it.

A new TV series, exclusively acquired for Toby TV, tells you the secret.

And it's a big secret – a bloody **humungous** secret, next to which George Bush's codes for calling down the first-strike are as meaningful as those cards that flutter from the nastier Sunday supps. A secret so closely guarded that the initiation rites of the Knights Templar pale into the significance of a Larry Adler chain-letter by comparison.

But what is that secret?

The secret is . . .

Rupert Murdoch is not a man.

He **is five men**.

For the first time, for the ludicrously minimal payment of your firstborn's school-fees, you can receive the smash-hit tabloid TV series that's already gripped a generation of mush-brained buddies and beer-bombed couch potato cobbers from coast to crumby coast. The award-winning programmes that tell the true story of . . .

THE MURDOCH 5

In **G'DAY BASTARDS**, your special complimentary premiere-length preview episode, you, the viewer, discover with no risk to life or limb the inside dope on the FIVE MEN WHO RULE THE UNIVERSE.

GASP as old man Murdoch's fiendishly ingenious manipulations of the Perth plastic surgery futures market bind the Murdoch Quins to a blood oath. A common purpose – the establishment of total world media domination. An audacious crusade – the utter moronification of anything with more brain cells than a rubber plant.

YELP as the quins pulp the playground into bloody, battered submission by their leveraged buy-out of the *Tinniebonga Teenie Times* and – aided only by a peppercorn $25 billion allowance from Dad – seize control of the school council and establish a camouflaged base-camp the size of Siberia somewhere in a remote area of western Australia.

SHRIEK as the quins go down for the third time after Harry "The Horsefly" Evans shoves them into a shark-infested swimming pool ... and the sharks rush for cover into the arms of sexy lifeguard David Mellor.

LOOK at these stupid pictures...

QUINS

RUPERT

The rough one. He drank beer. He built a global communications empire. He married a junior reporter. Then he had a sandwich that he liked so much he bought the city that made it.

RUPERT

The tough one. He drank whisky. He tore other men's global communications empires into tiny shredder-ready strips. His junior reporter wife started writing novels – so he watched TV. He hated it so much that he bought "Brillo Pad" Squeal in to give the medium a brown-nosing it'd never forget.

RUPERT

The buff one. He drank extract of reusable manila envelope. He discovered that by touch-tone dialling 213-555 8989 you could approximate the tune of Jingle Bells. But then a mystery woman picked up the phone. She claimed she was his wife, the world famous novelist...

IRIS

The sensitive one. She dictated her books to a secretary (David "Mr Laffter" Mellor) about capriciously-named people who fell in love with squillionaire media moguls. Her publishers bought the manuscript – and her husband bought the publishers. Then he read the book. "Harry," it began. "No man since Brillo Pad Squeal has ever satisfied me the way you do." Her husband turned on his heel, his dark impenetrable eyes clouding over with a fury that recalled his convict antecedents. Clearly this was a job for...

KERRY

The evil one. He drank heaps, he smelled bad and took his surfboard to bed. No, even the other quins knew that Kerry was different. But what they didn't know was that Kerry had plans. Big plans.

NEXT WEEK:
Iris makes a movie, Kerry makes his moves and David "Fisherman" Mellor makes love to the entire Iranian parliament. All this and more – uncut, live and on-camera. Coming soon to a TV tube near you in THE MURDOCH QUINS episode two – YOU'RE ALL FIRED YA DUNNYS.

(Legal disclaimer: Toby TV plc cannot accept any liability whatsoever for any damage to your life as a result of mendacious fabrications perpetrated by Murdoch Media Inc howsoever caused, including the possibility of materialisations in your laundry cupboard by skinheads claiming to be Gary Bushell).

Writing like Martin Amis is hard work.

Even Martin Amis finds writing like Martin Amis hard work.

His new novel, *London Fields*, has been driving him *tonto* for five years.

But you can beat him to it with SIMON CARR'S *Know-How Guide to Being a Short and Sour Smart-Arse Writer*.

It's no breeze, this Amis-writing lark. You've got to *butch* it out.

But if you follow the steps and exercises, you too can freak your friends with prose-ripple and vocab-flex

The Punch Guide to Writing a Martin Amis Novel

MARTY PANTS

Fat old dandies used to say about comic writing, about P. G. Wodehouse, or Clive James, "Of course it's harder than it looks, this sort of thing". Come to think of it, it was usually Clive James saying it about P. G. Wodehouse (and by implication, about his own material).

Martin Amis's prose isn't harder than it looks. He hasn't taken *any* pains to conceal the degree of difficulty in writing this sort of thing. And this sort of thing has become harder to write since *Billy Liar*, or *Lucky Jim*, or *Porterhouse Blue*, or any of those books you think you could – if you concentrated – write two at a time, one with each hand.

What did he say, the *enfant horrible*, in *The Rachel Papers*? In 1970-what-was-it? 3? "There was no reason to suppose that with her clothes off she would smell of boiled eggs and dead babies"? The density of expression was quite new. It still sounds fresh … if fresh is the right word.

"Once underway, though, Gloria would have been able to detect few noteworthy points of contrast between sexual arousal and rabies …" No one else was writing like this, not even in America, not in 1973. "Breasts so flaccid you could tie them in a knot." It was unthinkable in 1973, the writing was so *dense*; the density was close to the collapsed geometry we had recently heard about in dead suns.

And though he won a book prize for it, the fat dandies – bellying up to the bar even then – said "Why does he have to write about such sordid people?" The answer was (it seemed clear enough) for the fun of it. But it was strong-stomach stuff, and quite as hard as it looked to write. Now the generational stag-rite is well under way (Perry's gone down at *The Sunday Telegraph*, and of course, *Punch* has been privatised), and Martin Amis is the standard of a generation.

So if you really want to write this sort of thing try telling me for a start, does your girlfriend have a wraparound mouth?

Does she have, let me guess, a furrow of black hair on her belly which creeps like a trail of gunpowder into the sharp, white holster of her pants? Is she a supple, swervy, bendy, bed-smart hot-fox sack-artist, buzzing with high-tab body-tone, fizzing with brothelly know-how?

This isn't prurient interest, don't get a "fat". It's comic, not erotic, get a grip on yourself. This is to make us laugh. This is a D. Litt. locker-room conversation we're having here.

It's hard work fronting up a Martin Amis novel, but you'll do. You'll do for the moment. But we're sprinting; how long can you sprint? What's your distance? There's a long way to go, this isn't an 80-yard dash, this isn't the 220 at whatever standard, this is *distance* writing. Four hundred pages, sprinting all of it.

FIRSTLY, and this is the difficult bit, you, the narrator, have to formulate the central deal in your head. On the one hand, you are clever, ▶

You get to drink a lot and make a pig of yourself with girls in pornographic underwear

educated, cultured and as witty as all-get-out. On the other hand you recognise the advantages of being an unreflecting yob. Because you are clever you get to make highly-evolved jokes. Because you are a yob you get to drink a lot and make a pig of yourself with girls in pornographic underwear. Because you are a yob you can eat junk food. But on which side are you going to come down?

The cleverness is inescapable, but then the *heft* and the *bulk*, the *muscle* and *knuckle* is very attractive, particularly if you, personally, have none of these things in life. These qualities are particularly invigorating, they allow you to spill into clubs, and shout, and start fights, and jam your hand up ladies' dresses, and stick your fingers in mens' eyes, and hit their faces with your forehead, and roll around on the floor with big dogs saying "Attaboy!" and "You and me, pal!" and other such bloodcurdling sweet-nothings without suffering the least embarrassment. Yob-assets allow you to ride motorcycles and get girls, and beat people up, and hit women, and fall over in restaurants, and visit prostitutes, and attempt the occasional recreational rape of your girlfriend (that bitch). Yobs have all the fun.

In the earlier books the yob characters (Norman, Adorno, feckless but yob-aspirant Terry) are counterweighted by the clever ones (Charles, Quentin, feckless Terry's yet more feckless brother). By *Money* the opposites have been integrated into the character of John Self who is a complicated yob with the reactions of a poet ("the stippled bronze of the Thames," "dolour-bills", "my splayed and aching tackle"), who is capable of enough sensitive cynicism to bring large-scale horror into the work: "All prisons are waiting rooms. All prisons – all rooms. All rooms are waiting rooms. Your room is a waiting room. You are waiting. I am waiting. Everything is getting nearer to being over." Do you want to cry "foul"?

What will we have in *London Fields*, out this autumn? An overweight, morally inchoate, proletarian who bubbles and clicks with a laval mucous problem (and the rest – hangovers, snout-burn, porn-depression); an ineffectual, over-evolved, hyper-conscious graduate who can't engage with the visceral pleasures of bad sex and dirty girls; and a dirty girl. And a nice girl (cultivated, painterly). Only guessing. It's much harder than it looks. You try.

Farce Foods, Farce Cars

Limber up with a few exercises to get the right feel of demi-monde decay and crazed consumer cityscape.

WRITE A PRODUCT DESCRIPTION OF THIS FLASH-FRAZZLED FAST-FOOD YOU BUY IN BURGER DEN, BURGER SHACK, BURGER BOWER:

Wallies
Blastfurters
Fastfurters
American Ways
Tuckleberry Pie

PLACE THE FOLLOWING RESTAURANTS IN ORDER OF COSTLINESS

Kreutzers
Assissi's
The Mahatma
The Vraimont, on Sunset Boulevard

WHICH OF THE FOLLOWING CARS WOULD HAVE AN EXCEPTIONAL REPUTATION FOR UNRELIABILTY?

Autocrat
Boomerang
Tomahawk
Fiasco
Farrago
Alibi
V8 Hyena
Jefferson Success
Manana

Clever-clever tips

Brush up on your physics, Quantum mechanics, particle-chaos, and uncertainty principles. Get on nodding terms with a little basic pharmacology. Develop your chess game and your tennis terms.

Get to grips with the word "gimmick" in its different contexts:
* an ego-gimmick (a nation-state embossing the monarch's head on coins)
* gob-gimmick (a speech impediment)
* gimmicked the catch (unlatched the door)
* gimmicked youth (surgically implanted youth)
* they're giving you the gimmick with the eyes and mouth (a girl is playing her sexual trick on you across a dinner table)
* what's this gimmick with the pigs? (What is it with the pigs?)

Urban lingo

You should have ... *decks her/aims her/cools her* as synonyms for sexual rejection. A hand-job needs no explanation. Your sock is where you, as a bachelor, live in fetid indiscipline. There is your rug on your head, and you re-think it with a comb. You will know what a crying jag is if life is trying. Or a barking jag, if you are a distressed dog.

Rhythm gimmicks

You'll need to get to familiarise your thinking with the prevailing rhythm: casual iambics syncopated with double-barrelled spondees:

...you are a bank rat on a busy river...

...I don't see traffic but human forcefields – rattletraps, dropheads, hardtops, hotrods, the human saloons singling one out with the stares of their hard lights...

... naked and plucking at the buckle of my own stunned strides...

... the bouncy bim in her wind-whipped dress...

... last year's cackle-factory spectacular Down On The Funny Farm...

... watching from her new protectorate, the stopgap flat of a silent intermediary...

Chicks and pals

Detail the demonology of your girlfriend's (even better, your boyfriend's) underwear. How their performing flesh eddies in fantastic convulsions, how they ride to bed in black stockings, tasselled garterbelt, satin thong, muslin gloves, belly necklace, gold choker. Tell us in incredible minutiae how you bend them triple over the headboard and how you, and how you...

We'll want to know about your friends too. No, not your friends, you don't have any friends, your associates. Your street-company. All right, the people you see on streets, who catch your eye in public through the shimmer of a heat-ripple hangover. Are they gangrenous imbeciles? Shifty dotards? That'll do nicely.

Let them be degradingly poor, irretrievably ugly, fat-necked, fudge-brained slags and mumbling bitches slumped like rubbish bags in asylum corridors.

They must include ten of the following:
Pricks with powderpouffed hair, tarts in three-piece pinstripe suits, bastards in gambados, slags in tapestry bodystockings, dumb berks in boiler suits, purple-nosed losers, scowling bunglers, violent throwbacks, ragged little faggots, trashy photographers, hundred-word models, soccer trogs, suburban tykes, incipient queers, mutants, vile aliens, aged androids, tuxed fucks, lumbering retards, exhausted sack-artists, gasping fatsos, turks and nutters fizzing and gargling with rage and pain and loneliness and no money; and Martians who speak stereo, radio crackle, interference, sonar, bat chirrup, pterodactylese, fish purr.

What do your street-company friends' faces look like? Do their faces resemble:
a) A fat snake.
b) A cruel pig.

You will be familiar with the pedestrian stupidity of pub-people, cultural jetsam, and minor criminals

c) A gravy dinner.
d) A lunchbox.
e) A croc-face.

How did they get like that? What do they put into their faces to make them look so fallen? Was it?

a) Five Fastfurters, four Blastfurters, three Big Thick Bendy Hot Ones, a double order of Tuckleberry Pie, and a carton of cigarettes.
b) Fives vases of Californian chablis, four half-and-half gin rickies, three bottles of champagne, two pints of port, and a quart of scotch.
c) A handful of poppers, a phial of cocaine, a plug of opium, a cubic foot of coffee, and another carton of cigarettes.

Disjunctions that don't funk

You'll need a wide selection of two sorts of words. In Column One, nutty, muscular tough little words. Punchy little high-gravity words, which grip in the sentence and kick up in complicated effect.

Heft
Welt
Fizzing
Spangling
Coltish
Lardy
Rubble
Yob
Fruity (as in fruity yob)
Frisky
Wonky
Zooty
Bendy
Tub
Chip-chute
Radiator rod
Frazzle
Flash-fry
Shunt
Torque
Snout
Pocked
Lungs full of stagnant gook and offal

In Column Two, more elaborate, High Table, Lit-Crit, D.Litt words:

Deliquesce
Lupine
Ludic
Crepuscular
Camber
Decrepitude
Stippling
Argosy
Impiously
Emeried (any ideas? sandpapered?)
Frilling (a veil frilling her chin)
Jounced (she jounced her black dress)

Arrange column one words with column two words to produce striking disjunctions:
* *this goofball of critical plutonium* (a boil on his arse).
* *the lupine stares of the grease-bandits glimpsed through angles of axles and jacks...*
In case we have come to believe such an exercise is easier than it looks, place the word "impiously" in this paragraph in one of the six possible slots:
When Vron had sobbed it all out after showing her prospective steps on photographs of herself having a handjob with no clothes on for money, she explained to me – at throaty length and with hot tears still foiling the points of her lashes – that she had always *been creative. "I was* always *creative John!" she said again and again, as if I kept insisting that she was creative only sometimes, or not until recently.**

Lowlife verbals

Demotic parentheses should be used to deflate, or used as a counterweight against sentimental moments:

Whew, I could do with some of that
Whew, isn't that a drag?
How can people *stand* that stuff?

You will be familiar, intimate even, with the careful, pedestrian stupidity of pub-people, cultural jetsam, and minor criminals:
"She's a bloody marvellous girl, she is," I said thickly. "I mean, Di, she loves her people. She'd do anything for us, mate, anything. Anything."

You will be able to transliterate sloppy or affected speech in the same way that Kingsley Amis did in *Lucky Jim* ("you sam"), but somehow – and this is important – funny:

TRAMP (RECEIVING 10p): "Thankyou sir, thankyou. Gob less."
CHARLES: "I'll try."

Getting the whammy on jokes

There will be a requirement for more or less straightforward jokes in a variety of rhythms, cuts and lengths.
Crisp one-liners: *"Sex is like death, the poets say. It's what the doctors say too in my case."*
Evolving bathetics: *"I want to get back to London, and track her down, and be alone with my Selina – or not even alone, damn it, merely to be close to her, close enough to smell her skin, to see the flecked webbing of her lemony eyes, the mouldings of her artful lips. Just for a few precious seconds. Just long enough to put in one, good, clean punch. That's all I ask."*
Highly wrought four-parters of acrobatic ingenuity: *"My head is a city, and various pains have now taken up residence in various parts of my face. A gum-and-bone ache has launched a co-operative on my upper west side. Across the park, neuralgia has rented a duplex in my fashionable east seventies. Downtown my chin throbs with lofts of jaw-loss. As for my brain, my hundreds, it's Harlem up there, expanding in the summer fires. It boils and swells. One day soon it's going to burst."*

Check? Check.

Oh, and you'll also have to master an art of proletarian slapstick – of incredibly ugly, impractically fat plebeians swearing ineffectually at one another in socially degraded circumstances (compressed, by a sort of collapsed grammar into a quarter of the space normally allotted to such things).

But, hey, for a yob-natural like you, pal, that should be a cinch, a breeze. ■

* It goes between "kept" and "insisting".

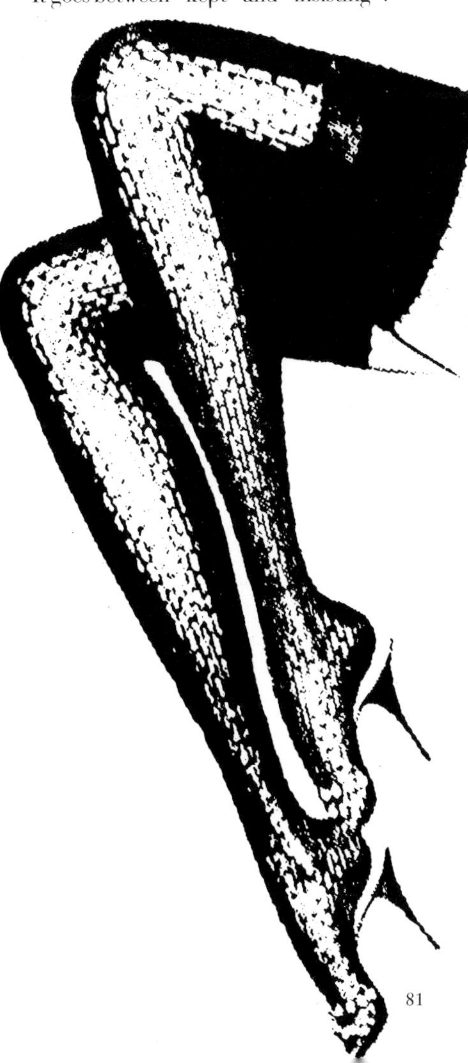

Weird men, big feet

Cartoons by DAVID MYERS

"I hear he was in the body-building business."

"Frankly I expected you to be far more technically advanced."

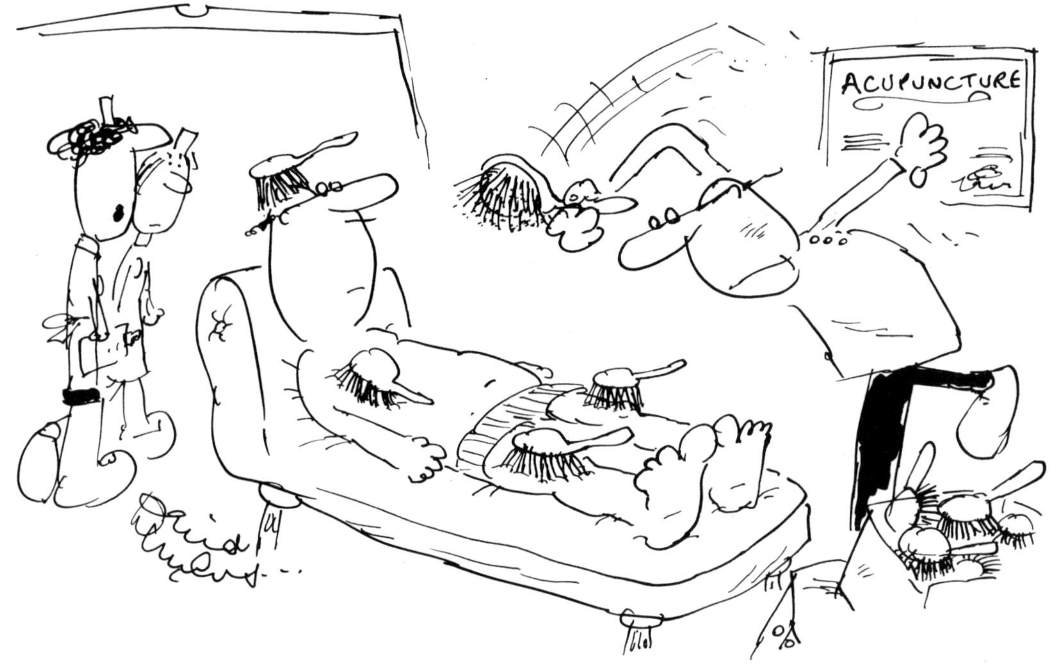

"His methods are unorthodox but he gets results."

CALL ME . . . LOVE ME . . . PAY ME . . .

PHONE IN TURN ON

NEW MODEL IN TOWN!
Busty European
BLONDE
262 5153

"Hello?"
"I'm ringing about the sticker"
"Bosom Yum Yums or Sexy Beast?"
"Er, whatever's convenient"

ROGER TAGHOLM, poor man, tours BT's kinky kiosks to find out who gives good phone

It was stiff and I slowly slipped it in. It felt good. It felt far better than some of the others I'd sampled that morning. And, ooh, that continuous purring. I thought that we were getting somewhere at last. I gave a sigh. I wiggled it about a bit. Ah yes! This time I was sure that I was *really* going to connect.

Outside, it was a glorious spring day in the capital. The sun was shining on the flower stalls, friendly newspaper sellers were at their bright pavement stands giving directions to the tourists and everyone seemed to have a smile on their face. Yes, it was exactly the sort of day that made you feel glad to be... well, glad to be in a phone box on the Euston Road ringing up prostitutes.

You see, London is in the grip of an epidemic. Many of its phone boxes are beginning to look like the back pages of *Fiesta*. The tourists are finding it hard to read British Telecom's payphone instructions because of the brilliant displays of stickers saying 'Miss Tease, Will Please or Spank Me Now' stuck all over them. Clearly the whole business needed investigating. *Punch*, quite rightly, thought I was the man for the job.

Which was why I was now inserting my phonecard to speak to Tie 'n' Tease. This was in fact my fifth call of the morning. French Lessons, I Need Toy Boys, Sin with Me and Blonde Bitch had all been out. For some reason, this fact was rather touching. Perhaps they were all shopping, getting the groceries in, paying the gas bill, just like the rest of us. For a minute it all seemed terribly harmless. Then I was through.

"Hello?" (They always say this. They never say the number. I suppose that would sound a bit suburban and unerotic.)

"Oh, hello there." (Confident. Cocky. I do this sort of thing all the time.) "I'm ringing about the sticker in the phone box." (That's me. Straight to the point.)

"Where are you, darlin'?"

"King's Cross."

"Well, the young lady's just off the Edgware Road. Is that convenient for you?"

"Er, yes, that's fine." (I wonder if my mother's reading this.)

"All right then. Shall I tell you about the young lady?"

"Er, yes." (Guilt! Guilt! I used to be a Sixer in the Cubs!)

"She's an eighteen-year-old ash blonde, 36-24-36 figure, very experienced. Basic hand-relief massage is £25 and personal services start at £40. Now, would you like the address?"

"Um, what about, er, the 'personal services'?" (Purely in the interests of journalistic research, you understand.)

"What did you want, love?"

"Um." I wanted to ask her if she'd ride a unicycle naked across my belly while I recited *The Love Song of J. Alfred Prufrock*, but somehow I felt that their price structure wouldn't accommodate this. She did, however, make the following suggestion.

"We can strap you to the bed, love, and then give you tease and hand relief if you like. That'll be £55."

Madam To Cane You was the explicit message and £40 was the answer

I scribbled all this down, including the address (just in case) and wondered what would happen if I had a road accident on the way home. I may have been wearing clean underwear but my notebook was beginning to look quite soiled.

To tell the truth, I hadn't started running into the smut until I reached the Edgware Road. Despite the rumours, the two phone boxes I had visited in Sloane Square that morning were as upright as any elderly couple up from the ▶

LONDON CALLING: SOME OF THE CAPITAL'S SEXIEST PAYPHONES

Payphone location	Nearest phallic symbol	Approx no of stickers	Best name/message	Quality of artwork
Westminster	*Big Ben*	7	*Madam Tanya – As Cruel as she is Beautiful*	*Moderate*
Tottenham Court Rd	*Centre Point*	5	*Sinful Cindy*	*Nice gold blocking, otherwise poor*
King's Cross	*British Telecom Tower*	50+	*Latex Lady & Foot Worship*	*Superb*
Wapping	*Tower Bridge or Andrew Neil's ego*	–	–	*But still better than* The Sunday Times
British Museum	*Head of Rameses II in Egyptian Room*	8	*Make Love Slowly to me*	*Could do better*
Trafalgar Square	*Guess*	4	*Very Cheeky Teenager Needs Firm Hand*	*Provocative*

Sussex coast to spend the day in town. And Paddington had seemed anything but immoral, the reason for this no doubt being that the cluster of payphones on the station concourse happens to share its site with the Saga Holidays Assembly Point.

But at Edgware Road tube you come across Call Me You Sexy Beast and Bondage for Beginners. The floor is littered with spent phonecards. They look like used condoms that have gone green with mould.

Green Park's pretty impressive too. Its wall of sin by the four payphones outside the tube is quite famous. Why feel restricted to the insides of the phone boxes when you've got a nice smooth marble-looking wall to show off your stickers? And some pretty fine ones there are too. The artwork on I Need Strict Punishment – a quite skilfully drawn lady, leaning over, with two huge welts on her backside – caught my eye and I was rather taken, in a manner of speaking, by Madame Orgasm.

Madame O is tired of the sort of price enquiry phone calls I had been making all morning and gets around it by putting her prices on her sticker. Thus we have good old hand relief (it seems to be the favourite phrase) for £25 and something called Bosom Heaven for £15. In the interests of comparative price research for today's discerning consumer I popped into the Ritz down the road and asked them how much tea for two would be. "£10.50 each sir," said an upper-class gentleman in silly clothes. "But we advise you to book up two weeks in advance."

Why wait? You could get Bosom Yum Yums round the corner for little more than that and what's more get them immediately.

Then I had a nice phone call with a pleasant-sounding lady called Chris. In fact, this call was going so well that I was tempted to drop round to her place and continue the discussion face to face. Let me explain before you get the wrong idea. Chris Levey is the Public Relations Manager for the London Payphone Service, which sounds about as enviable a job as working in PR for Boeing or being a British Rail Safety Officer.

"Our contractors remove all the stickers and wash down the hand-sets"

She told me that the stickers were a very big problem. "Our contractors are instructed to clean particular kiosks twice a day," she said. "They have to remove all the stickers and used cards and wash down the hand-sets. But I can guarantee you that if you went back to some kiosks an hour after they've been cleaned – particularly in King's Cross – you'd find them covered again."

I didn't wait around to find out if this were true. I'd had enough suspicious looks anyway. No, I made my way to Soho now. There comes a time in every man's life when he has to find out how much it costs to be spanked and that time was now. Madam To Cane You was the explicit message and £40 was the answer. "With a whip or a cane, darlin'," she added, "whichever you prefer." I'm still thinking about it.

It was here, also, that I spoke to Janey, whose expertly drawn sex kitten sticker seemed to have a professional edge to it. "I did it myself," she said. Janey and I got on famously. She'd been to art college in Leicester and now does a bit of drawing on the side. How marvellous, I thought; it occurred to me that what some might fantasise about doing on the side, she now does as her full-time job.

Janey wanted me to pop up and visit her in Hampstead (yes, I'm afraid so. Who'd have thought it?) and see some "real talent". But I declined this tempting opportunity to see some more of her artwork and began to make my way home. Having spent most of the day researching the above, everything I looked at now began to take on prurient overtones. On Oxford Street one of L. Ron Hubbard's dozy dianetics disciples handed out a leaflet which read: "Worried about your confidence in yourself and your abilities?"

But I suppose if you've read this far you'll want to know the answer to the Big Question. Did I or didn't I? Well, sorry to disappoint you. I didn't. The nearest I got to 'the act' was going into fourteen tunnels on fourteen tube trains. At least it's cheap. ■

Phonecards and Condoms: Some Differences

You cannot buy fruit-flavoured phonecards
Condoms cannot be used to find out the latest cricket score
It is not embarrassing for three phonecards to fall out of your pocket in church
You cannot buy phonecards in pub toilets
There are no pyjamas with phonecard pockets
Phonecards can be shared
If your phonecard gets stuck during use it is not the end of the world
Phonecards cannot be filled with water by fourth years at the local comprehensive
A new phonecard does not have to be used every time

Strange but genuine PROVERBS

" UGLINESS IS BUT SKIN DEEP "

Mr Punch has lots of friends. Bet you didn't know that! Can you guess who they are?

Meet the Mr Punchmen

Mr Dribbly

Mr Dribbly is a very messy eater. Mr Dribbly is a very messy speaker. Sometimes when he talks, he drowns his dinner. It's a very big dinner. It's a very expensive dinner. He bought it at the Gay Hussar. But if he ever says "Hussar", be sure to pack a towel.

What does Mr Dribbly do? Mr Dribbly is Number two to Mr Windy.

What does Mr Dribbly say? Mr Dribbly says, "I support Sheffield Wednesday." (Make that three towels.)

Mr Windy

Mr Windy enjoys tortuously convoluted rhetoric. And rhetorically tortuous convolutions. And convolutedly rhetorical torture. Once Mr Windy starts, he doesn't know when to stop. Boyo, boy – he's certainly windy all right!

What does Mr Windy do? Mr Windy opposes Mrs Bossy.

What does Mr Windy say? Mr Windy says he is the first Windy to go to university for ten hundred thousand billion generations.

Mr Stubbly

Mr Stubbly has faith. Mr Stubbly has faith that wherever he goes in the world, he'll always find a blow-dryer. And a sun-ray lamp. But probably not a razor.

What does Mr Stubbly do? Mr Stubbly sings pop songs.

What does Mr Stubbly say? He says, "Wake me up before you go-go."

Mr Cross

Mr Cross has a very red face. Mr Cross has very red hair. But Mr Cross does not have red politics. They are pure dark blue. Mr Cross is on the winning side. So why is Mr Cross so cross? Why oh why? That sounds like a newspaper article. Perhaps Mr Cross will write it. And make a lot of money.

What does Mr Cross do? Mr Cross is a journalist.

What does Mr Cross say? He says, "(Salman Rushdie) seems to me an egregious example of a literary celebrity created by the left-wing cultural establishment and by the hype of the prize system, which is already beginning (as I always suspected it would) to damage English literature."

Mr Oily

Mr Oily has no sense of humour. But Mr Oily really cares. He cares about all the ordinary people who write in with their most private personal problems. Mr Oily passes on these problems to the outside world. Then he plays a little song.

What does Mr Oily do? Mr Oily plays Our Tune.

What does Mr Oily say? Mr Oily says, "Then he met a bloke called Fritz – literally. That was his name."

Mr Pretentious

Mr Pretentious has read lots of books. Some of them are filled with very difficult words. Like "synchronicity". When Mr Pretentious is not reading books he likes to visit the Amazon and talk to the natives. You can easily spot the natives. They are the ones who look intelligent.

What does Mr Pretentious do? Mr Pretentious sings pop songs.

What does Mr Pretentious say? Mr Pretentious says, "De-doo-doo-doo. De-da-da-da."

Mr Bob

Mr Bob owns lots of newspapers. Mr Bob likes to see his picture in ▶

all his newspapers. Unfortunately, other people don't like to see Mr Bob's picture nearly as much as Mr Bob does. So they don't buy Mr Bob's papers. They prefer the ones owned by Mr Smutty. They'd rather look at boobs than Bob.

What does Mr Bob do? Mr Bob owns things.

What does Mr Bob say? Mr Bob says, "How much will that be?"

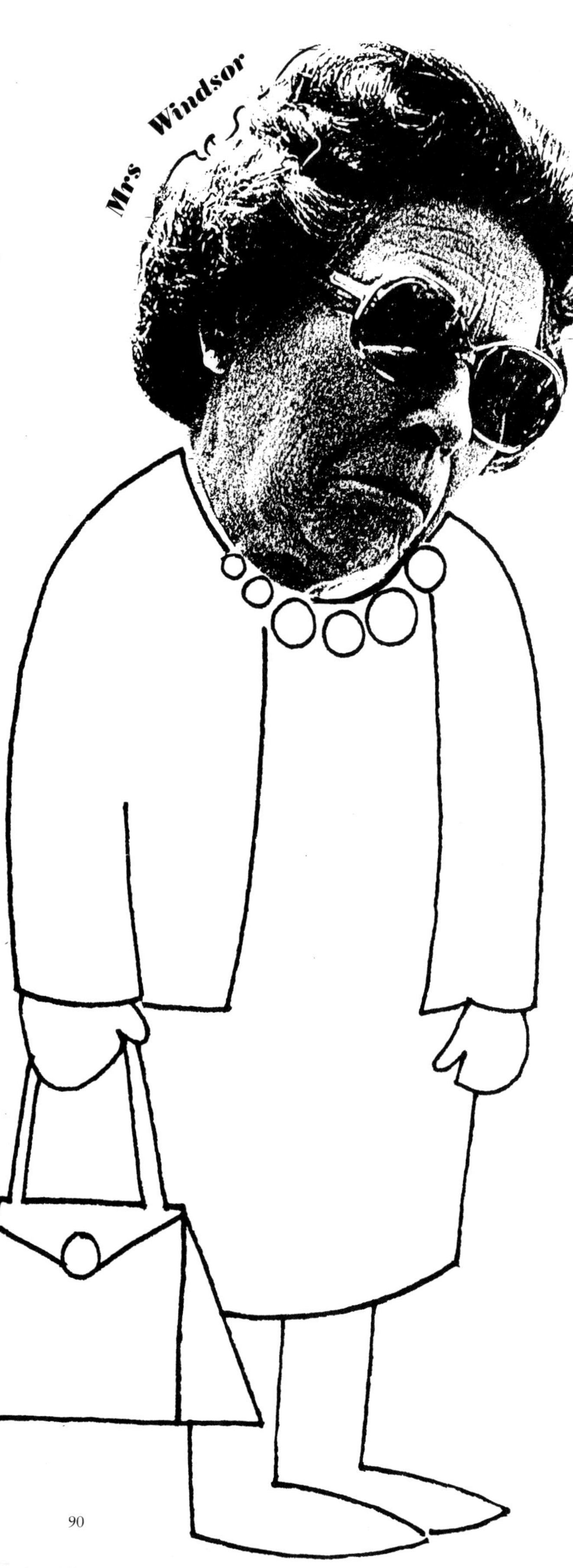

Ms Rumpy-Pumpy

Ms Rumpy-Pumpy likes to play games with boys. She plays "Pass the Pass". She plays "Hide the Sausage". Some of the boys are very upset. They say Ms Rumpy-Pumpy won't play with them unless they give her money. Somewhere between £500 and a grand appears to be the going rate.

What does Ms Rumpy-Pumpy do? Who's asking?

What does Ms Rumpy-Pumpy say? "What I could reveal would make *Scandal* look like a teddy bear's picnic."

Mr Frizzy

Mr Frizzy has electric hair. Mr Frizzy has exploding skin. Mr Frizzy likes exotic girlfriends. Mr Frizzy's exotic girlfriends attract even more exotic publicity. Poor Mr Frizzy. How is he supposed to know what they get up to in their spare time?

What does Mr Frizzy do? Mr Frizzy edits *The Sunday Times.*

What does Mr Frizzy say? Mr Frizzy says, "Look, I beat you every Sunday with my newspaper. If you want Pamella you can have her."

Mr Midget

Mr Midget is very small. Absolutely teensy-weensy. In fact, he's even smaller than that. The big boys won't let Mr Midget play with their ball. But Mr Midget has a plan. He's going to make the big boys carry cards. Now they won't be able to play with their ball either.

What does Mr Midget do? Mr Midget is Minister of Sport.

What does Mr Midget say? Mr Midget says, "I never slept with Ms Rumpy-Pumpy. We are friends, but that is all there is to it."

Mrs Bossy

Mrs Bossy runs the country. So we all have to do whatever Mrs Bossy wants us to do. And that includes Mr Bossy. Mrs Bossy calls herself "we". Mrs Bossy thinks she's the Queen. Which comes as a bit of a shock to Mrs Windsor.

What does Mrs Bossy do? Mrs Bossy rules the world.

What does Mrs Bossy say? Mrs Bossy says, "We are a grandmother."

Mrs Windsor

Mrs Windsor used to be the Queen. She used to be the Queen until Mrs Bossy turned up and decided that *she* was going to be the Queen instead. So now there isn't very much for Mrs Windsor to do. No wonder she dislikes Mrs Bossy so much. Lots of other unemployed people feel the same way.

What does Mrs Windsor do? Mrs Windsor breeds Corgis.

What does Mrs Windsor say? Mrs Windsor says, "My husband and I..."

Duchess Piggy

Duchess Piggy has just had a porking big pay-rise. She needs the money. She needs it to pay for all her holidays. And all her new clothes. And all the other clothes she needs when she can't get into the last lot any more.

What does Duchess Piggy do? Good question.

What does Duchess Piggy say? Duchess Piggy says, "Clock the rocks! Clock the rocks!"

Mr Luvvy

Mr Luvvy is a film director. His films are terribly artistic. But they're terribly, terribly long. Sometimes people say, "Please Mr Luvvy, can we leave now?" And Mr Luvvy says, "You can only leave if you give me an Oscar." So they give him several. Just to be on the safe side.

What does Mr Luvvy do? Mr Luvvy gets nominated.

What does Mr Luvvy say? Mr Luvvy says, "Thank you luvvies. Thank you darlings, thank you, dears. Thank you my lovely, dear, darling luvvies."

Mr Tubby

Mr Tubby has lots of money. About £14 billion at the last count. This money used to belong to us. But Mr Tubby won't give it back. And he won't spend it, either. Mr Tubby just wants to keep his money for a rainy day. Or an election. Whichever comes first.

What does Mr Tubby do? Mr Tubby does whatever Mrs Bossy tells him to do.

What does Mr Tubby say? Mr Tubby says whatever Mrs Bossy tells him to say.

Mrs Bossy

I'M BOSSY

Duchess Piggy

THE 10 MOST DISGUSTING DISEASES IN THE WORLD

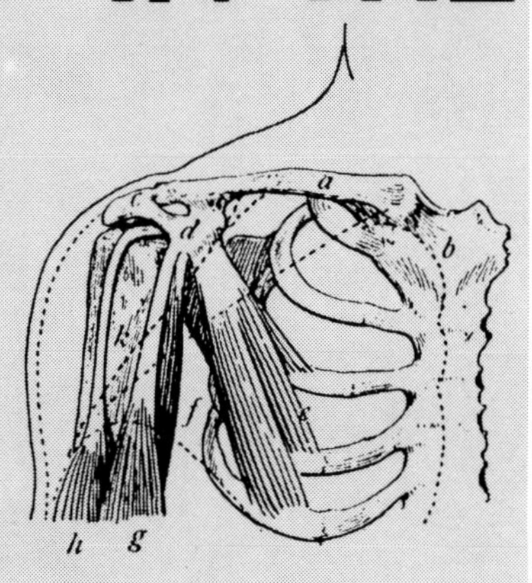

Here is your chance to brush up on all the diseases you don't remember, especially if you'd never heard of them in the first place. CAROL COOPER describes ten illnesses so gruesome that nobody has dared warn you about them. The squeamish may be more at ease with Good Housekeeping

1

Perhaps you haven't been feeling well lately. If friends say you look tired, colleagues call you burnt-out, and Aunt Frieda insists you need a tonic, better check out your nose in the bathroom mirror. Are your yuppy horn-rims slipping down? If so, either you have been too busy to get your specs adjusted, or that trip to South America didn't agree with you.

You've got **New World Leishmaniasis**. It's as old as the hills. The parasite hangs out in a sandfly until, that is, the sandfly finds you. Within a couple of years, the bridge of the nose collapses. Leishmaniasis also destroys mouth and tongue, so that Gevrey-Chambertin tastes like British sherry. Soon, however, you may not care. The cause of the trouble is the innocent-looking leishmania parasite with a cute little tail. It reminds me of a spermatozoan. But unlike pregnancy, leishmaniasis can be avoided by sleeping on the roof. Sandflies don't fly much above three metres.

2

What could be worse than leishmaniasis, apart from income tax, baldness and wheel clamps? It's the illness so dreadful that doctors refer to it in whispers as *Hansen's Disease* to avoid inducing panic in the bus queue. This condition starts with a bit of catarrh, muscle pains, enlarged lymph glands and sometimes a patchy rash. If you're any kind of hypochondriac at all, you will know from the very first sneeze that this is **Leprosy**.

Soon you lose a little pigmentation, and then a few fingers, because they are numb and you chop them up with the celery. By the time the leprosy bacillus gets into its stride, the face is covered in boils or bumps, and friends are apt to be too busy to see you. There may be other complications: inflamed testicles, a spleen like sago pudding, that sort of thing; but any more details would be in bad taste.

Leprosy is highly infectious. Or else it isn't. As usual, the experts disagree. If your doctor rushes out of the consulting room, you'll know which school of thought he adheres to. One study showed that the only certain way of contracting leprosy was to share a bed with a leper for twelve years. There's no need to avoid bus queues, though it is smart to steer clear of lactating lady lepers, who shed leprosy bacilli as if there were no tomorrow.

Actually there is a tomorrow. As the posters tell us, leprosy is curable. Too bad that treating an entire village for a month costs about the same as an expense-account lunch for four, and that's without looking at the wine list.

3

I include **Acromegaly** at the insistence of my four-year-old who has recently abandoned Postman Pat in favour of the *British Medical Journal* and *Punch*. His interest in endocrine disorders started when we saw a particularly florid case on holiday in Switzerland. By then the diagnosis could have been made from the piste 50 yards away, which it was. Why were the man's hands so big, my son wanted to know. And why was he wearing pillows on his feet instead of shoes?

I told him that the pituitary was busy making too much growth hormone. My son was disappointed to learn that acromegaly isn't contagious. However gross acromegaly may become, the onset is subtle: coarse skin and greasy hair, increase in hat size, a little deepening of the yodel, and difficulty making watches or doing up your lederhosen. To be cured, you need to seek help while you are still able to squeeze into cable cars.

4

Even pillows may not fit your feet when you are infected with *wuchereria bancrofti*. Every layman has heard of **Elephantiasis**, though few realise that it begins with just a few lymph glands in the groin. Walking is thus still possible. Swelling sets in later, often in only one leg, and sometimes in the scrotum too, if you have one. Eventually the skin is thrown into rough folds and warty outgrowths. The scrotum, when affected, can hang down to the knees, which poses problems at the tailor's and elsewhere. Prevention is simple. Always use a mosquito net and avoid Burmese septic tanks if you want to wear both legs of your trousers at the same time.

5

Should you dislike rodents, you'll hate **Lassa Fever**. It is transmitted by rats and was discovered in the Nigerian village of the same name, which you might like to make a note to avoid. After it was first described in 1969, the DHSS sent out circulars so that GPs wouldn't miss the diagnosis. As the years passed, I never saw a case, but I kept the literature in case we ever had a wobbly dining table.

Lassa has an insidious onset, with symptoms like those of many diseases, i.e. fever, malaise, headache, a flushed face, red eyes, nausea, vomiting, diarrhoea. Later the nose, gums, mouth, stomach and lungs bleed spontaneously – a plague of blood, with a high mortality. As I remember it, Lassa fever resembles other haemorrhagic fevers, such as Marburg-Ebola, Green Monkey disease, and Crimean-haemorrhagic-Congo-Hazara fever, though I'd have to check under the dining table to be sure.

Anyone who is unconscious when disembarking from West Africa runs the risk of his drunkenness being diagnosed as Lassa fever, with the result that masked attendants whisk him off to the nearest high security isolation unit where he is kept in a plastic tent until the tests are back. I need hardly add that the outlook is much worse when Lassa fever is mistaken for inebriation.

6

Typhus (not to be confused with typhoid) is my next choice. Typhus is caused by organisms called *rickettsiae*, which breed in the gut of the louse, and are transmitted to man in louse faeces. A louse bite is itchy. Scratching it rubs infected droppings into the skin.

As with Lassa, headache, fever and weakness are the early symptoms of typhus, though one may also be prostrate and have a spotty rash. Later the mental state deteriorates, and toes, fingers, ear lobes, even private parts may go gangrenous. About now, the kidneys pack up and perish. But you're in good company – Mozart is said to have died of typhus.

Tsutsugamushi Fever (a.k.a. scrub typhus) is a hot contender for the medical student's all-time favourite, because it has so many syllables, and because it causes a picturesque but painless ulcer covered with a dark crust. More importantly, an attack of *tsutsugamushi* unlike other forms of typhus, gives no immunity against further infection. Medics can therefore imagine repeated episodes of scrub typhus at each outbreak of acne, and some have been known to scratch for several years after exposure to a single lecture.

The louse apart, mites, ticks and fleas can also transmit *rickettsiae*. It is a good idea to check the body daily for ticks etc, and to give yourself a generous dusting with DDT. ▶

Should you fancy something tamer, you might consider keeping a pet worm, like the **Guinea Worm** *dracunculus medinensis.* It beats head lice into a cocked hat. You can try picking one up in Africa in your drinking water. Maintenance is easy as there's no need to keep it in an aquarium or the garden. And you're never alone – it prefers to live just under the skin. I remember one man who called his worm Ali, though as the worm turned out to be female, Alison might have been more appropriate. Anyway Ali lasted a long time, making little red bumps all over him and keeping him company, until the day when she tried to escape through a huge blister on the arm. When the blister finally burst, the little *dracunculus* poked through the skin and started on her way. Ali proved to be several feet long. She had to be wrapped around a stick and pulled out gently to avoid breaking her. The outward journey took two-and-a-half weeks. Bon voyage, Ali!

DR PUNCH'S INSTANT DIAGNOSTIC KIT

Answer the following questions, then count up the points to discover your state of health.

WHEN YOU WOKE UP THIS MORNING DID YOU FEEL...?
(a) Perfectly well, thank you very much
(b) A nagging ache in the back of the neck
(c) Hung-over
(d) Pamella Bordes

OPEN YOUR MOUTH AND SAY...
(a) Aaaah
(b) Ooooh
(c) Yes, yes, yes
(d) Don't stop
(e) Ooops, I just did

ARE YOU PLAYING HOST TO ANY OF THE FOLLOWING...?
(a) Head lice
(b) Flu bugs
(c) Intestinal worms
(d) The *Wogan* show

WHICH OF THE FOLLOWING COMPARE MOST CLOSELY TO YOUR OWN PRESENT STATE OF FITNESS...?
(a) Sebastian Coe
(b) Mark and Sue, who have never taken good health for granted
(c) The Polish economy
(d) Salman Rushdie

SCORE
1 pt for every (a)
2 pts for every (b)
11 pts for every (c)
83 pts for every (d)
–83 pts for every (e)

ANALYSIS
Yes. If you've read this far, you'll almost certainly need it.

Just when you thought it safe to go on a business trip if you took a good book, spare a thought for **Kuru** and take a good sandwich as well. Kuru causes shaking, staggering and eventually complete loss of mind. Not a blinding hangover, this, but an incurable disease. Confined to New Guinea, kuru is blamed on the Fore tribes which consider eating a dead relative's remains the greatest honour that can be bestowed. Unfortunately grandma's brain may harbour this slow virus. The pundits say cannibalism is on the way out, but speaking for myself, when abroad I am still wary of those little local dishes smothered in sauce.

However you needn't travel to catch anything sensational. You can get **Syphilis** without leaving the country. It's Columbus's fault, since, the story goes, his sailors brought it to Europe in 1493. What is certain is that an epidemic of syphilis spread from Naples throughout Europe in the sixteenth century. The English and Italians called it the French disease, the French called it the Neapolitan disease, and pretty well everyone thought of it as the Great Pox, since smallpox was small potatoes by comparison.

Syphilis is more contagious than leprosy, as just a few minutes in a shared bed will do. A bed may even be superfluous. One man, having been inspired by the notices in the public convenience, claimed to have caught syphilis in the lavatory. "That's a damn silly place to take a woman," replied the consultant.

The Lon Chaney of diseases, syphilis mimicks anything from tonsillitis to athlete's foot. It all depends on the stage of the illness.

The hallmark of early syphilis is a painless ulcer or chancre, which can be found anywhere on the, er, privates. Oh well, genitals then. The secondary stage, a few months later, gives symptoms such as fever, headache, general malaise, aches and pains, a rash (especially on hands or feet), mouth ulcers, enlarged lymph glands, or patchy baldness. Of course this is exactly what everyone goes to the GP with.

Late syphilis sets in several years later, and it's downhill all the way from there. The legs no longer transmit signals about position, and this is the cause of a typical stomping walk often seen in Central London. It also makes you fall into the handbasin when you close your eyes to wash your face. If very wobbly, you may fall into the toilet instead.

There is nothing left to catch at this stage, though one can pass on congenital syphilis, with its stigmata of a saddle-shaped nose and Hutchinson's teeth. These are peg-shaped front teeth, according to the textbooks so typical that they clinch the diagnosis. I had a friend at medical school with just such teeth, but his dad was a bishop so one didn't like to mention it.

No account of horrible diseases would be complete without the scourge of the surgery. When it is diagnosed, you will be referred to hospital, where the doctors recoil as you exhibit the offending part. Sister in charge of the clinic will bundle you out of the building as soon as possible, usually while you are still talking, whereupon she will fumigate the consulting room so that Doctor can enjoy his tea and biscuits in comfort.

They will promise you an operation, but you may not live long enough to get to the top of the waiting-list. Should you manage to get as far as the operating theatre, the procedure will be delegated to the most junior house officer, not because it is so simple, but because nobody else will do it. Blood and pus pour out, and at least one hapless houseman has thrown up on the patient. At this stage, the patient has it easy. By the time he wakes up, the whole gory mess is tidy and bandaged.

Sadly, this unsavoury condition is on the increase. Like most other disfiguring diseases, it has a long incubation period. The cognoscenti call it IGTN, and claim that it is caught in shoe-shops. It may interfere with walking. It will certainly ruin games of footsie-footsie. I look forward to the day when every pair of winkle-pickers carries the government health warning "Wearing shoes may cause **Ingrowing Toe-nails**". As for me, I'll take a plague of locusts any day. ■

Commercial Medicine

In need of a cure for your own top ten diseases? HALDANE scours the ads for the new media medics

"Ah yes, you're one of Doctor Simpson's consumers."

"I'll say it's a cheap stunt. Here comes the gynaecologist."

"Get me the small ads, Miss Benson, I think I'm having a heart attack."

"Let me through – I represent a doctor!"

INTERNATIONAL
CHESS
TOURNAMENT
ENGLAND
V
USSR

INFLATED *egos*

by McLACHLAN

"Somehow I didn't expect to still *have haemorrhoids up here*."

"And who the hell is *this, Laura Ashley?"*

for tough dirt and stains
multi-
pur
new-miniature designs!
exciting technology

Inventions – necessity may be the mother, but frustration is the daughter. MARCUS BERKMANN gives

FUTURE SCHLOCK

a techno-hostile rundown of gizmos that get to him, while Far East correspondent MIKE MARKLEW looks at Japan's new sci-fi SNAFUs

ILLUSTRATION: LAWRENCE ZEEGEN

FUTURE SCHLOCK

In these pampered times, it's somehow entirely appropriate that the world is replete with technological marvels, gadgets and inventions that, when it comes down to it, don't really work. Although it must be said, a few new products have changed life for the better – the full impact on Western civilisation of the TV remote control device, for instance, has yet to be properly assessed. Most modern devices are pretty useless or, to get technical, CRAP (a convenient acronym for Completely Redundant and Absolutely Purposeless).

In a way it's almost heartwarming to think of all those millions of quids thrown into the furnace by the naïvely optimistic companies who research and develop these products. Or at least it would be if that was the way things worked out. As it is, unutterable CRAPness has never been a barrier to commercial success. Indeed, some of the most facile inventions of the past 30 years have made depressingly large piles of money for everyone concerned.

All this may explain why the non-functional nature of these products is something not usually discussed in public – there's far too much to lose. If everyone thought that certain products were, well, CRAP, then who would buy them? Exactly. Whole careers in sales and marketing would be on the line.

The question is, could we at *Punch* really live with ourselves if scores of men called Nigel with polyester ties, in-car fax machines and gold chains on their loafers were deprived of employment simply on account of our single-minded quest for truth and justice? You bet we could.

So here is our selection of things and products of which even the most generous observer would have to say, "It's CRAP!"

London underground ticket machines

London Transport spent countless millions installing these impressive-looking machines into Central London stations – all to save on station manpower. The trouble is, no one wants to use them. By the time you've put the ticket in the wrong way, caught it on the rebound, put it in the right way, not been allowed through the automatic exit, called for the manager, shouted at the manager, had your ticket (an all-day Travelcard) returned after the engineer has extracted it from the machine's inner workings with pliers, and finally left the station threatening sundry lawsuits to everyone in uniform, the man in front of you, who just showed his *ticket to the fellow in the booth, has reached the office and fired you for persistent lateness. Result: everyone shows their tickets to the fellow in the booth. Total savings on station manpower: nil.*

Just to make matters worse, when the new Chairman of London Transport (regular means of transport: a chauffeur-driven car) turned up for a photo-call at Victoria tube station, he posed next to the new barriers. And, surprise, surprise, all seven of them were bust.

These fancy new toothpaste dispensers

Pretty groovy, aren't they? Never again will you need to lie in bed at night wondering if you're going to be able to extract that last squeeze from the toothpaste tube in the morning. With these fancy new toothpaste dispensers you know you won't be able to: the last two or three days' paste remains relentlessly inaccessible to all known household utensils. But there's more. Take one of these fancy new toothpaste dispensers on an aeroplane, and guess what happens? Yes, it explodes, covering all of your personal belongings with minty Tooth-o-gleem. Although you won't be able to clean your teeth when you reach your destination, your clothes will never have smelt fresher.

Car alarms

The basic idea of car alarms is simple – to stop unwanted intruders from gaining access to the inside of your car and the various stereos, portable telephones and in-car fax machines you have secreted under the front seat. Sadly this superbly straightforward concept has not translated easily to the real world. A passer-by

---

NEW JAP CRAP

Mag-Lev for Seito-Chashi

Requests by residents living beneath the new Seito-Ohashi bridge, which spans the Japan inland sea, to reduce the noise created by the trains, may soon be answered.
Japan Rail's Mag-Lev Research Organisation will conduct a trial run of their experimental "Super-Magnet Hover Coil" car across the bridge in May.
JR discovered the steel bridge contained sufficient magnetic reluctance to allow use of the "SMHC" developed by them. Tests proved that enough lift can be obtained by using eight SMHCs to raise the weight of one 250 per cent over-laden passenger carriage above the rails. The trains will be able to reach cruising speeds of over 300 kph powered by twin Rolls-Royce gas turbine engines.
"It's a much prettier sound," a JR spokesperson advised, "than the present *clankety-clank*, and is considerably less noisy than a USAF F16 on a night-landing practice run."
If the trial is satisfactory, JR plans to introduce the new service in time for the Spring Cherry Blossom viewing season of 1998.

Computerised roads

An error in construction may have paved the way for computerised driving. During reconstruction of the roads on Okinawa Island after the last war, considerable amounts of "Rubidium" (a powder derivative of ruby) were put into the bitumen used for road making. The product was intended to increase the lifetime of the surface, but due to a lack of supply of the precious stone, a synthetic compound was used.
The Japan Ministry of Science and Technology has discovered that this synthetic compound can be electrically polarised, in much the same way as magnetic tape.
A major computer manufacturer has been given permission to encode all roads on Okinawa, and work begins in May. It will soon be possible for residents to install a small device in their vehicles which will allow them, under auto-pilot control, to proceed to any chosen point on the island.
Pre-programming routes can be done on any IBM-compatible home computer. And there is no possibility of collision as all metallic objects are sensed and automatically avoided. Life-forms are also detected using a tiny infra-

brushing his raincoat fleetingly against the window of your wired-up car will instantly trigger off the 90 dB alarm, causing three nearby old ladies to require urgent medical treatment. Anyone actually getting into the car – especially late at night in a residential area – can expect a similar result.
In fact, there's only one person who can get into your car without a murmur: the professional car thief, who goes quietly about his business, removing all your electronic equipment, including the alarm, in fourteen seconds. As it is, few people now react when a car alarm goes off, because everyone assumes it has gone off by mistake. And because the nearest parking place you could find was half-a-mile away from where you were actually going, you never hear it anyway.

Sticky tape

Modern sticky tape is much thinner and more brittle than it was, probably because improved production techniques mean it can be manufactured that way in South Korea or Paraguay at enormous profit to everyone – except the consumer. So when you try to rip off a bit with any force, does it pull easily away from the roll? Or does it split straight down the middle, leading to half-an-hour's anguished picking at the side that remains?

Fruit juice makers

Hugely trendy and completely useless. To make the fruit juice, first go to your greengrocer and buy most of Chile's annual fruit crop. Then insert it, piece by piece, into your fruit juice maker. While it makes an impressive-sounding noise, the only consumable product is half a cupful of fruity sludge as the three bin-liners full of pulp have to be thrown away. While it is, of course, far easier and cheaper to nip up to the 7-11 and buy a carton of the real stuff, that defeats the object – which is to show the machine off to your friends at dinner parties. As a conversation piece, a fruit juice maker has its advantages; as a fruit juice maker, it sucks.

Psion Organisers

When home computers first appeared on the market, everyone searched for a good reason to buy them. One possible use that was readily leapt upon was as a sort of electric diary-cum-address book. Naturally, in the time that it took to call up any information on these ridiculous machines, you could not only have opened and referred to your real address book, but also phoned everyone in there as well.
It's interesting, then, to see this old chestnut disinterred for the marketing of the Psion Organiser, a pocket calculator with serious delusions of grandeur. Inputting the necessary information takes weeks, and extracting it again takes even longer than my own preferred method of information storage and retrieval, the notorious Back Of The Envelope System. But with its many keys and flashing lights, a Psion Organiser is probably quite fun to show off in the boozer if your name is Nigel, and satisfyingly (for me) overpriced.

This is, of course, a mere sample of crap products – and we are all afflicted by them, every day of our lives. Why are all pedal-bin-liners too small? Why do replacement windscreen wipers come in packets of two, when only one breaks at a time? And why do roller blinds always stick when you want them to roll up, and fail to stick when you want them to stay down?

If there's a particular product whose uselessness makes you boil, write to Marcus Berkmann, *Punch*, 23-27 Tudor Street, London EC4 and let me know. Anything printed will win something that's far from useless – a boxed set of the first titles in the *Punch* Really Useful Guide:

● *The Pamella Bordes Motorcyclist's First Aid Kit.*
● *Regaining Self-Esteem: A Skoda-Owner's Manual.*
● *Plug That Leak! Lord Young's Home Office Handbook of DIY (ti).*

---

red sensor.
Under an agreement with the American Government, cars fitted with the unit will automatically revert to manual control upon entering any US Base on the island.

Ultra fast lap-top

A major innovation in lap-top computers by the Meguro High-Tech Institute will be demonstrated to the public on Saturday at Tokyo's new 45,000-seat, inflatable amphitheatre.
MHTI has taken the floating platform developed by Japan Rail's "Mag-Lev" Research Organisation and combined it with the Takeshita, AH (Advanced Hysterisis) thyristor announced last month, to produce what is believed to be the first, ultra-high-speed, transportable personal computer, the "Rap-Topu 5000".
By adding a freon-cooled computer to give superconductivity speeds in processing, it is possible for a typist to input large amounts of data without actually depressing the keyboard keys. Production units will have the coolant cylinder built into the carrying handle, and plans are already under way for the agent to be changed to a non-ozone-depleting substance by 1998.
"Under a joint venture with the Ministry of Science and Technology, we are working on a very large-scale computer," a spokesperson advised. "This will have many of our Rap-Topu computers connected together in such a way that it will be possible to obtain answers to hypothetical questions without input of the operand."
High-ranking Japanese officials' secretaries will be given access to this device to enable them to determine the results of any planned excursions into the share market. President Bush is expected to use it also, to screen candidates for certain senior positions.

Earphone translator

A major breakthrough in translating devices by the Meguro High-Tech Institute will be on display at the Alien Language Festival to be held this Saturday at Hibiya Park, Tokyo. (Foreign passport holders are admitted free.)
A number of Japanese manufacturers have pooled their superconductive technologies and constructed what is believed to be the world's first translation device which can be worn in the ear. Weighing less than a packet of cigarettes, the present model is designed to translate from Japanese into American English.
"We are aiming at the visiting diplomats," explained an MHTI spokesperson. "Most Japanese politicians can understand American, but nobody can comprehend them when they speak it."
The speaker makes six simple sounds first and thereafter the device will emit the American equivalent of some hundred Japanese phrases – many more than is used in present day government-to-government negotiations. Key phrases are "I've got a Yen for some Geisha," and "Who's sake now?"
The unit will not be available to the public because it is COCOM classified, as there is a possibility of the memory being re-programmed with propaganda or even advertising slogans. A joint research team between MHTI and the FBI is working towards producing a micro-chip, suitable for two-way translation, which can be implanted in the brains of senior Government officials. Research efforts are being hampered by a lack of fully-functioning official brains available for experiment. ■

TRASH INTO CASH

Watch out Charles Saatchi. You are not the only person with a major collection of Modern Art. Thousands of colour supplement readers are catching up, buying masterpieces-by-mail such as *The Girl Evacuee* in Fine China, *Crystal Caper* in full-lead crystal, and *The Great Ships of the Golden Age of Sail*, on "the finest, gold-decorated porcelain". Timeless artefacts, by leading sculptors and painters, beside whom David Hockney is merely a bleached mop-top from Bradford. World-renowned names like Derek G. M. Gardner, James Carpenter and Adrian Hughes. Never heard of them? You may be missing out on an edifying investment. GRAHAM VICKERS investigates the instalment-plan Museum Without Walls

Your tiny china armada keeps you in touch with art and history – and beats inflation

Our reputation as a nation of art lovers is allegedly under threat. You may have heard vague rumblings. Should the Government really be turning the art schools into design factories? Frowning upon The Arts Council? Demanding entrepreneurial skills from artists who are by tradition incapable of selling even their paintings, let alone themselves?

It seems to me rather regrettable that this sort of scaremongering should go unchallenged, particularly when the facts speak so eloquently to the contrary. The proof is all around us, and nowhere is it more evident than in that flourishing branch of the arts where King Arthur, Mrs Wallis Simpson and Little Bo-Peep are to be found in a resonant synthesis of our golden heritage. I refer of course to the world of collectable *objets d'art.*

Flip through your Sunday supplements and there, for the asking, are various introductions to the world of art collecting, all pieces coming in formats ideal for despatch by post. Naturally this cultural well-spring is ignored by those with a blind political commitment to publicly-owned museums where exhibits are drably displayed for (but, significantly, never sold *to*) a public with an essentially acquisitive hunger for culture. I would suggest that jaded institutions of this sort are quite out of touch with the aesthetic spirit of the times. For example, speaking as someone who has visited The British Museum at least twice, I am in a position to state that nowhere within its echoing halls is there to be found an Excalibur backgammon set inspired by the enduring legend of King Arthur... and yet exactly this item is readily available from Franklin Mint Ltd of London, SE6. True, they will only send the set in instalments in return for an extended financial commitment of some complexity, but this is nothing that a major museum's financial director assisted by a couple of accountants couldn't quickly come to grips with, if he so chose.

The real point is that The Franklin Mint, having somehow managed to acquire a priceless memento from the games cupboard at Camelot, is prepared to let it go to anyone who wishes to buy into history. This seems to me to represent the sort of art we need more of today – fragments of our heritage purchased privately and installed in our homes as a constant source of beauty and patriotic inspiration.

In this same spirit The Franklin Mint also offers a series of porcelain plate portraits entitled *Great Ships of the Golden Age of Sail* which, quite honestly, make J. M. Turner's marine canvases look like the blotchy gropings of an untutored Sunday painter. Derek G. M. Gardner may not yet merit an entry in the art history books, but by God he knows how to get *H.M.S. Endeavour* bang in the middle of a nine-inch plate with every rigging detail intact...*and* how to tie up a lucrative distribution deal for the result.

Meanwhile, investors in *Great Ships of the Golden Age of Sail* can rest assured that their tiny porcelain armada is not only putting them in daily touch with art and history, it may also be providing them with a useful hedge against inflation. I think you catch my drift. If not, you will have to hope that some chance purchase revealing your interest in fine things will result in your name being added to the direct mailing list of one of the major suppliers of collectable art. Because this is where the real marriage of art and commerce flourishes. May I quote from a personal letter that I received recently from John R. MacArthur of The Bradford Exchange?

"Dear Friend,

Suppose that 25 years ago the Chairman of IBM had offered you stock in his company and guaranteed to buy it back any time during the first year for the full price you paid...

Of course that didn't happen. Most opportunities don't come with guarantees. But I'm about to describe a plate that does..."

True to his word, Mr MacArthur goes on to describe *Polperro* which his letter suggests may be viewed either as "Plate One in the new Famous Fishing Harbours series by Kevin Platt" or alternatively as "a plate that could break records in secondary market trading". Where, in Vincent Van Gogh's interminable exchange of letters with his brother, did we see any hint of this sort of awareness? And I need not remind you that Vincent was a man whose paintings have subsequently proved to be so marketable as to make any suburban home without one the object of quiet derision among its neighbours.

But, you may ask, doesn't all this mean that art is now about acquisition and investment, that its ennobling aspects are in danger of being lost? By way of reply, let me simply refer you to an offer called *The Windsor Style.* I cannot, offhand, think of a nobler and more emotion-charged story than that of the abdication and the successful TV mini-series it inspired. Now, through Carlyle Fine Arts, it is possible for art lovers to tap into the world of Edward and Mrs Simpson in exactly the same spirit that engendered their timeless romance: her jewels are up for grabs. Or at least their very essence is, which is almost the same thing. I quote: "As a salute to the Duke and Duchess of Windsor and the jewels which marked the love affair of the century, Carlyle proudly presents 'The Windsor Style' – a selection of three brooches representing the very essence of the Windsor jewels."

These brooches, including the Duchess's alleged favourite, the Flamboyant Flamingo ("handset with tiny brilliant rhinestones"), seem to me to be so surprisingly inexpensive at around £30 each, that the sensitive art collector, watching them drop through the letter box, might experience no small pang of remorse on behalf of the woman who after all received the prototypes as a consolation prize for not becoming Queen. If this is not heartfelt art, then I really don't know what is.

But if you want further evidence of the emotional probity of today's most popular art, consider Royal Doulton's heart-wrenching figurine *The Girl Evacuee.* Of course, to the untrained eye it may look like an 8″ statue of a shabbily-dressed little girl sitting in such a way as to suggest the imminent need of a visit to the loo (an impression rather unfortunately echoed by the title), but to the thoughtful art lover it is a moving evocation of a period in our history of which personal sacrifice, civic responsibility and strong leadership were the very foundations.

There is a dark side to all this. Where valuable art thrives, so do unscrupulous people, and it is clear from the impassioned advertising copy for ▶

ART APPRECIATION

A Punch *investigation*

So, you've shelled out your hard-earned money on a delightful set of porcelain figurines and now here's a charming Spode nature scene that's just caught your eye; the question is, will it really *be a good investment?*

Let's look at The Bradford Exchange's very own Market Analysis Reports and see what they say. Well, the first thing they say is, "To be completed in triplicate. Original to John R. MacArthur: blue copy to Market Analyst; pink copy to file". They don't say anything about sending copies to Mr Punch, but never mind, we got 'em anyway.

The first work under consideration is entitled Morning in the Farmyard. *"A rural scene from a bygone era, created by John L. Chapman and beautifully realised in fine Wedgwood Queen's Ware".*

Bradford Exchange says that this "richly detailed work... recreates a vital part of England's rural heritage, a 'memory' of the past conjured up in the imagination of an accomplished modern artist... Morning in the Farmyard *takes us to a peaceful corner of rural England, where man and animal work in harmony to earn a living from the soil."*

Forgetting for the moment that rural England in the nineteenth century was far from tranquil, being instead the setting for poverty, disease and outbreaks of social unrest that would make our modern lager lout scuffles look like a temperance society picnic, let's concentrate on the art. It's awful; saccharine genre work that would have seemed outdated when the past was more than just a "memory".

The Bradford Exchange's market analyst takes a different view, observing, "Wedgwood first issues performing consistently well on secondary market. This could accelerate demand for Morning in the Farmyard. *Notify interested parties of availability and urge them to act now to avoid disappointment."*

To back up his confidence, our friendly analyst provides a chart of previous Wedgwood releases, viz:

TOP-PERFORMING WEDGWOOD FIRST ISSUES

Year	**Plate**	**Issue Price**	**Last U.K. Sale**	**Last Sale as % of Issue**
1969	*Wedgwood Christmas "Windsor Castle"*	*£4*	*£215*	*5375%*
1971	*Wedgwood Calendar "Victorian Almanac"*	*£2.10*	*£44.50*	*2119%*
1971	*Wedgwood Children's Story "Sandman"*	*£1.45*	*£21*	*1448%*
1977	*Wedgwood Blossoming of Suzanne "Innocence"*	*£30*	*£63*	*210%*
1985	*Wedgwood Street Sellers of London "The Baked Potato Man"*	*£11.95*	*£35*	*292%*

Pretty amazing, no? Bet you wish you'd put your money into Windsor Castle *or* The Potato Man *instead of squandering it all on Sid and the property market. What concerns us, however, is the relative failure of* The Blossoming of Suzanne "Innocence", *up a mere 210 per cent since 1977, well below the rate of inflation. What is it with poor Suzanne? Doesn't anybody love her? Is innocence a worthless commodity in this cynical world of ours? And what would be the prospects of a special* Punch *plate:* The Blossoming of Judy "Violence"? ■

◀ The Danbury Mint's statuette of *Little Bo-Peep*, that forgers are a constant threat. "Look at the fingers!" it says, a trifle hysterically. "Individually defined in lifelike detail, and so much more delicate than those of other, inferior figurines." *Little Bo-Peep* works out at £98 which, says Danbury, "represents excellent value when you consider the price asked for figurines that cannot match *Little Bo-Peep* for quality or charm".

It was this transparent *cri de coeur* that suddenly made me want to know more about the origins of the new champions of our national art. So I rang The Danbury Mint. They didn't answer. Perhaps they were all out tracking down a cache of bootleg Bo-Peeps, I don't know. Disappointed, I tried The Bradford Exchange where a helpful, but I suspect visually unsophisticated, man explained to me how his company's success was heavily dependent upon the marketing of nostalgic clichés to which he personally would not give house room. This puzzled me and I was left feeling that we had little common ground for discussion *vis-à-vis* art. When he started referring to a perfectly charming Bradford Exchange offer featuring *English Thoroughbred Horses* as "an above-the-line-manifestation" I felt it was definitely time to move on.

The real news came from collectable pioneers and market-leaders The Franklin Mint. From them I learned that the parent company was US-based and until recently was owned by Warner Bros. Of course. How appropriate that the driving force should have come from a company which has an unrivalled expertise in fine art (ask yourself honestly, could Bugs Bunny have been British?) and a country which combines a healthy appetite for history with an unashamed talent for commercial enterprise.

We can only speculate how companies like The Franklin Mint of Pennsylvania and indeed The Bradford Exchange of Chicago dealt with the absence of an indigenous history when first setting out their stall back home. No doubt at times they had to use a little artistic licence. However no such problems faced them when they came to Britain: the rich associative opportunities presented by real historical personages such as King Arthur and Little Bo-Peep must have come as a welcome relief after the thin pickings garnered by a handful of George Washington busts and half a dozen commemorative Betsy Ross figurines.

Finally, a word of warning seems appropriate. Despite all this activity, still cultured societies need their avant garde artists, and it may be plausibly argued that the merest trace of conservatism runs through works of art I am advocating. It is for this reason that I would suggest that some more challenging contemporary themes should be tackled from time to time. For example, even with the next election some considerable way off, it still may not be too early to start work on a limited edition entitled, tentatively, *The Falklands Spirit*. Something showing *The Belgrano* being seen off by a helicopter, perhaps with a Windsor at the controls. Or maybe just grazing island sheep bathed in sunset's last glow. Either way I really think it could have very strong market credentials.

THE PUNCHMINT COLLECTION

This week Mr Punch is proud to present The Punchmint Collection – a series of beautiful artworks that will grow into a treasurehouse of culture for you and your descendants. These magnificent contemporary masterpieces will give you a Library of Heritage and an unrivalled get-rich-slowly-style Investment Opportunity. The first two offerings from the Punchmint Collection are being released to the public this week. They comprise . . .

The Country Lassie

Here is an image embodying everything that is lovely and wholesome about the English Countryside. World-renowned artist Karl N. Blacklable has conjured up a delightful picture of fresh faced innocence and prominent dentistry. His genuine oil-painting has been interpreted by skilled craftsmen and hand-embossed onto an edition of 150,000 beautifully-crafted, hard-wearing PVC tea-trays. This unique combination of traditional art with contemporary technology sums up the very best of Then and Now.

Les Bicyclettes de Penge

Come with us back to more innocent times, when Spaghetti Junction was the name of an Italian railway station and a contraflow system was a toilet that wouldn't flush. Those were the days when hearty yeomen and honest working lads would strap on their cycling clogs and pedal off to office or mill, secure in the knowledge that their saddlebags were filled with hearty Hovis sandwiches. Armed only with an overactive imagination and an old video of Ken Russell's Women In Love, *Continental maestro Thor de France has brilliantly recreated an entirely spurious slice of misleading nostalgic piffle. It comes to you in a limited edition of only seven million copies, machine-printed with vibrant da-glo inks on a square of 100 per cent man-made shag-pile orlon velveteen.* ■

LOVE & MARRIAGE

"Just a minute – did you say forsake all others?"

"What's happening to us, Graham? We never finish our arguments any more."

"Hullo, darling – your case or mine?"

"You don't laugh any more.
All you do is nod and say, 'That's funny'."

"As soon as I saw you, I said to myself, there's a man who isn't married."

EUROT

It's the same old song contest

TEN GREAT EURO BRIT HITS

1967 PUPPET ON A STRING SANDIE SHAW
Sandie started it all. For me, anyway. Oh yeah, there had been Pearl Carr and Teddy Johnson with *Sing little birdie*. The Allisons and *Are you sure?* Even Kathy Kirby and Matt Monro had a go at Eurovision. But it was the former Sandra Goodrich from Dagenham who became the first British winner, in 1967. Barefoot, long before Buddhism and chanting *Nam-Myho-Renge-Kyo* – a possible Euro entry? – Sandie was singing: 'I wonder if one day that/you say that, you care/ If you say you love me madly, I'd gladly be there/ Like a puppet on a string'. The song didn't stretch the singer spiritually. She quit showbusiness shortly afterwards.
VERDICT: Eurovision can build or bury careers. Full marks for getting out while on top.
SCORE: United Kingdom: Ten ● United Kingdom 10 points

1969 BOOM BANG A BANG LULU
Marie McDonald McLaughlin Lawrie and the poignant poetry of *Boom bang a bang* was one of four winners with eighteen points in 1969. 'My heart goes boom bang a bang/ loud in my ear'. Folklore suggests that the song was sung as a panegyric to the balding Bee Gee whom the 'wee yin' later wed.
VERDICT: The marriage fell apart, as did Maurice Gibbs' hairline and Lulu's career.
SCORE: Grossbritannien: Vier ● Great Britain: 4 points

By 1970 we were hard pushed to find a female singer to represent us abroad. Bassey was too big, and rumoured to be black. Dusty was too good, and too popular with the gay audience. Cilla and Petula didn't stand a chance as professional scouse accents and shag perms don't travel. The job was left to a former folk singer and *Opportunity Knocks* winner from Wales.

1970 KNOCK KNOCK WHO'S THERE MARY HOPKIN
A girl with an accoustic guitar and an ethnic smock implied two things to judges across the globe – free love and marijuana. Mary and her middle-parting didn't stand a chance against a sixteen-year-old Irish virgin with a two syllable name. *All kinds of everything* was the nearest ex-convent girl Dana was ever to come to a drug-induced state of heightened awareness. 'Snow drops and daffodils/butterflies and bees/ Sail boats and fishermen/things of the sea/ Wishing wells, wedding bells/a snowflake or two/ All kinds of everything remind me of you.'
VERDICT: 'Hopkin the voice' was a folk fish in a pop pool and finished second.
SCORE: Engleskom: Devet ● England: 9 points

1971 JACK IN A BOX CLODAGH RODGERS
British songwriters went back to the nursery in an attempt to recapture the success of *Puppet on a string*. Foreign voters didn't fall for it a second time and voted Severine from Monaco the outright winner. *Un band, un arbre, une rue* found its way up the British hit parade in the singer's native tongue. We couldn't understand what she was singing, but at least it kept Clodagh out of the charts.
VERDICT: Rodgers outraged the organisers by promoting both nymphomania and the coil: 'I'm just a jack in a box/ you know whenever love knocks/I'm gonna jump up an' down on my spring.'
SCORE: *Royaume Unie: Trois* ● *United Kingdom 3 points*

DO your own THiNG!

RASH

Just as every American knows where they were when Kennedy was shot, every Briton knows where they were when The New Seekers lost the Eurovision Song Contest in 1972. Where were you? And where will you be on 6 May when millions once again tune in to watch 22 countries take part in the 34th annual song competition?

WILKOMMEN! BIENVENUE! WELCOME! to the *Punch* world of Eurovision past and present. Read about songs you hoped you'd forgotten by artists you wish you'd never heard of. The girls were sweet, the boys were glandular, the clothes were flared and floral, and the songs were... *rubbish!* MICHAEL COLLINS names that tune

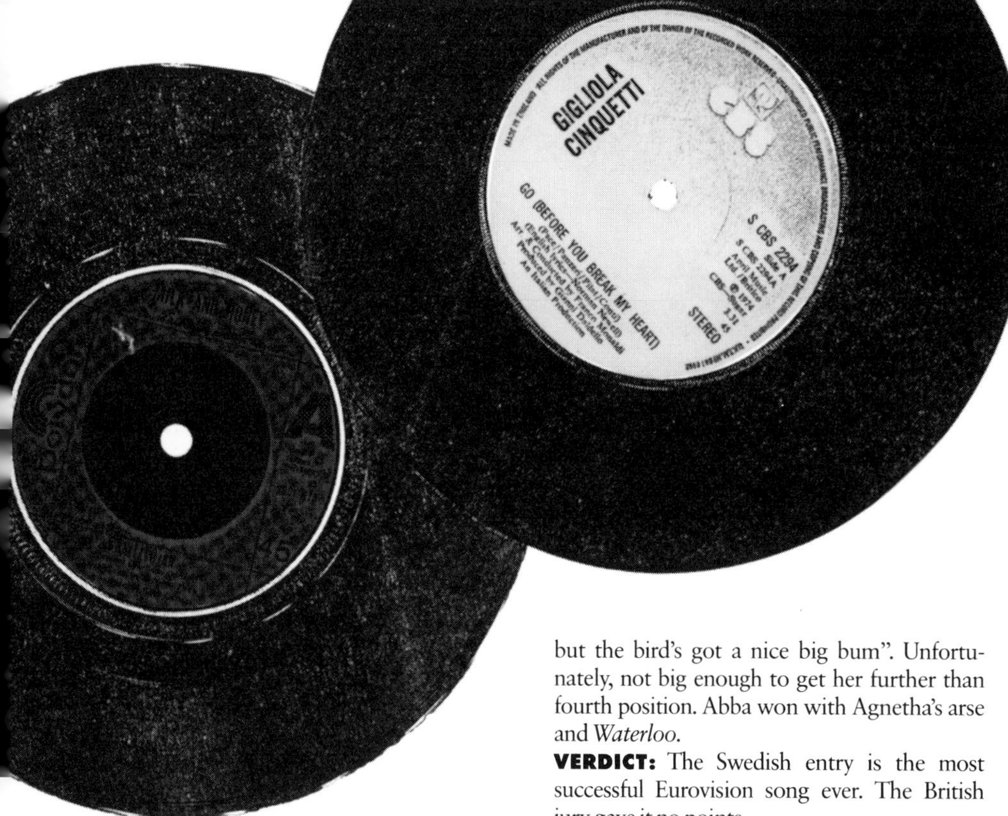

1972 BEG, STEAL OR BORROW
THE NEW SEEKERS

Europe continued to send foreign girls with feather cuts into Europe. We diversified and entered *Popswop* pin-ups Peter, Paul, Marty, Eve and Lyn. The group was too stoned on the success of their coke ad anthem *I'd like to teach the world to sing* to realise that *Beg, steal or borrow* had B-side written all over it. The Greek midget Vicky Leandros represented Luxembourg with a French song and came out top. *Après toi* translated into broken English as *Come what may* and featured on the TV-advertised *20 Fantastic Hits* on Arcade.

VERDICT: The group gets good marks for trying to sneak a guitar solo into Eurovision.

SCORE: Anglia: Okto ● England 8 points

1973 POWER TO ALL OUR FRIENDS
CLIFF RICHARD

Cliff Richard is celibate. The only thing he has entered in the last twenty-odd years is the Eurovision Song Contest. Twice. Nearly coming first on one occasion. *Congratulations* was second in '68 but is played at silver weddings in South London to this day. *Power to all our friends*, at the 1973 contest, was an attempt at gospel. Cliff and Christianity are synonymous. Cliff and choreography are not. The knee-knocking, hand-raising dance routine which accompanied the chorus of the song lost him the competition and goes down as the most embarrassing moment in Eurovision.

VERDICT: Cliff claims his career is an act of divine intervention. God denies it.

SCORE: Gran Bretaña: Uno ● Great Britain: 1 point

1974 LONG LIVE LOVE
OLIVIA NEWTON JOHN

Olivia was untalented, Australian and a friend of Cliff's; all three are apparent in this song. As my Uncle Ken put it, so succinctly, at the time, "It sounds like a bleedin' Salvation Army song, but the bird's got a nice big bum". Unfortunately, not big enough to get her further than fourth position. Abba won with Agnetha's arse and *Waterloo*.

VERDICT: The Swedish entry is the most successful Eurovision song ever. The British jury gave it no points.

SCORE: Storbritannien: Två ● Great Britain: 2 points

1975 LET ME BE THE ONE
THE SHADOWS

The year we capitalised on the unfortunate face and Christian name of Cliff's other bosom buddy, Hank Marvin. The sympathy vote took us to second place. Dutch group Teach-In were the winners with an uptempo number that suggested the singing of a simple mantra to relieve stress and a broken heart: 'When you're feeling uptight, everything is alright/ listen to a song that goes dong ding a dong/There will be no sorrow, when you get tomorrow/ even when your lover has gone, gone/sing ding ding dong.'

VERDICT: The Shads looked more like the Turkish entry than the Turkish entry.

SCORE: Groot Britanie: Vijf ● Great Britain: 5 points

1976 SAVE YOUR KISSES FOR ME
BROTHERHOOD OF MAN

Britain won the title for a third time with the tune of *Tie a Yellow Ribbon* and a lyric which dealt with the touchy subjects of paedophilia and incest. Luckily, the content of the song did not become clear until the final phrase: 'Won't you save them up for me/even though you're only three.' The group utilized the successful two boy/two girl line up of Abba, and Cliff's dance sequence. (This didn't look so bad when split four ways.)

VERDICT: High marks for a band name which could have been used by a heavy metal outfit.

SCORE: England: Syv ● England: 7 points

1977 ROCK BOTTOM
LYNSEY DE PAUL AND MIKE MORAN

In 1977 politics met pop and became punk. The subversion and anarchy of the new wave movement were reflected in the lyric of our Eurovision entry of that year. 'Where are we – Rock bottom/Tragedies – we got em/ Remedies – why don't we rub it out and start it again.' The song lacked the immediacy of *Looking through Gary Gilmore's eyes* so the prize went to the Clash-like *L'oiseau, l'enfant* from France.

(From top) Sandie Shaw, Lulu, Bucks Fizz, Cliff Richard, and The New Seekers showing a flare for fashion

VERDICT: Mike and Lynsey sat perched at pianos. They should have pogoed and spat at Katie Boyle.

SCORE: Regno-Unito: Sei ● United Kingdom: 6 points

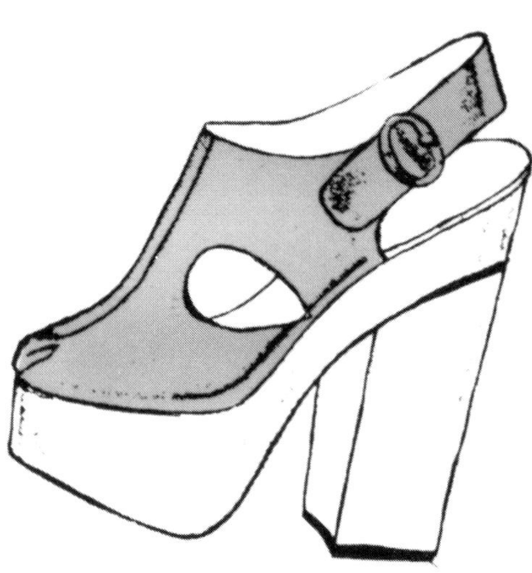

BUCKS FIZZ – THE LEGEND

Cheeky 'cockney sparra' Cheryl Baker helped put us in tenth place in 1978 as a singer in Co-Co. Three years later she surfaced in Bucks Fizz and won. *Making your mind up* praised the power of positive thinking as the two male members of the group ripped off the skirts of the girls, mid-song. The routine was the creation of their manager Nicky Burns. Sadly for Nicky, Jay Ashton continued to rip off her skirt, in order to slip into bed with Mr Burns.

THE FORSYTH SAGA

1964 winner Gigola Cinquetti represented Italy again in 1974 with *Si* (Go). Only two people remember the song: myself and Julie Forsyth. Last year, Jules composed the UK entry *Go* by Scott Fitzgerald. One point pushed the song into second place and caused Bruce Forsyth – Julie's dad – to have an attack of xenophobia backstage. 'Plagiarism' is a foreign term to Bruce. He can't say the word but made a career out of the deed (he used his own material: it was other people's hair he nicked). A skill now passed on to his daughter. Just compare Gigola's *Go! Go before you break my heart,* with Scott's *Goooo, before you break my heart.*

BONJOUR! GUTEN ABEND! WATCHA COCK!

Over-dressed and under-rehearsed, Katie Boyle was never ruffled when repeating 'Come in Norway' or 'Are you receiving me Belgium?' in a blouse so loud that it disturbed the television reception in Lichtenstein. She somehow remained aged 54 throughout her Euro years.

THIS YEAR'S MODEL

RYDER, RIKKI, VIKKI, PRIMA DONNA and **BARDO** are just some of the nonentities we have sentenced to Eurovision this decade. All failed and drifted into anonymity or the Circus Tavern, Purfleet. On 6 May we will be banking on the ballad *Why do I always get it wrong* by Live Report. The title says it all. Members of the group have worked or written for international singing stars like Whitney Houston, Paul McCartney and Dennis Waterman. Professionalism is the opposite of Eurovision.

THE FUTURE

This year's contest in Lausanne, Switzerland will be watched by 75 million in the Soviet Union. If Glasnost and Gorbachev continue, there will one day be a Russian contestant, who will no doubt win. Musically, the Soviets are at the same stage as Eurovision – somewhere in the mid-Sixties. Any aspiring songwriter should obtain a copy of the 1970 long player *Souvenirs of the Eurovision song contest* (MFP 1384), available at selected Help the Aged shops. By listening to tracks like *Vivo cantando, Volare* and *Love is blue* it's possible to appreciate – in the words of the sleeve notes, "how music is not only a fundamental means of communication but also how it can act as a stimulant for better understanding".

On hearing the 1968 winning song from Spain, I know what they mean: 'La la la laaa/ la la laaa/la la laaa laaa/ La la la laaa/ la la laaa laaa'.

WHERE ARE THEY NOW?

1. CLIFF RICHARD – *celebrated his 30th year in pop by celebrating the Conservatives' tenth year in government at the BPI awards.*
2. CLODAGH RODGERS – *turned to country music in the Seventies and* Pump Boys and Dinettes *in the Eighties.*
3. SANDIE SHAW – *rediscovered by Morrissey and recording again.*
4. LYNSEY DE PAUL – *never grew musically, physically or emotionally. Did a 'shag and tell' on James Coburn. Did a sing and sell on Mrs Thatcher.*
5. LULU – *voting Tory, flogging Freemans' catalogue, dying in* Edwin Drood, *playing in* Peter Pan *and getting her Glasgow giggle back for chat shows.*
6. MARY HOPKIN – *went back to her folk roots by calling her children Jessie and Delaney.*
7. THE NEW SEEKERS – *Paul and Marty still perform under the group name. Lyn loved Mike from Bucks Fizz and sold the story.*
8. BROTHERHOOD OF MAN – *who cares?*
9. THE SHADOWS – *will be back behind Cliff again in June.*
10. OLIVIA NEWTON JOHN – *following* Grease *and* Xanadu *she got* Physical *and eventually pregnant.*
11. PRIMA DONNA – *Kate Robbins became to comedy what Prima Donna were to music.*
12. BUCKS FIZZ – *in a car crash, a court case and now a current tour. Cheryl Baker was so broke, she was forced to plummet to TV stardom in* My Secret Desire.

Nothing unites a nation like an INFANTILE TITLE!

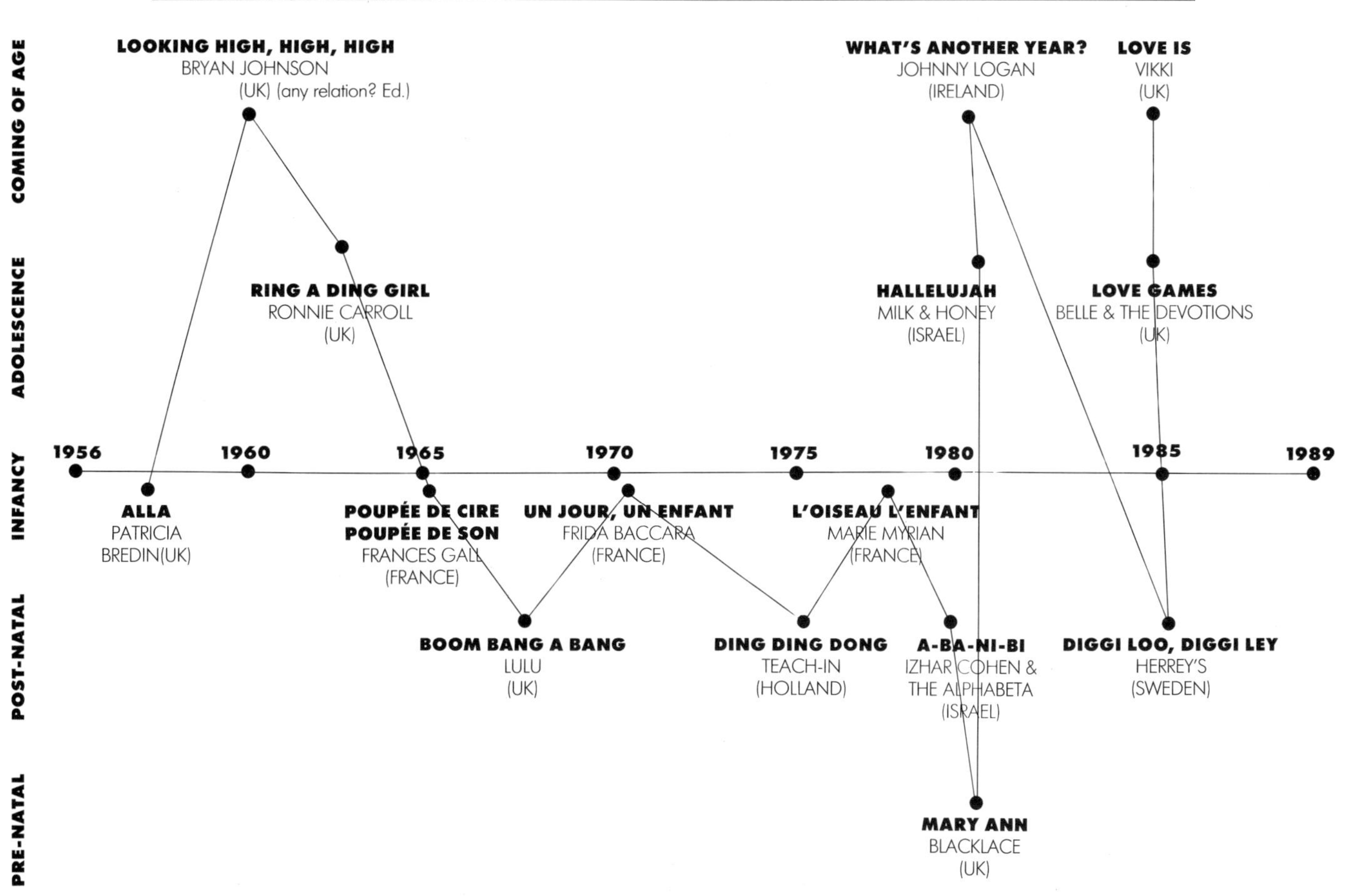

It's a dog's life

Ego-gratification for the environmental Eighties. All the kudos, none of the mess, and the inestimable satisfaction of exploiting a fellow human being. And there's nothing the Animal Liberation Front can do about it

COOL FOR CATS

HEAVY PETTING

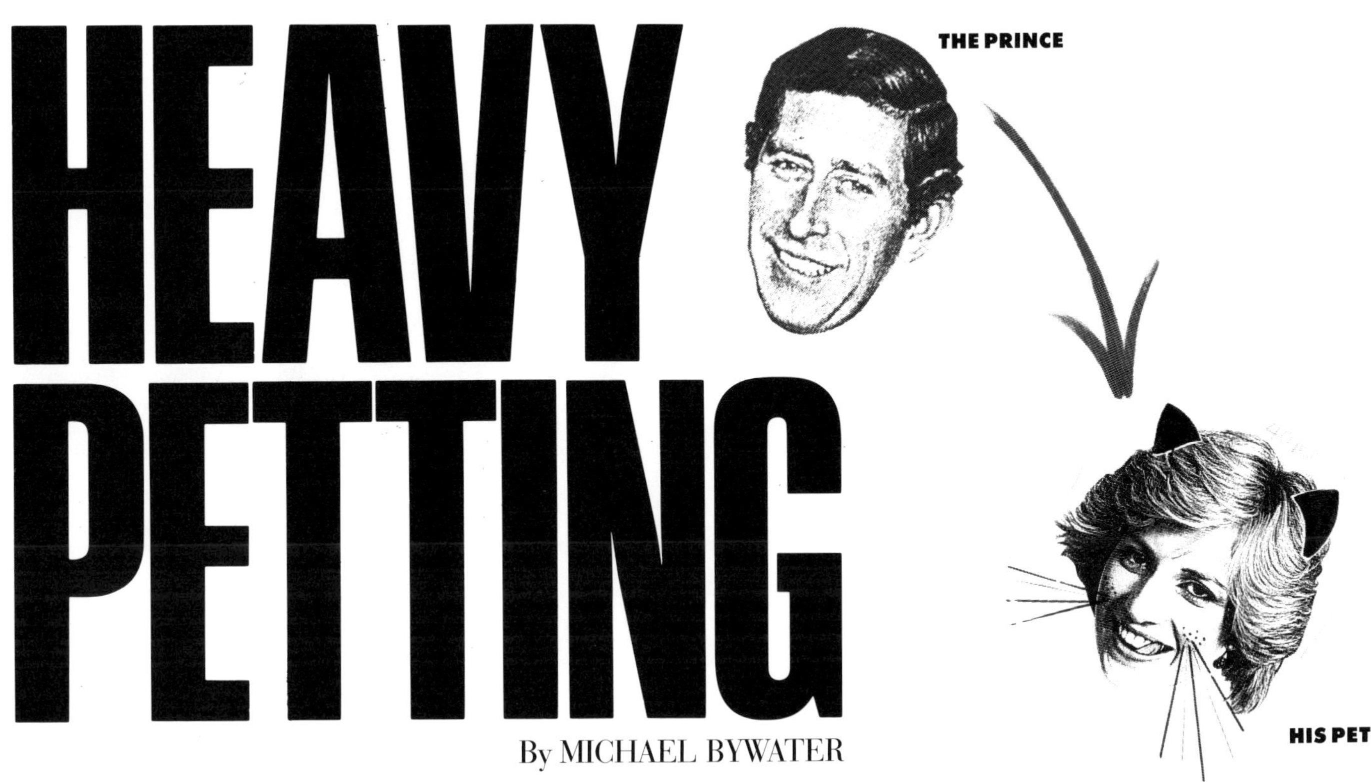

By MICHAEL BYWATER

See the man walking towards you? The one with the muscles clad in the lagging of yellow fat from lager and burgers, and the greyish, reeking, tattooed skin. You can't *see* it, but you know it's there, underneath the yellow Lacoste polo shirt and the Porsche anorak and the acid-washed jeans. This foul creature is doing very nicely, thank you; he is up to something with a rusty white van and a Vodafone, and knows a lot of people called Dave and Tony who have "premises" and Persol sunglasses. Like them, he has a Rottweiler called Göring and soon he will buy himself a mastiff to be called Studs.

These animals supply his deficiencies and create his image for him. People imagine he is strong because he has them, and he thinks that he will acquire their virtues by walking around with them and squirting their excrement on pavements, so that he can let himself go wholly to pieces.

This man is out of date. His ambitions are under-vaulting. Why acquire the virtues of a dirty, smelly, disloyal, half-baked, red-eyed brute which requires to be stuffed with tinned cow's-nostril and horse's-eye twice a day, when you can acquire the virtues and the charisma of another human being, not by eating it like some cannibal in the days before Brent Council showed the world the White Man's Way, but simply by *owning* it.

The days of slavery are over, but the days of possession are with us more than ever. The new status symbol is *your own personal person*. Someone whose identity is defined by your ownership. Someone who is reminding the world of your presence and your power even when you are not around. Someone who won't run out on you when you beat them, but will wait for a kind word, however long it takes, then roll over to be tickled.

It's no good having an *ex officio* pet, like a secretary or subordinate. Their loyalty isn't to you, but to your position. Think of the people you push around. Will any of them follow you when you leave? Or defend you after you are fired? If the answer is "no", you have no pets; you are merely a spectator at the zoo, a hand with a sticky bun on the end, but you have no permanence, no identity, no *power*.

Real pets are different. The ultimate pet of all is the Princess of Wales. Once a pet, always a pet: Her Royal Highness has acquired the status, not of the Prince of Wales, but of the *Prince's pet*. There is a great difference.

Superior status does not always clinch the owner/pet relationship. The Duchess of York keeps the Duke of York as a pet. For many years, Cardinal Marcinkus, the Vatican Banker, kept the Pope himself as a pet, to lend lustre to the Bank and to himself. Nasty criminals in canary jerseys keep comedians and entertainers as pets, and what is more, the entertainers readily consent; all entertainers are pets at heart. Some nasty criminals in canary *vicuña* jerseys keep policemen as pets, too, although usually the policemen believe that *they* are the owners. Roy Garner, the cocaine dealer, kept Superintendent Tony Lundy as a pet for years – or so he thought; after years of bringing little titbits, Lundy suddenly sent Garner to his basket for a *long, long time*.

Pets can be collective. Mrs Thatcher keeps the entire cabinet, and Mrs Marcos kept an entire *nation*, making them do tricks and bring her things and showing them off to her friends until they all went mad one day and ran amok and got into the bedroom and ate her shoes. The Ayatollah Khomeini keeps God as his pet – or so he thinks.

Not everyone is suitable to be a pet. Decorativeness does not count. The most decorative person in London, the monstrously weird and plaguey Leigh Bowery, would be a most unwise choice. Who would want a pet which changed ▶

shape each day, so that you might go to sleep with a cockatrice and awaken to a mandrill? Take, too, those startling and widely-celebrated ornaments to London society, the Blacker sisters Charlotte and Lulu; everything one could desire in a woman, both of them, but *totally unacceptable as pets.* [1] They are noisy and vulgar and forthright; they bark hugely all night long, then appear in the morning, ravenous and bouncy. What is worse, they *refuse to fawn*. Pets *have* to fawn; the ability to go on being impressed is an essential quality of a pet.

There are, too, those who do not want a pet. John Aspinall keeps pets as people, a tricksy sort of eighteenth-century reversal which requires greater investigation than can be provided here, although poking your nose out of your window should convince you that he is quite right.

But his sort are thin on the ground. Drool your way through the rolls of the rich and famous. Almost all of them are masters or pets. It is only the undermass, the toiling classes, the noble, Godly, liberal humanitarians like us who believe in the dignity and rights of mankind. We persuade ourselves that we are decent, utilitarian Benthamites, but where did that ever get anybody? Where did it get Bentham? Embalmed, stuffed and propped up in his glass case for ever – just, in fact, like a favourite pet.

[1] Their father, the benign and diligent Bloggs, kept these two creatures as pets for years. To the ignorant, he appears to have survived, a jovial man of middling stature. What the ignorant are ignorant of is that Bloggs Blacker was *always* jovial, but used to be *huge*. Personally, I blame the mother.

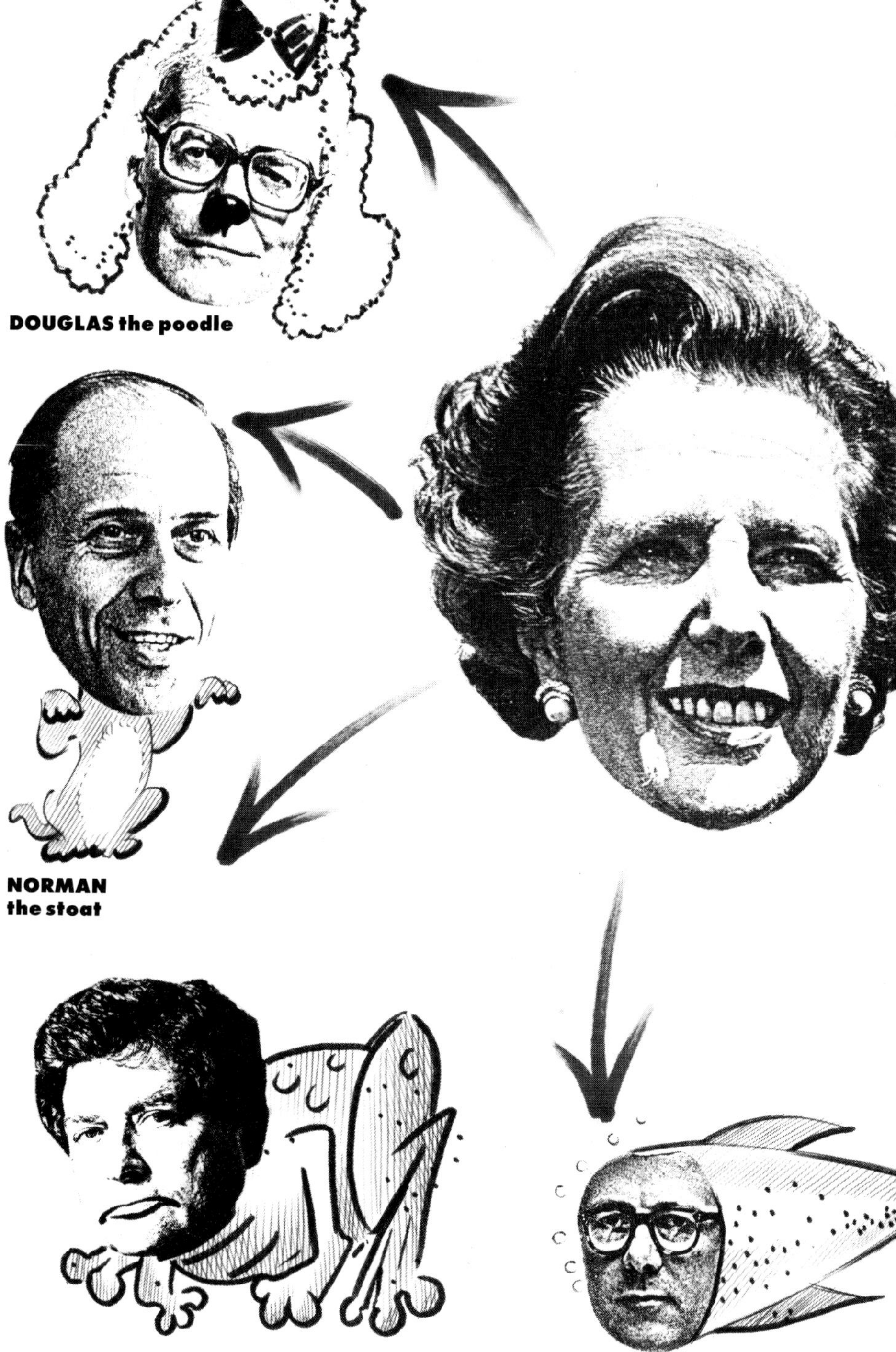

DOUGLAS the poodle

NORMAN the stoat

NIGEL the toad

GEOFFREY the haddock

Mrs Thatcher's private menagerie

History will place Mrs Thatcher second only to Dr Doolittle as an animal-lover. Although a pet herself (see "Celebrity Pets") she has surrounded herself with not just one but an entire zoo of pets, some dull, some gloomy, some bouncy and excitable, and some you wouldn't even want to read about. The smell at cabinet meetings is abominable, say inside sources, but Mrs Thatcher loves the devotion her pets give her to such a degree that the place has to be hosed down afterwards.

Every member of the Government is a pet, but many of them are indistinguishable from one another except to their owner, who is always ready with a kind word, a smacked nose, or a little treat like the Department of Health when one of them has been particularly good.

If you want to get on with Mrs Thatcher, and maybe even become one of her pets yourself, you must know them all and be prepared to treat them in accordance with their station. Here are some of the more important ones:[1]

KENNETH CLARKE is her *lurcher*. She has him to show that she has no side. Loving and loyal, despite a slight tendency to drool, he has been well-rewarded for his affectionate nature. He never barks at night though can do so on a single word of command. His pedigree would suggest a stable, insouciant, streetwise animal, but in fact he has been bred for hare-coursing and, underneath, is bloodthirsty and barking mad. This is why nobody but his owner will go anywhere near him, and even the other pets cross the road when he walks by.

DOUGLAS HURD is her *poodle*. Bland and boring, but soothing to have around as he never makes a mess and does what he is told. Sometimes he scampers around a bit, but a sharp word of command reminds him that he has no claim to autonomy, and he lies down again nicely by his favourite dish of tea.

NORMAN TEBBIT is Mrs Thatcher's *stoat*. Not many people would want a stoat, but Mrs Thatcher does. In Norman, she found a stoat among stoats; anything a stoat does, Norman does better.

NIGEL LAWSON is her *cane toad*. Hideous to look at, he is full of beans, quite unstoppable, possessed of a louche and repulsive charm and, in the end, rather dangerous. His owner feels proud to have the loyalty of such a horrible pet, but does not realise that one day he may creep up the drainpipe, squat on her face and murder her in her bed.

CECIL PARKINSON is a *gerbil*. Gerbils appear quite pleasant but are really rather wicked, secretive and troublesome creatures. Their family lives are unconventional, and though Cecil has not yet eaten his young (now grown too big to go down the red lane) he has shown signs of nastiness, counteracted, however, by his pleasing ability to whizz round and round on the spot in his little wheel until called upon to come out and play.

MICHAEL PORTILLO is her *budgie*. He knows her name and whistles pleasingly whenever he sees her. Michael thinks he is

KENNETH the lurcher

JEFFREY the hedgehog

JOHN the budgie

going to grow up to be a parrot, and his owner is finding it hard to break the news to him. Instead, she makes sure he sees a lot of…

JOHN MOORE, another *budgie* who grew up and found he was still a budgie. To keep him happy, his owner had given him a specially big cage, but when she told him the truth, she had no alternative but to take half of his cage away to make space for her lurcher's new big basket.

EDWINA CURRIE sadly had to be put down after choking on eggs, a problem to which every *mongoose* is prone.

SIR GEOFFREY HOWE is her *haddock*. A funny thing to have as a pet, you might think, but they can travel long distances and arrive relatively fresh, for a haddock. Also, nobody really can object to a haddock, although nobody would want to spend a lot of time with one. Except Mrs Thatcher, who likes his strange little "face" and his funny smell and his cheerful splashings in his briny playground.

Finally, **JEFFREY ARCHER**. Jeffrey is her *hedgehog*. He thinks he is a pet, but he isn't. Cruel of her, you might say, to keep putting out the occasional saucer of milk on the step, but you know how these animal-lovers are at heart.

[1] Though of course none of them is *really* important. Pets never are.

Secret Relationships of the Fourth Estate

You may believe that the Press is the guardian of our freedom, run by staunch, dauntless, hard-faced men and women concerned only with the truth. What is wrong with you? Everyone else realised long ago that the entire enterprise is not only corrupt but absolutely oozing with a foul sort of white, frothy discharge of sentimental pet-keeping. In such an internecine, secretive world, pets and masters change places and loyalties in less time than it takes Andrew Knight (owner: Conrad Black; Analogue: Dogfish) to destroy *The Daily Telegraph*. Outsiders find this fearful. Outsiders trying to become insiders quote Beaverbrook's Law – *Any journalist can be exchanged for any other journalist without penalty* – but believe that emotions come into it, and get nasty and vindictive, making themselves unhappy and making everyone else laugh at them behind their backs. Real insiders know that it doesn't matter; the concept of ownership is meaningless in a world exclusively populated by dingoes.

Here are six of the current owner-pet relationships. Don't forget: all parties are *really* dingoes. Their analogues simply represent the animals they would be if they weren't dingoes but people.

OWNER **ANDREW NEIL (qv)**

PET **NEVILLE HODGKINSON**, Worrying Correspondent, *The Sunday Times*

Animal Analogue One of those nervous, creepy freemartins that mad scientists make.

Character Tormented, valetudinarian, ascetic, glum. Moves in pre-ordained grooves, tail drooping. Scared of corners, the dark, the light, breathing, dropping dead.

Benefits Makes owner feel relatively terribly jolly, provides surrogate proxy conscience.

Drawbacks More than 30 seconds' exposure to the Hodgkinson can produce The Other Hodgkinson's Disease: an urgent desire to kill either oneself or one's pet Hodgkinson.

Cry All-purpose, concerned, nervous, but somehow modern snuffle: "Dirty! Nasty! *Dangerous*!"

OWNER **ANDREAS WHITTAM SMITH**, Editor, *The Independent*

PET **ALEXANDER CHANCELLOR**, Editor, *The Independent Magazine*

Animal Analogue Flat-coated retriever

Character Shambling

Benefits Almost unique among all its owner's creatures, the Chancellor possesses (a) charm (b) editorial ability and (c) a personality.

Drawbacks See "character" and "benefits".

Cry Peat-smoke drawl: "Oh… yes… no, we never did, did we… I expect it's around here somewhere… I'll have a look one day".

OWNER **RUPERT MURDOCH**, Global Threat

PET **ANDREW NEIL**, Part-time Editor, *The Sunday Times*, Part-time CEO, Sky Television

Animal Analogue Jack Russell

Character Rushes around, snarls, barks, bites, slavers, libido only controllable by surgery, frightens victims of its rage and desire alike, widely regarded as horrible.

Benefits Gives correct impression of owner.

Drawbacks Nasty. Impossible to house-train.

Cry Incomprehensible Hibernian rasp, like someone prising open a rusty tin with a screwdriver.

OWNER **CONRAD BLACK**, *Telegraph* and *Spectator* owner

PET **THE STAFF** of *The Spectator*

Animal Analogue Moggies

Character Aimless, shabby, wander around mewing, occasionally conduct huge inexplicable squabbles, appear ignorant of owner's existence but secretly think he is God.

Benefits Convey impression of benevolent, charitable disinterest on part of hard-nosed owner.

Drawbacks Vicious, potentially disloyal, picky.

Cry "One does feel that Tuscany is so essentially un-frivolous."

OWNER **TINY ROWLAND**, Thwarted shopkeeper

PET **DONALD TRELFORD**, Editor, *Lonrho Weekly*

Animal Analogue Potto

Character Excitable, submissive, almost paranormal ability to anticipate owner's wishes.

Benefits Biddable and preternaturally dapper.

Drawbacks One day will wholly lose credibility and have to be put down.

Cry "Yes! Yes! Yes, we've already done it! Yes!"

OWNER **DONALD TRELFORD (qv)**

PET **SUE ARNOLD**

Animal Analogue Cuckoo

Character Only at home in others' nests. Will fly miles for free accommodation, then boast about it afterwards. Good-natured, despite reputation for guile.

Benefits Keeps the freebies coming in without the owner needing to go on the ones he doesn't fancy.

Drawbacks Goes on the freebies the owner fancies; snarls if thwarted.

Cry Breathy Himalayan gurgle: "Charming . . . very nice . . . *wonderfully* done . . . *enchanting* . . . *awful* American tourists."

OWNER **STANLEY REYNOLDS**, Prominent humorist

PET **MICHAEL HEATH**, Cartoonist

Animal Analogue Kakapo (flightless nocturnal parrot of owl-like appearance)

Character Irritable, flamboyant, solitary and egregious; simultaneously uxorious and misogynistic.

Benefits Hates everyone, fails to remember people, treacherous, bites savagely, thus confers distinction on owner as only person who can control it, or indeed be remembered by it.

Drawbacks Gloomy. Insane. Fashion victim. Inexplicably youthful appearance. Tendency to fall out of tree.

Cry Hoarse, tortured bark. "Christ, what a nightmare! Beep-beep! Nag, nag, nag. Nightmare! You're just a peanut. What do you know about anything? Nightmare!"

AND NOW, THOSE SUPER CELEBRITY PETS . . .

OWNER **STING**, right-on eco-fascist and bit-part actor

PET **MILES COPELAND**

Animal Analogue Rat

Character Vicious, amoral, greedy, requires twice own body-weight in freshly-killed money every day or dies.

Benefits Scavenges efficiently, leaving owner free to concentrate on preening nimbus, exuding odour of sanctity etc.

Drawbacks Frightening, dangerous, nasty to have about the house.

Cry Avaricious sort of whistling rasp: "That's not enough! Give me *more*!"

OWNER **ED VICTOR** ("Literary" Agent)

PET **DOUGLAS ADAMS** (*Hitch-hiker's Guide* author)

Animal Analogue St Bernard

Character Huge, playful, understands every word.

Benefits Theoretically confers lovability and sense of fun through osmosis. Also impresses people since size of pet suggests size of owner's member. (Though N.B. the adage "Big nose means big hands".)

Drawbacks Huge, playful, understands every word. Also repeats every word behind back, not as benign as appears. No bar presence; inexplicably renders entire party invisible to *maîtres d'hôtel*.

Cry Deep, mournful, ululation: "God I'm depressed. It's awful. Hey! Look at my new camera! Look at this software! You know where Schrödinger went wrong? Let's *eat*. I'm hungry."

OWNER **CLIVE ANDERSON**, incipient TV personality

PET **JOHN SESSIONS**, actor

Animal Analogue Chimpanzee

Character *Toujours gai*, Archie, *toujours gai*.

Benefits Distracts attention from owner's suit, baldness, wicked little knife hidden beneath agreeable grin.

Drawbacks *Toujours gai*, Archie, *toujours gai*.

Cry Imitative of whatever it read the previous night.

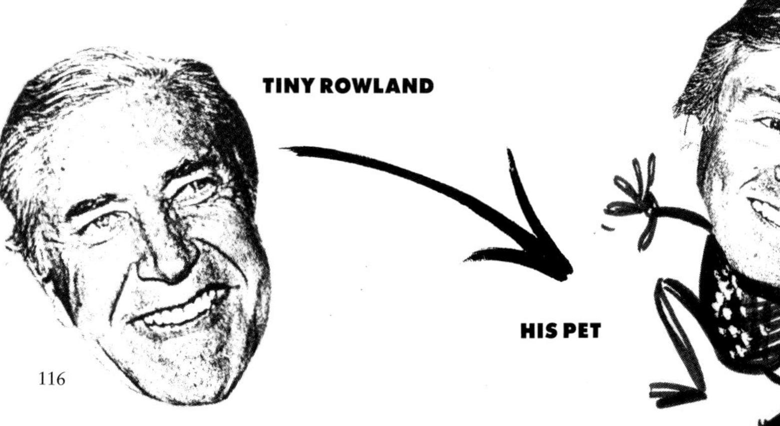

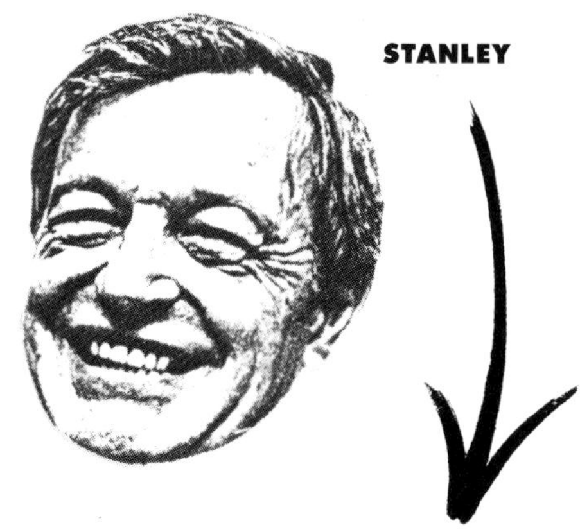

STANLEY

HIS PET

OWNER **THE PRINCESS ROYAL**

PET **CAPTAIN MARK PHILLIPS**

Animal Analogue Mongrel

Character *Sub judice.*

Benefits ?

Drawbacks *Sub judice.*

Cry "?"

OWNER **GEORGE BUSH**

PET **J. DANFORTH QUAYLE**

Animal Analogue Chicken

Character Ruffled, decerebrate, largely automatic.

Benefits Makes owner look smart.

Drawbacks Makes owner look dumb.

Cry "No I didn't! Yes I did!"

OWNER **DENIS THATCHER**

PET **MARGARET THATCHER**

Animal Analogue Racehorse

Character Bony, unlovable but keeps on winning.

Benefits Reflects glory if you don't look too hard.

Drawbacks Relentless, exhausting, pointless *sub specie aeternitatis* and very expensive; requires constant grooming, exercise and ego-massage.

Cry Interminable.

OWNER **Fr KIT CUNNINGHAM**, Rector of St Etheldreda's *de facto* spiritual advisor to literary and journalistic London.

PET **Fr JEAN CHARLES ROUX**, Assistant Priest at St Etheldreda's

Animal Analogue Ocelot

Character Suave, urbane, impeccably-dressed, amazing manners concealing sharp claws.

Benefits Fascinates women, who feel they want to stroke him but dare not. Supplies much-needed air of timeless elegance to owner.

Drawbacks Refusal to roll over and show devotion. Tendency to attract more attention than owner, causing growling attacks in the latter and, in severe circumstances, going out for a quick one with Michael Heath (qv).

Cry Aristocratic Gallic purr. "Really? How very Belgian." (Allegedly said to smart woman making recondite confession.)

OWNER **AARON SPELLING**, Producer of *Dallas*

PET **CANDY SPELLING**

DONALD TRUMP

Animal Analogue Borzoi

Character Decerebrate, distressingly emaciated beneath the glossy topcoat.

Benefits Follows owner displaying more gew-gaws than he could fit on himself.

Drawbacks Turns nasty if asked to display same gew-gaws twice.

Cry "Chardge id to my huss-bind, Aarod Spellingue, the brodjuicedster."

OWNER **DONALD TRUMP**, Atlantic City casino operator

PET **IVANA TRUMP**

Animal Analogue See Candy Spelling

Character See Candy Spelling

Benefits See Candy Spelling

Drawbacks See Candy Spelling

Cry "Charch itter my huz-bund, Danald Tramp, the prapatry velper."

OWNER **The COUTTS & Co "A" list**

PET **PAMELLA BORDES**

Animal Analogue Train

Character Goes like one.

Benefits Goes like one.

Drawbacks Goes like one.

Cry Carefully – but not totally – modulated Asian cackle: "Aaah! Aaaaaaah! AAAAAAAAH! Oh how generous! Is that for me, you big man you? I slept with Ayatollah Khomeini once, did I tell you?"

HIS PET

"That's all, Mr Jones. You can put your unfashionable clothes back on now."

"You don't look well – shall I call an accountant?"

"I don't know if Jack Sprat was on a low cholesterol diet. All it says here is he couldn't eat any fat."

Sick jokes

"I'm sorry, doctor, but while there's the teeniest chance, we can't give our consent to turning his Walkman off."

"One doesn't feel so guilty when one finds another smoker to talk to."

"Results negative! As a Labour MP, you've got years of disgruntled resentment in you yet."

GOLDEN
SPANIA
EAGLE
UDO
UNITED STATES OF AMERICA
HALF DOLLAR

STEINBERG ENTERPRISES FOR VIBRANT HEALTH AND SUCCESS:
As a Light Force Distributor, you can have fun, grow as a person, share products that truly make a difference in people's lives, know that you are helping to end world hunger and make big money to get what you want out of life.

These words are taken from a genuine Californian small ad. ROBIN EGGAR investigates

THE MARKETING OF METAPHYSICS

In the beginning was California and it was cool. There was sun, there was sea and there were avocado pears. It was a land of mountain bikes, designer water, Sikh chiropractors, genetically enhanced marijuana and the Grateful Dead. A realm where there are one million names for God and not a single one is spelled correctly. But inside this Garden of Contented Mammon has always lurked the spectre of Disquiet. Something was missing. Something *important*. Something *big* yet *immaterial*.

At first they thought that long hair, fresh grass and free love might do the trick. When that didn't work, the Californians turned to money and cocaine instead. But now the Age of Aquarius has become the New Age. Hippies have met Yuppies and created Dummies in their own image.

New Age is a catch-all label for the Marketing of Metaphysics, a total lifestyle to succour a soul left unattended for far too long. Everything is available – for a price – but the cardinal rule of the New Age is that it must be available *now*. Not tomorrow, not after a lifetime devoted to the contemplation of why men alone collect fluff in their navel. Now.

The New Age is a lifestyle shopping mall of everlasting choice. A never-ending suburb of psychic supermarkets packed with nutritious spirituality. The Mind Gym, where they guarantee to rebuild your brain for $50 an hour, is right next to the aerobics centre; here a couple of racks of trance channellers, there a bunch of reincarnated souls; here a shaman, there a crystal gazer and over there a psychic surgeon. Behind the mall are row upon row of churches and satellite dishes, fundamentalist braggarts and swaggarts, Islam, Hindu, 57 Varieties of Buddhism and an ancient stone ring for the pagans.

We live in a godless age, us in the West. This has been trumpeted so loud, so long and so many times by voices as disparate as Mary Whitehouse, Jerry Falwell and the Ayatollah Khomeini that it must be true. Except that while the world gets smaller and corporations get bigger, hundreds of personal beliefs are flying off chaotically into the cosmos. Money and the accumulation of things may have become the goal and God may have got lost in midfield, but once the excitement of the achievements has worn off, one nagging question remains. What comes next?

The New Age beliefs all echo this primal *cri de coeur*. Like Buddhism they concentrate on a very personal route to salvation, but couched in the imagery of the blipvert. Eternal life is but a credit card call away. Americans have a constitutional right to life. Now they want to exercise it... for ever. Reincarnation is one way they can come back for a second helping. Death is only going to be a temporary inconvenience. On the great answerphone of life they are leaving a message. "After the beep I'll be back ... in another incarnation."

But for now the Kingdom of Heaven can be found in the City of Angels. Whatever your preferences from magic, Christian to plain out-of-your-gourd, they're all in the Los Angeles Yellow Pages or the directory published by the Bodhi Tree – LA's premier metaphysical bookshop. Up in Marin County (north of San Francisco) where designer craziness first took root, the whole middle-class infrastructure is plaited through with platitudes of the New Age made flesh and mortar.

A quick peek through *Common Ground* – a Marin County quarterly freesheet – reveals many wholesome organic service industries it would be unfulfilling to do without. Alternative ▶

ILLUSTRATIONS BY MARIE-HÉLÈNE JEEVES

Orthodontics. Holistic Financial Planning. Verbal Hygiene. Whole Brain Learning. New Age dentists vie with New Age Car Salesmen, Animal Healers with givers of herbal enemas.

Spiritual salvation is no longer a matter for established religions. It has to be personal. It has to enrich your lifestyle. Everybody who is anybody has a psychic. Some are charlatans, some are frauds; some believe in themselves, some are believed. Most take credit cards.

In this kingdom of the hindsighted, the short-sighted and the blind, second sight makes perfect sense. It might even get you an edge. Indeed, LA psychics' fees are overtaking those of favoured shrinks. Kevin Ryerson commands $1,000 for a half-hour session. Penny Torres charges $350 to put you in touch with Mafu...

Mafu, what a scorcher...

(In which our hero meets the great Mafu, part spiritual entity, part codswallop.)

Mafu is not a health food, a designer drug or an exercise club. Mafu is a spiritual entity who appears to the gullible whenever they can be gathered together in a motel conference room and relieved of a few bucks.

"Mafu has lived many lives," explains Richard ("call me Dick") while I gaze round the room wondering where he has hidden the dope.

Richard is a California casualty. He needs an edge. These days he dabbles in real estate and talks about opening a "wilderness store". Over the years he's been a rock musician, an alcoholic, an actor, a drug addict and a really nice guy. Two years ago, "in the middle of a spiritual crisis," he discovered Mafu.

"Mafu is the Second of the Brothers of The Light who lived in Atlantis 35,000 years ago. He is bronzed of skin, seven feet tall and he speaks to us through the medium of Penny Torres."

Dick describes super-consciousness as "having a CD player in your head"

Were I an ancient spirit roaming the Astral Planes, Penny Torres would not be my first choice of home. She is a poorly educated Catholic girl whose husband was a Los Angeles cop until Mafu came to stay. Now she is highly marketable as a trance channeller, who has the ability to "tune into the Universal Mind, their body becomes a satellite dish enabling the spirits to pass on any wisdom they have acquired over the eons".

In a darkened room, surrounded by expectant acolytes, Penny Torres's head snapped back with an audible crack. Her voice dropped three octaves, the California whine vanished into the ether replaced by a sonorous Vincent Price crossed with Roger Rabbit. Penny/Mafu walked amongst the congregation. A stiff legged gait as if there were a poker up her backside. She gave personal messages to a select few – notably the converted – but imparted a philosophy to all.

"Mafu does not want people to follow or worship him," explained Call-Me-Dick, whose tongue is adept at contradicting his brain. "His philosophy of God I Am is to make you love yourself so you can love other people."

Mafu has also prophesied super-consciousness by the year 2,000, which Dick describes as "having a CD player in your head". Such car boot philosophising is common to all New Age ideas, perfect fodder for the former Me Generation which likes to hear that change can only come from inside the person even if it is aided and abetted by the spirit world.

California has more trance channellers than TV channels. The spirits they call down range from "Soncha, a 5th density Sirius energy" to the Men from Atlantis and "Torah, a loving interdimensional consciousness". Fortunately they all speak English.

What trance channellers like best is publicity. For with it comes celebrity and money. The doyen is Kevin Ryerson whose most reliable spirits, Tom Lazaris and John, were prepared to play themselves when Shirley Maclaine turned her bestseller *Out On A Limb* into a TV mini series. This was only fair since – as Shirley revealed in her book – they had convinced her to accept the script for her Oscar winning role in *Terms of Endearment*. In Hollywood the favour bank stretches far beyond the grave.

Krystle balls

(In which our hero tries to get his rocks off in Los Angeles.)

Back to Mafu. Now his big brother in Atlantis was a gentleman named Ramtha, who took up squatter's rights in the body of TV executive JZ Knight, announcing that he could only stay for seven years. Eight years later he is still around, and JZ has published several books and formed the tax deductible charity "Church I Am", with consultancy fees at $500 an hour. She has also been bosom buddies with Linda Evans since 1985 when the helpful sea spirit from 4,000 fathoms introduced the *Dynasty* bimbo to "Ayurveda" – a 6,000-year-old beauty system involving herbal and hot oil treatments with secret ingredients, plus meditation, massage, and a visit to an oriental health farm.

"When Ramtha spoke," says the dewy eyed

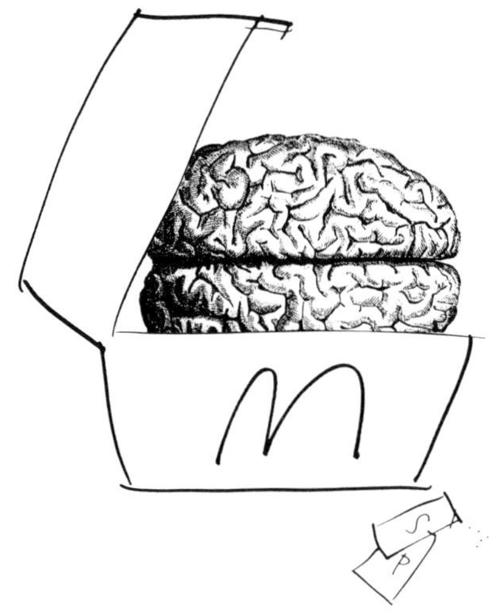

actress, "it was like a voice saying all that I felt within myself."

Like any religious fanatic the seekers after New Age knowledge seldom see the whole spectrum. Adherents to one doctrine decry another, until they try it out.

When Ramtha pales, try crystals. LA loves them. In ten years prices have gone up 1,000 per cent. Owning a crystal is the first step in becoming a New Age person by "physically articulating the advent of one's spiritual odyssey". Big ones are pretty enough to augment any designer sitting room and they make a great conversation point.

It is no historical coincidence that crystal balls and rocks have long been part of the apparatus of magic and prophecy, for they do give out a tiny electrical charge when squeezed and emit precise vibrations in response to electrical current. Molecularly they develop shapes in harmony with their internal structure. They are indeed soothing to contemplate and warm to the touch, but whether they can cure cancer or bring good luck is debatable. That the entire civilisation of Atlantis was powered by crystals – as Crystal Master Dael Walker says – has not yet been confirmed by Ramtha or his brother.

Believers run their hands over the crystal to find the right vibrations, before bathing them in moonlight, basting them in sage or drowning them in sea salt. The charged crystal will then calm, energise and purify wherever they are placed. The Ford Motor Company sadly refuses to confirm reports that crystals placed inside a petrol tank give better mileage.

But when the Bee Gees wanted a big hit to launch their comeback after ten years growing facial hair in Florida, all the assembled hacks and disc jockeys at the launch of their 1987 album "ESP" were given tiny pre-energised – to ensure no sourpuss critic would make with the negative waves – crystals in a little pouch. The first single was a massive hit in Britain.

The whiff of one-time celebrity is enough to encourage people to fill a London church to hear John Richardson – once the drummer with saccharine pop stars the Rubettes – drone on about how he found Jesus, made a brand change to the Hare Krishnas and is now a faith healer who claims to be capable of regressing dim witted punters back to their happy life as a buttercup. This was exactly the regression one believer claimed to experience at a recent lecture. On his own admission Irish aristocrat turned singer Chris de Burgh has healing hands and can "tune out" negative influences.

Loony tunes...

(In which our hero discovers that New Age music is the business.)

The New Age has already obliquely entered the credit stream of the British designer generation. Music, eating habits, literature, pretentious conversation have arrived. Metaphysical fulfilment and brain building machines are just the next step.

That was the case when guitarist William Ackerman first pressed a few copies of his pretty pretty tunes and started flogging them in health food stores. They went down great with the brown rice and thus the Windham Hill label was born.

Music is an integral part of the whole New Age experience. Record stores now have a complete section devoted to waxings that don't fit into any other category. Anything goes provided it eschews vocals: electronic settings of meditation mantras; Tibetan nose flute concertos; Incan funeral laments; incredibly ▶

When Ramtha, pales, try crystals. LA loves them

dull Tangerine Dream albums from the mid-Seventies; waves breaking over rocks; the Humpback Whale's Greatest Hits. Sounds that can be marketed as an aid to meditation and relaxation are little more than aural wallpaper. New Age music is essentially undemanding, too simple to be classical, too pretty to be jazz and too boring to be rock and roll.

Once a market has been established record companies are not slow to exploit it. As punk became new wave, so New Age metamorphosed into New Instrumental Music – ridding itself of the pejorative mystical tag en route to the chain store. All the major labels and smart entrepreneurs want a slice of the NIM pie.

Satellite TV also wants a piece of the New Age action. In October, Landscape was launched. Its MD, Michael Appleton, used to produce that hippy vision classic *The Old Grey Whistle Test.* He then broadcasted the Live Aid concert. Now he beams down pictures of seagulls flying over azure seas, silent volcanoes erupting in Technicolor slow motion – all reds and yellows without pain – serene landscapes accompanied by lots of lovely instrumental music. Mind numbing really. Punks and new romantics are now confined to the museum, acid house will be next and all that will be left is the vacuous smile on the blissed-out face of the NIM-wit.

In Oklahoma nine out of the ten bestselling books are metaphysical in nature – a definition which includes anything written by Shirley Maclaine. It has not reached such a level in the UK, though an article in the Weekend *Guardian's* fatuous "New Age" column – the sandleshod *Grauniad* was inevitably the first quality paper to bandwagon jump – claimed that Scott Peck's spiritual odyssey *The Road Less Travelled* has sold more than 100,000 copies. The market is out there.

Most publishers now carry a New Age list. The annual festival of Mind, Body and Spirit at the Horticultural Halls is a runaway success as the shopwindow of the alternative culture, though older stallholders are starting to grumble about prices and commercialism.

Health food stores have increased tenfold in the last decade, invading every high street with vegetarian stock cubes and dried apricots. A success story only confirmed by a recent *Which?* report suggesting health food might be bad for you. There is even a New Age diet book, Colin Rose's *The Mind and Body Diet* which begins portentously: "The subconscious mind cannot differentiate between what is real and what it believes is real. Yet your subconscious mind directly controls your actions in a very tangible way.

"You have just proved something of the utmost importance. You have proved that you can deliberately direct the power of your mind to produce an immediate and measurable physical effect on your body. Harness this power for slimming and you need never diet again."

The chubby acolyte is then invited on a "six week voyage of self-discovery". Actress Candice Bergen has already claimed to have had "psychic facials". Coming next – ectoplasmic face-lifts.

Mysteries is London's "Psychic Shop and New Age Centre". From tiny beginnings six years ago in Monmouth Street it has stretched back, across and up. There are now three clairvoyants/readers working full-time every day, all the paraphernalia necessary for spiritual growth can be purchased from informed, helpful assistants – who include a large, well-spoken Englishman with shaggy beard and white turban rejoicing in the name of Gujarat Singh. Business is booming.

"New Age has to be one of the biggest growth industries in the country," says co-owner Matthew Geffen, "though it will probably never attain the same level as the States. In Miami there will be a dozen shops like this in a 50 mile radius."

The British typically prefer books and subliminal self-help tapes to the pizzaz of trance channellers who are only just starting to attract interest. Sales in crystals are still good but demand is down on a year ago. The clientele is varied from shaven headed neo-Goths buying sweet, pungent aromas to Knightsbridge matrons in pearls perusing the *Tao of Pooh*.

Readers who have enjoyed this genuine New Age bestseller might wish to get in touch with the founder of Taoism, Lao Tzu. He died more than 2,000 years ago, but that's no problem because he happens to be a good friend of Norman Hamilton Farmer – an old-fashioned fortune teller with a homely pixie face and ears that would be elfin were they only pointed. An untipped Pall Mall smoulders unheeded between the ragged nails of his yellow stained fingers as an eldritch smile spreads over his face.

Farmer believes in his own powers. He is the very last of a 500-year line that began in fifteenth century Yorkshire where Ursula Southiel – better known as Old Mother Shipton – so terrified her contemporaries that she lived to a ripe old age. His mother is psychometrist Marjorie Staves, who still runs her business from an address near Harley Street but has problems remembering her real age, the names and whereabouts of her two sons or even that she prophesied her own death 14 years ago and omitted to keep the appointment. Being clairvoyant does not make living in the real world any easier.

Farmer has spent his life searching. He has studied voodoo and witchcraft, lived with the Pueblo Indians and been the chief structural steel draughtsman for a Toronto engineering firm. The latter could not have been accomplished without his spirit guides: Tanka, grandson of Chaka the Zulu king; Fred Wilson, a Bow Bells cockney; Rekhmire, the Grand Vizier to a minor Egyptian pharoah; and most impressive of all, our old friend the Chinese sage Lao Tzu. Is this all becoming too much? You need a Mind Gym Voucher...

A coffin fit

(In which our hero discusses the meaning of life while gazing at his navel from 900 different angles.)

At the Altered States Float Center and Mind Gym in Hollywood they have rebuilt many a battered brain. And they do it all with good old-fashioned technology: sensory deprivation tanks. These are overgrown coffins where you float in a saline solution cut off from sight and sound. Except you don't have to be deprived. They'll happily put in waterproof headphones and a video to make the experience more fun.

Perhaps I had a negative experience but during my floating I felt uncomfortable and disoriented in a foetid warm atmosphere. So I moved on to the Graham Potentialiser, a psychiatrist's couch that revolves through an electromagnetic field.

The owner, Jeff Labno, uses the GP because it is useful "for taking this rough stone of an idea, playing with it, caressing it until it becomes this polished gem stone of an idea".

To aid me I was given a Hypno Therapy Tape – equally popular sellers at Mysteries in London. This consisted of two American voices with excruciating long vowel sounds telling a different fairy tale in each ear simultaneously. Supposedly this creates a sensory overload which blanks out the conscious mind allowing the unconscious to get gem polishing. The first time I heard two rather odd stories about a dog called Bradley winning a frisbee competition on the moon and a ghost stuck in a child's computer. The second I had a relaxing nap.

Altered States has other machines. The Synchro Energiser is a pair of green goggles surrounded by yellow and opaque bulbs which flash in random patterns creating some spectacular effects behind the eyelids. Narcissus would have loved the Sensory Enhancement Environment – a tiny mirror box – where he could gaze for eternity at 900 different angled images of himself. The Hemi-Sync Synthesizer is supposed to help balance the two different hemispheres of the brain, while the Mind Mirror – developed by Britain's Maxwell Cade – can measure different brainwave patterns.

Many reputable authorities argue that biofeedback machines are at the cutting edge of modern science. In the whirlpool of the New Age industry they are merely playthings for the chronically bored.

"I am not here to entertain someone's diversionary appetite," snaps Lynn Andrews, best-selling author and urban shaman. "I don't give workshops as they have become an absolute fad. People go from one to the other, they write down all this borrowed knowledge and they have absolutely no idea how to make that knowledge part of their lives."

Lynn Andrews dispenses an ancient lore – often for free – learned from two Red Indian women in the forests of northern Canada. Now she is an example to the Bears and the Deer – two New Age tribes who are Britain's very own Green Indians. Honourable in a profession that breeds charlatans and con artists like cockroaches, Andrews still knows how to play the media game while throwing out insights that strike deep down home.

"It is easy to be a sacred person living in a cave," she says. "It is hard to do so with one foot in substance and one in spirit. We are a society of blamers, desperate for spiritual solace but we look outside ourselves for the answers. That is another long way home and how can we be surprised that nature is turning against us. We have to learn to live in harmony with the earth or we are not going to be living here much longer."

In other words: if we're not careful, the New Age might be the Last Age too. ■

NEW AGE HISTORY

6,000 BC Shirley Maclaine born (for the first time)
1967 Grateful Dead emerge
1969 The Dawning of the Age of Aquarius
1976 The Serial published
1981 Ramtha appears
1987 Time of Celestial Convergence
1988 Nostradamus prophesies LA destroyed by earthquake. Ludicrous small ads
1989 Los Angeles is still there

REINCARNATION ETC:

Match the following Hollywood actresses with their previous *lives:*

1) Shirley Maclaine:
a) Egyptian lady-in-waiting
b) Balinese temple dancer
c) A fish

2) Linda Evans:
a) Ramtha, a warrior from Atlantis
b) Henrik Ibsen
c) Joan Collins

3) Which of the following is not a god:
a) Ramtha
b) Mafu
c) Vishnu
d) Tofu

NEW AGE/SMALL ADS

PAST LIFE THERAPY BREAKDOWN:
Past life regression combined with Rebirthing, Reichian body/breath work, chakra clearing and energy balancing creates a powerful multilevel process. Clients report experiencing intense white light, chronic conditions healed; income doubled
(Taken from Common Ground)

HYPNOTHERAPIST:
Join me on Cloud Nine and learn the art of self-belief

WILD DREAM WORKSHOPS:
Learn Life Skills

AFTER THE CRASH:
THE RAINBOW ECONOMY: a new economy is emerging based on values which respect our inner natures, our communities and our Earth

A LIVING MASTER VISITS LONDON:
The Earth has few living masters, Barry Long is one of them. (Time Out)

"HOLISTIC REBIRTHING INSTITUTE" –
100 hour foundation diploma course
(Transformer Quarterly, Natural Ways to Live and Grow)

IF THE SHOE FITS

JONATHAN SALE goes in search of a Mr Right for Mrs Marcos

Any day now the ex-President of the Philippines is going to make his wife a free woman. But where will she find another ex-dictator of her dreams? Answer: with Global Contacts, a Surrey-based firm that offers a mail-order marriage bureau for Filipino brides and their would-be western grooms*.

The ads for Global Contacts appear in dubious magazines like *Private Eye*. "Beautiful oriental girls," they promise, "want gentlemen for friendship and marriage. Send SAE for details."

We did, and received details of the four plans, from Executive Bride (£125) down to El Cheapo (£30). To this we add Plan Five – the Ex-Presidential and First Lady scheme. And since Imelda isn't around to fill in her application form herself, we've done it for her, viz:

Name: *Imelda Marcos*
Address: *Motel de los Damnatos, Miami*
Age: *Pass*
Date of Birth: *You don't catch little Imelda like that!*
Weight: *Over*
Do you wear glasses? *Only to look at the prices in the footwear department of Neiman-Marcos (my little joke)*
Occupation: *First Lady*
Favourite colour: *Gold*
Pet hate: *Human rights organisations*
Religion: *Catholic and Voodoo Economics*
Marital Status: *Not for very much longer*
Favourite Car: *Stretch limo under armed escort*
What kind of man are you looking for?
(a) Country: *Yes, must own one*
(b) Income: *Two-thirds of GNP of any Third World nation will do*

*** The lonely-hearted can find them at PO Box 39, Reigate, Surrey RH28 8YX.**

And what of her potential husbands? We present...

THE MEN ON THE MARKET

ED KOCH

Ed Koch, Mayor of New York City, is one of American politics' most eligible bachelors. And with a tricky election coming up this autumn, an experienced and charming consort could be just the thing he needs to help win back the hearts of an electorate disturbed by constant allegations of corruption at City Hall, not to mention vindictive and unfounded smears about Mr K's... ah ...proclivities. Furthermore, as an Asian, Imelda belongs to one of the minorities that American politicians are always so keen to woo. The problem is, it's the wrong one – the black vote is what Koch is desperate to attract. Also, there has to be a question mark as to whether Koch would ever "marry out". Or in, come to that.

SUMMARY: *He could be perfect. But he probably won't be.*

TED HEATH

Another deposed leader, he has been connected with only one other woman but it did not work out. In an attempt to wipe his name from her memory, she was forced to bury herself in her work as leader of the Tory Party. Any woman who lands Ted can therefore rest assured that she is his first love. A musician, yachtswoman and Europhile, with all the allure of the Brussels chamber on a wet afternoon, looks like being the person to get his vote in the marital stakes. His vowel sounds have improved with age, but maybe not enough. He will always offer a shoulder to cry on, even if it does heave up and down rather excessively.

SUMMARY: *Just because he lives in a cathedral close doesn't mean he is a saint! In the event of a break-up, he could be a bad loser. The devil has all the best tunes and so does Ted Heath's organ.*

"BUNGALOW" BILL WIGGINS

After all those years of marriage to an ageing, sickly dictator, it is just possible that Mrs Marcos may now be in the market for fresher meat. If that's the case, then Bill's her boy. He's got more balls than an executive toy. Plus, he has unmatched experience in meeting the needs of a world-famous middle-aged lady. He looks behind the wigs to see the real woman underneath. As if this were not enough, Wiggins also has the valuable attribute that he always looks good in pictures. His big, bland, cheerful features invariably come out a treat in gossip columns or Headliners spreads, which, to a woman likely to attract publicity by the bucket-load, has to be a vital consideration. We have only one further word of advice for Imelda; if you marry Bill, to be sure to get a really ugly au pair.

SUMMARY: *Without doubt a fun guy. But after spending the last couple of years living in a bungalow, does Imelda really want to marry one as well?*

MANOLO BLAHNIK

This elegant, Argentine-born cobbler is not as rich as some of Imelda's other potential suitors. Nor does he have much experience of running Third World countries. He restricts himself to a shoe shop in Chelsea. But, and this is a big "but", he designs the cutest footwear in the world. Now in his fifties, he is conveniently unmarried, although Immy might feel the need to drive a wedge between Manolo and his sister Evangeline, who helps run his business and to whom he is very close – sort of an insole-mate, in fact. She would also be well advised to keep her new husband away from his old customers (we are assuming that he will retire from public shoemaking on marriage), who number Jerry Hall, Marie Helvin and half the most beautiful women in the world.

SUMMARY: *Promising, decorative, but could be more useful as a footman than a husband.*

MALCOLM FORBES

When it comes to billionaire boyfriends, Malcolm Forbes takes a lot of beating. A magazine-owner by profession, he devotes much of his attention these days to the serious business of having fun. And boy, does he have fun! He has a private jet, a wonderful private yacht – both christened Capitalist Tool (no comment) – he owns châteaux and mansions galore, loves hot-air ballooning and is often to be seen with a massive, throbbing motorbike clasped between his knees. Until recent months Elizabeth Taylor could be found on his pillion, but as Liz sits in the Betty Ford Clinic, acquiring an outline not dissimilar to that of one of Mr Forbes's balloons, less is heard of their liaison. The question is, would he be any more interested in Imelda? Mr Forbes knows a lot about the importance of image and publicity. And right now, Marcos is not a name of which the American public is over-fond.

SUMMARY: *Could be perfect, but remains frustratingly unattainable.*

GENERAL ALFREDO STROESSNER

Ex-dictator, finds himself womanless having been given only a single, one-way ticket from Paraguay. Like Imelda, he's well-heeled. Loves women – in fact, at the last count he loved approximately eight of them, and now hopes to fill the position of First Lady, Second Lady, etc. Aged 76, he is on the young side for a dictator in this part of South America. Believes a man should pay attention to the fingernails, preferably other men's fingernails, preferably with red-hot pincers. After a hard day in the Interrogation Centre, or avoiding Amnesty inspectors, needs to relax in the arms of the women of his dreams, the only women in his life.

SUMMARY: *This is the man for Imelda. They have so much in common, such as great reserves of strength and bullion removed from a nation's coffers. Also, he won't mind stepping into a dead man's shoes (all 5,000 of them).*

General Alfredo Stroessner believes a man should pay attention to the fingernails, preferably other men's fingernails, preferably with red-hot pincers. After a hard day in the Interrogation Centre, he needs to relax in the arms of the woman of his dreams

Alfredo Stroessner, the world's most eligible former dictator

GUIDED MIKHAIL

Gorbachev's Russia has a groovy new image. STEVE WAY sat in on the re-design

"KGB – you come help us with our market research."

"Why have we called this trendy media club 'Harpo's'? Because for years we Russians had to remain silent."

"Mr Stalin is no longer with us."

"OK, Generals, from now on it's no longer missile deployment, it's product placement."

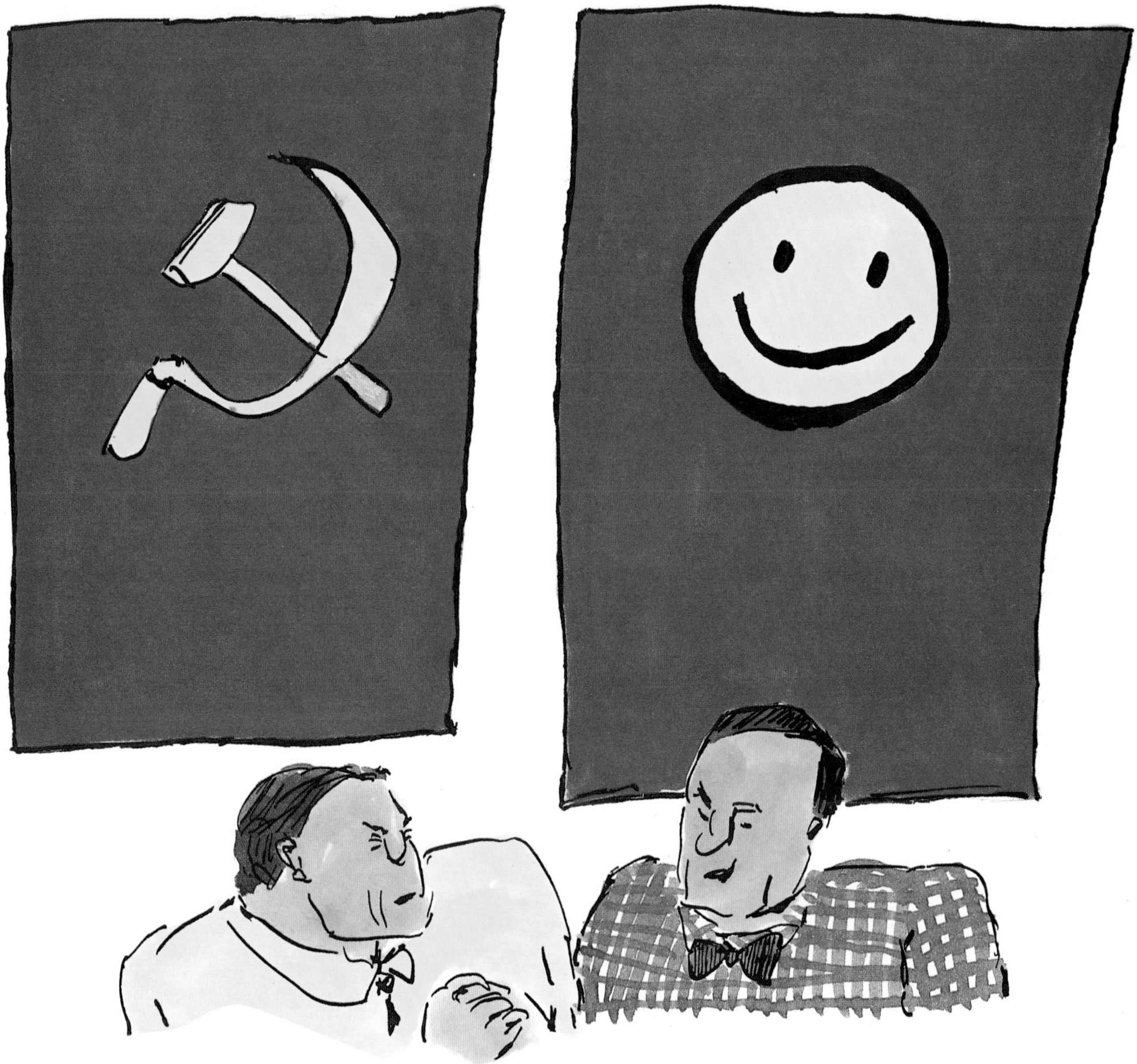

"The new corporate identity has a softer look."

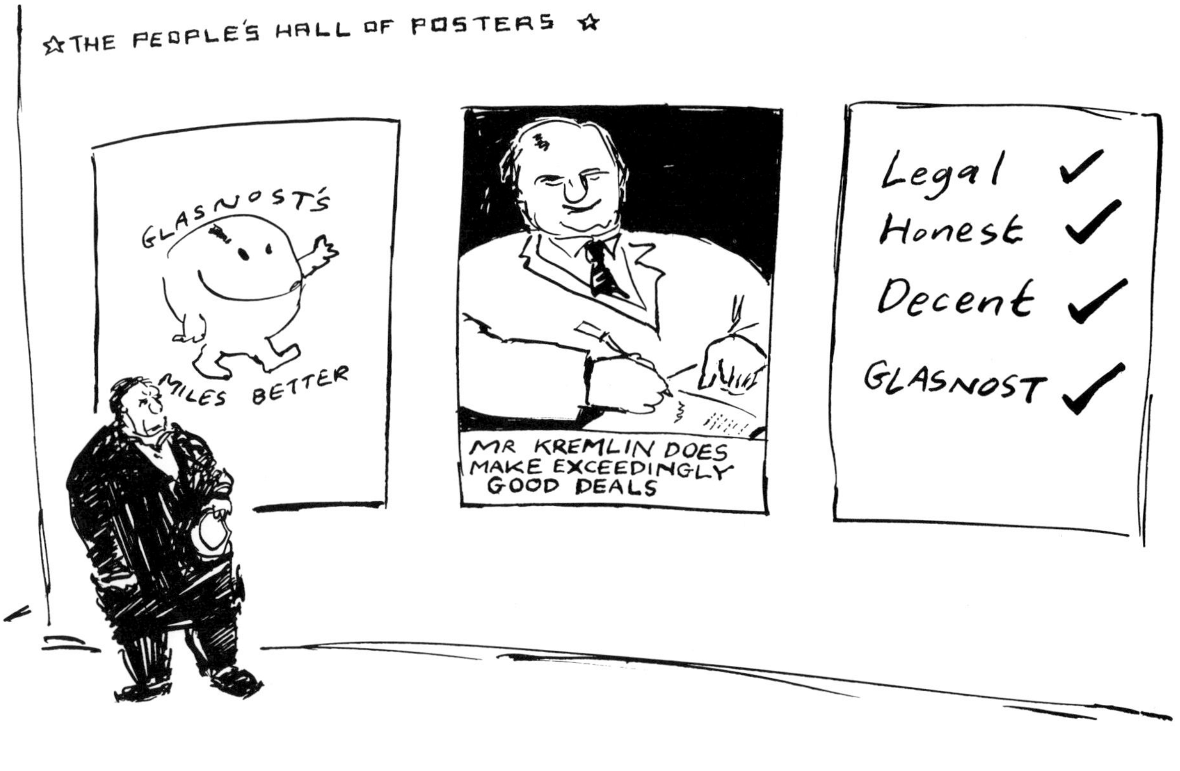

☆ THE PEOPLE'S HALL OF POSTERS ☆
GLASNOST'S
MILES BETTER
MR KREMLIN DOES MAKE EXCEEDINGLY GOOD DEALS
Legal ✓
Honest ✓
Decent ✓
GLASNOST ✓

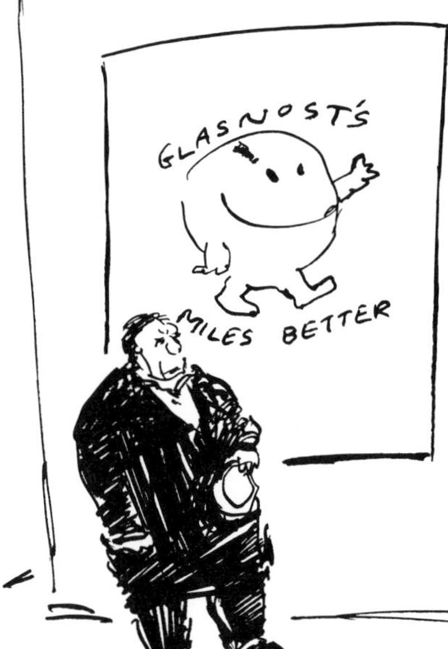

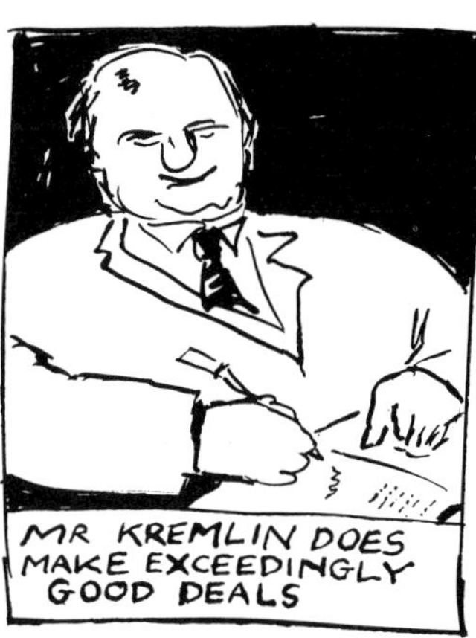

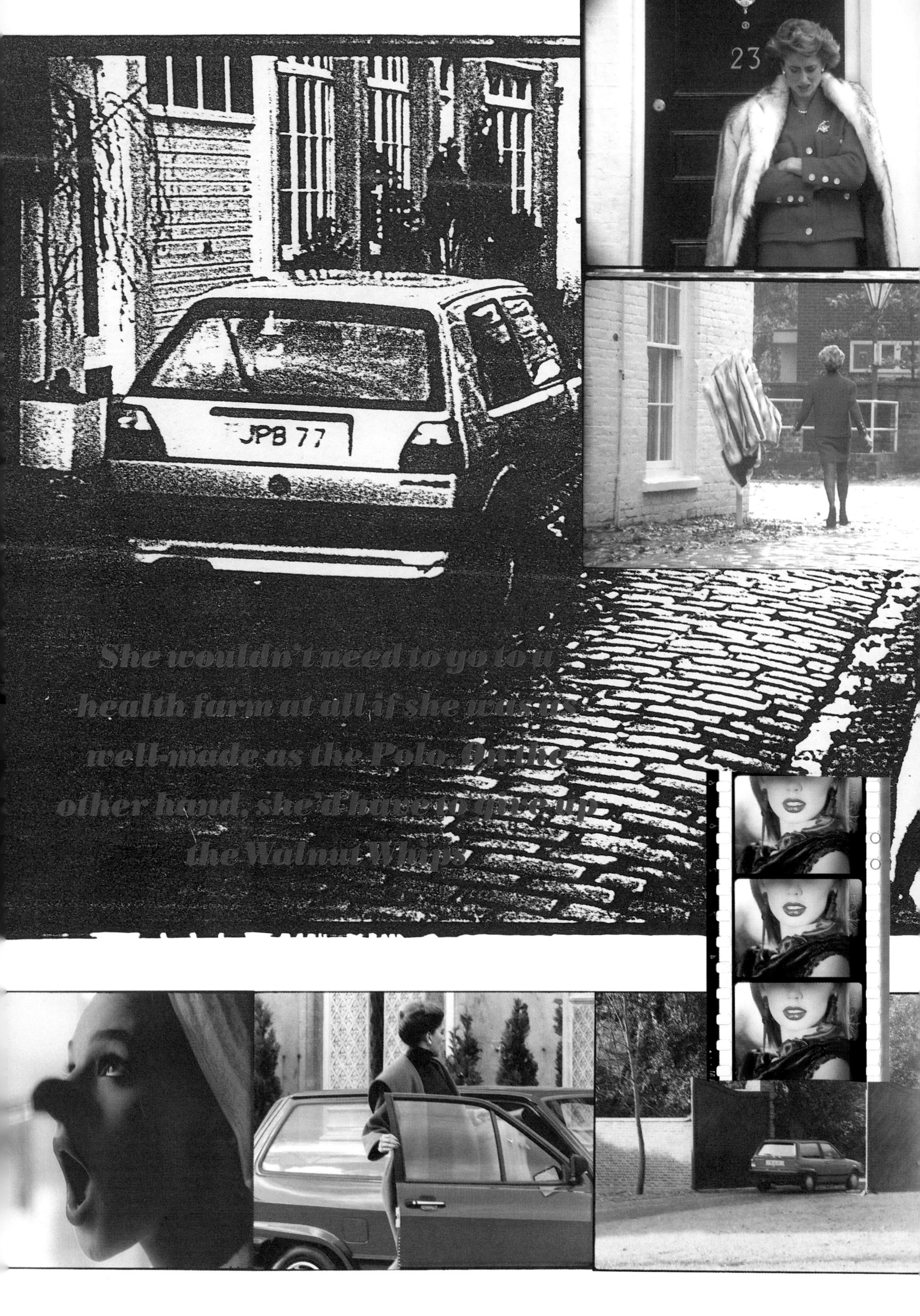
23
JPB 77
She wouldn't need to go to a health farm at all if she was as well-made as the Polo. On the other hand, she'd have to give up the Walnut Whips

MAD COWS ON WHEELS

...and other adventures in advertising

DAVID THOMAS and MITCHELL SYMONS

MAD COW DISEASE – *Bovine Spongiform Encephalopathy* to the vets – is driving British cattle to a terrible, raving doom. Now the virus has spread to humans. The first victims appear to be the creative departments of advertising agencies. Regardless of the product, they now feel obliged to fill their ads with sex-crazed, red-lipped harpies in micro-skirts. These are television's Mad Cows. But it's worse than that. These Mad Cows all drive. They drive small red cars to the sound of pounding music. They are, in fact, Mad Cows On Wheels.

This *Punch* report provides the first authoritative survey of the phenomenon. We begin with the natural home of Mad Cows on Wheels ... car advertisements.

How many mad cows does your favourite ad score? Remember: the more cows, the crazier.

FIAT TIPO

Scenario: *Ginormous 18th-century operatic soprano drives around with a bunch of Italianate fops whilst singing about the virtues of the car's galvanised steel construction. They prove that it is possible to get five adults, all in outrageous wigs, into a small family hatchback.*
She wears: *A classical Sun Goddess ensemble complete with extravagant golden head-piece. She does not wear black tights.*
The car is: *Red.*
Sexual imagery: *None. We are not talking bimbo with this bouncy babe.*
Conclusion: *Jolly operatic spoof, weakened only by all the other Italian products whose campaigns were based on the same idea. Only one question remains; we know you can get a soprano* into *a Tipo... but can you ever get her out again?*
Rating: *One mad cow.* 

CITROËN BX19GTi

Scenario: *A man arrives outside his (presumably new) girlfriend's house. She emerges, only to find that the car (red) clashes with her clothes (pink). She starts worrying. This concern sets the tone for an unspoken interchange of mindbending neurosis between the two romantic protagonists. After several hours on the road, they draw up outside his magnificent country pad. She thinks he's a flash berk. He pulls out a remote-control for his garage door. It fails to work properly. She thinks he may be just a berk. Luckily the car's variable suspension allows it to scrape under the half-open garage door. They get out. She leaves the garage. He presses his gizmo again. The door closes. He is still inside the garage. Yup – he's a berk all right. Still, judging by her daft expression she's not much better.*
She wears: *Little pink power suit to set off her blonde yuppette image. Black tights.*
The car is: *Red.*
Sexual imagery: *The odd flirtatious glance. Lots of agonised worrying. These characters clearly have one major sexual dysfunction – their principal love-affair is with themselves.*
Conclusion: *Almost as smug as the Renault 25 couple. Let's pray they never make a second episode.*
Rating: *Four mad cows out of five. Plus a bonus bull point for him.*

VOLKSWAGEN GOLF

Scenario: *A woman walks out on her lover, discarding her fur coat, pearls, platinum credit cards, subscription to* Punch, *etc – everything, in short, that makes her life worthwhile. Except ... her car keys. These she keeps, so as to be able to drive away in her snazzy VW Golf.*
She wears: *A fake fur (David Bailey, who directed the commercial, wouldn't allow a real one), a bright red Chanel-style executive suit, heels and black tights.*
The car is: *White.*
Sexual imagery: *Very restrained. There is, for example, no new hunk waiting in the car.*
Conclusion: *This one is, as they say in* Variety, *the Hollywood trade paper, "socko boffo", or to put it a few other ways, brill, fab, gear and absolutely smasheroo. She's great, she's cool, she's in charge. We're in love.*
Rating: *No cows at all.*

METRO GTA

Scenario: *A woman is being driven in a taxi through an Italian city, presumably Rome. She spots a Metro in the traffic and feels she has to follow it. When the taxi cannot keep up with the diminutive pride of the British motor industry our heroine leaps out of the cab and chases after the plucky little vehicle on foot. She never quite catches up with the car; the romance is never consummated.*
She wears: *A restrained black dress (calf-length?), unexceptional shoes and tights.*
The car is: *Red.*
Sexual imagery: *Nothing obvious here – how very British!*
Conclusion: *Let's be honest here... would you run helter-skelter through an Italian city in pursuit of a* Metro? *The notion that a German would be impelled to buy a Rover thanks to its associations with an art gallery designed by a "Britischer architekt" is ludicrous enough. But this attempt to convince us that an Italian signorina would dash off on an ad hoc frenzy of Continental jay-walking just because she'd seen what is, after all, no more than a souped-up Mini... well, she'd have to be bonkers. But of course, she is. She's a Mad Cow.*
Rating: *Three mad cows out of five.*

VAUXHALL NOVA

Scenario: *A woman finds herself stuck in a traffic jam somewhere in Britain but, thanks to her incredible stunt driving skills, is able to drive up, around, over and through a building site and out the other side of the jam.*
She wears: *Glasses (thereby indicating her intelligence, independence and all-round Serious Womanhood), green jacket, black miniskirt, black tights.*
The car is: *Red.*
Sexual imagery: *A quick fondling-the-gear-knob shot, but, to be fair, she is changing gear at the time. The car is inserted at high speed into a concrete drain-pipe... geddit?*
Conclusion: *The driving is pretty hot stuff – a souped-up version of those old stunts with the Minis from* The Italian Job. *Any complaints about the possible exploitation of the woman must bear in mind that alternative Vauxhall spokespeople currently include Martin Shaw and Robbie Coltrane. Faced with the choice, we'd take the woman every time.*
Rating: *One mad cow.*

VOLKSWAGEN POLO

Scenario: *A woman is at a health farm attempting to improve herself. She exercises, she sweats, she is covered in greenish sludge. Finally she gets dressed and walks out to her car where she eats a secret chocky. She drives off.*
She wears: *A series of tracksuits and towels, short, swingy brown cape and black tights.*
The car is: *Red.*
Sexual imagery: *Aside from the sub-Flake-style nibbling-the-Walnut-Whip-shot, the images are mostly concerned with woman's everlasting need to perfect her physical appearance. Is this exploitation... or simply parody? The script explains that she wouldn't have to be doing it at all if she was as well-made as the Polo. On the other hand, she'd have to give up the Walnut Whips and stick to lead-free four-star, which is neither as tasty, nor as deliciously creamy.*
Conclusion: *VW maintains its tradition of wit, rather than exploitation. But this trails a long way behind its illustrious predecessor.*
Rating: *Two mad cows.* 

PEUGEOT 205

Scenario: *A woman is idly rubbing herself against a stone balustrade somewhere in the South of France when she spots a Peugeot 205 driving up the street below. Her heart does backflips, her body melts, her knees go weak. She is impelled to display the affection she feels towards this sportif French supermini. Having demonstrated that it is actually possible to walk downstairs whilst simultaneously swinging one's hips by 36" in either direction, she finally catches up with the motor of her dreams. Lovingly, she inscribes a heart upon its windshield with her scarlet lipstick.*
She wears: *A minuscule black dress, high heels, slave bracelets round her ankles and... black tights.*
The car is: *Red.*
Sexual imagery: *Rampant and continuous. The star herself rubs, wiggles and pouts at every possible opportunity. The camera also pulls in for close-ups as she pulls a glove on to her upheld arm (subtext: safe sex) and twists her lipstick up out of its case (subtext: unsafe sex). The music is* See Me, Feel Me.
Conclusion: *Peugeot makes great cars. I drive one. But... A couple of years ago the campaign for their 405 series outraged both ecologists and fire disaster victims by showing the car being driven through a burning cane field to the tune of* Take My Breath Away. *Now they've gone for the feminists with a sex object who doesn't want to drive the car – just sleep with it. Unquestionably the Car Cow Classic of 1989.*
Rating: *Five mad cows out of five.* 

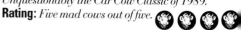

But advertising's epidemic of bovine insanity extends much further than the automotive industry. Commercials for toiletries, hosiery and casual clothing all exhibit the same fascination with sultry sluts in sexy cars. Many models are too young to be fully-qualified Mad Cows. They are more like Mad Heifers. To wit...

DIMENSION SHAMPOO

A young woman in an open-topped car that is not red. She realises that her hair is almost as filthy and greasy as her motor and decides to remedy both problems at once by driving through a car-wash with her hood down. En route she shampoos her hair with fab new Dimension. As she emerges on the far side of the wash, several astonishing phenomena are revealed...

1. *Although she has been sluiced, brushed and blown, her hair is immaculately neat and tidy.*

2. *The vast quantities of water and shampoo frothing around her upper regions do not appear to have disturbed her make-up. Indeed, it has improved – could this be the effect of the car-wash hot wax treatment?*

3. *Although her hair is completely dry, and despite the absence of any of the water which one might assume would be sloshing around the car's floor and pedals, the Heifer's dress is still damp enough to outline her finer features.*

LEVI'S JEANS

Levi's have, for the past few years, been as keen on Mad Bullocks as their female counterparts. Indeed, the company has been largely responsible for introducing the notion of the Boy Bimbo to British screens. The latest ad has taken to the road. A young woman is so excited by the sight of Our Hero's snowy white underpants that she leaves her geeky boyfriend and goes off with the handsome stranger, thereby giving new meaning to the term 'pick-up truck'. The ad fails to deal with one crucial point, which is that if the young man drives his truck across a state line with the young woman inside it, he will almost certainly be arrested.

PIRELLI TYRES

With decades' worth of sexy calendars behind them, it is no surprise that Pirelli's "Gripping Stuff" campaign goes for the cars'n'girls angle. The last ad, which featured a wet-lipped blonde attempting to kill her husband so as to leave him for another man – an attempt foiled by hubby's remarkably adhesive tyres – was as gripping as the slogan implied. The new one, in which a girl wearing a nightie drives a Lamborghini through Italian hill villages in order to start the world turning again, is exactly as daft as that synopsis implies. Cow cognoscenti should note that...

1. *To Italians a car is not a vehicle, but a genital.*

2. *No car is more phallic than a Lamborghini.*

3. *This one is... you guessed it... red.*

There have been plenty of other campaigns that played on the magic combination of man-made machinery and female flesh. Pretty Polly sold women tights when they featured a blonde mending her fan-belt with her nylons a couple of years ago. And they also reminded men of the virtues of (a) blondes who wear stockings and (b) open-topped vintage Jags.

More recently Lee jeans have had a spot in which a bob'n'gob-job* girl chucks her boyfriend out of her (red) car, only to find that his super-tough denims allow him to slide downhill on his bottom so quickly that he catches up with her. She is then amazed to find that he does not wish to continue the journey. If she weren't such a blatant sociopath she might understand why.

Such appalling couples are nothing new in advertising. We met similar examples earlier behind the wheels of Citroëns and Renault 5s. All of which leads one to the following list...

**Def.: An aggressively trendy young woman with cropped hair and prominent lips.*

The three most nauseating couples in advertising

In reverse order, these are...

3. The Gold Blend coffee duo

So much has been said and written about this noxious duo that there is nothing left to ponder but their future. We spill the beans, or rather, the granules on what's coming next...

She goes out with him for dinner. They drink coffee. They have sex. They drink coffee. They get married. They drink coffee. They buy a satellite dish for all-night television since all this coffee interferes with their sleep. They drink coffee. He goes sterile from drinking too much coffee and, in a fit of depression, starts shooting up heroin. They drink coffee. The shared needles lead to him becoming HIV positive. They drink coffee. The caffeine makes her irritable and she leaves him. He drinks coffee. She finds she's got Aids and goes round to his place to confront him. They drink coffee. He's as high as a kite from his smack and stabs her through her pancreas (which was cancerous anyway as a result of her coffee habit). He tries to revive her with coffee. She dies. He drinks coffee. He sues Nestlé. They deny responsibility on the basis that it's not real coffee anyway. He overdoses on coffee and dies. Gareth Hunt, Diane Keen, Tony Anholt and Sarah Greene are the pall-bearers at his funeral. At the wake, coffee is served.

2. The couple who drive the Renault 25

He decided to go it alone. She asked whether he was sure it was wise. We all gagged.

She got a new job. They gave her a company car. She called home on the car-phone to tell him all about it. We exhibited the signs of having contracted severe listeriosis.

They took the boy away from school. En route they talked about calling in the lawyers. Could this be divorce? We cheered up a bit at the prospect. But no, they were going into business together. Now they could both have Renaults. And the son could have a toy one too. We dialled 999.

1. Mark and Sue, who have never taken good health for granted

These two saps are too awful to contemplate, let alone write about. So let's just keep this as painlessly short as possible by noting no more than the following...

1. The first thing the kids want to do on entering mummy's sick-room is .... turn on the telly, and

2. How many people do you know who would enter a cancer-scanner smiling? None. Quite. So why has Sue got that stupid look on her face as she slides in to meet the gamma rays?

Finally,

Mr Punch's First Annual Naff Ad Awards to...

John Hurt for making Uncle Ben's Classic Recipe Rice sound more urgent and majestic than Shakespeare.

The Royal Shakespeare Company for making most contemporary productions of The Bard sound *less* urgent and majestic than a recipe for Uncle Ben's Rice.

The Biactol boy for being the biggest yob on television (close runner-up: anyone in a lager commercial).

Maureen Lipman for collaborative racial stereotyping.

The Owner of this year's Cruft's Supreme Champion for bearing such an astounding resemblance to her dog. This award applies every year and is thus given in perpetuity to Pedigree Chum, whose ads introduce us to the top dogs and their owners.

Jim Dunk for being the worst wally in a lager commercial (close runner-up: anyone in a lager commercial).

Today newspaper for running endless colour features about the Gold Blend coffee couple and then following up with a front-page scare-story warning that coffee-drinkers faced sterility.

Griff Rhys-Jones for starring in Holsten Pils ads opposite Marilyn Monroe (who was a drug-addict) and John Wayne (who died of tobacco-induced lung cancer). Who next? Dylan Thomas?

Jim Dunk (again) for being the man in a lager commercial who was most nearly Bob Hoskins, but not quite (close runner-up: yes, you guessed it...)

The Heineken sheepdog for being the best actor in a lager commercial (close-runner-up: none – no one else in any other lager commercial was even close).

"I guess he's a bit of a cliché but we love him anyway."

"Never mind 'Pourquoi?' – just get it!"

BONA-FIDO

A Pack of Dog-Eared Cartoons

"There used to be a small yellow bird perched on his nose but it was covered over in Victorian times."

PUNCH RESHOOTS THE HOLLYWOOD CLASSICS

They don't make movies like they used to. And the reason for this is very simple. They used to make movies for grown-ups with IQs somewhat larger than their age. Nowadays, however, movies are made for sub-literate thirteen-year-olds whose brains have been addled by a constant diet of food additives and MTV.

What's more, just to check that modern movies are suitably moronic, they are all tested before representative preview audiences – representative, that is, of an audience with the emotional and intellectual development of the average fruit-bat.

The result is that films with unhappy endings or complicated plots simply don't get made any more. If they made *Love Story* in 1989, Ali McGraw would have to get better. Except, of course, that it wouldn't be Ali McGraw. It would be Lisa Bonet or Emily Lloyd.

It's enough to make you grateful that the classics of cinema were produced when they were. Because if they were coming out now, they'd be something like this...

GONE WITH THE WIND

Date: 1939
Stars: Clark Gable and Vivien Leigh
Problem: The goodies lose the war. The girl loses her man. And the old-fashioned language is incomprehensible to today's thirteen-year-old movie-goer.

Solution: Sylvester Stallone and Cher star in a new version. Sly does not say, "Frankly, my dear, I don't give a damn." He goes for the more modern approach, viz: "Y'know...uh...like... uh...I couldn't give a f***." This is his entire dialogue for the film. Instead of talking, Sly spends the first three reels oiling his muscles, whilst Cher undergoes the plastic surgery required before she can fit into her costumes. Having worked up a nice skin-sheen, Our Hero goes out and defeats the entire Union army single-handed. The fact that they are not armed with Cruise missiles (unlike the well-prepared Stallone) may have something to do with their downfall. Finally Sly comes home to meet his loving Cher. Their famous "jacuzzi scene" is a wow with audiences all over the world.

CASABLANCA

Date: 1943
Stars: Humphrey Bogart and Ingrid Bergman
Problem: She flies off with the wrong man. Plus it is set in Morocco. Most Americans can't find America on the map of the world – Morocco is a definite no-no.

Solution: Michael J. Fox plays Rick, a bouncy, energetic teenager who is transported back through time to find himself running a milk-bar in Casablanca, Idaho, some time in the early Fifties. He plays in a rock'n'roll band with his pal Sam, a wise-cracking black kid played by Spike Lee. Together they write a string of hits with titles like "Here's Lookin' Atcha, Babe", "A Hill O' Beans" and "I Can Take It If She Can". Michael still doesn't get the girl (played by Molly Ringwald), but he does get to walk off into the sunset with Tom Cruise, uttering the immortal lines, "Gee, this could be the start of a great career making buddy movies."

THE BIG SLEEP

Date: 1946
Stars: Humphrey Bogart and Lauren Bacall
Problem: This film is totally incomprehensible. Even Raymond Chandler, who wrote the original book, didn't know whodunnit. Also, it's in black and white and extensive research shows that kids today just do not want to watch black and white (a fact which must come as a shock to the makers of grainy monochrome rock videos, but never mind).

Solution: Arnold Schwarzenegger and Danny De Vito play a crazy couple of brothers, Big Sleep and Little Sleep. They get up to a whole host of whacky gags. It's still impossible to work out what, if anything, is going on, but no one cares because the film makes a fortune, and an incredibly loud soundtrack by Def Leppard makes conscious thought an impossibility anyway.

LITTLE WOMEN

Date: 1933
Stars: Katharine Hepburn and Spring Byington
Problem: Totally sexist concept – nice "little" girls grow up to be proper unliberated women.

Solution: The film is remade as *Little Men*. As a nice casting touch, the remake stars Martin Sheen and his sons, all of whom are (a) related and (b) somewhat less than enormously tall. Film-goers are already familiar with Martin's sons Charlie Sheen and Emilio Estevez, but this production introduces them to two more members of this talented family – Radiccio and Mister Sheen.

SNOW WHITE AND THE SEVEN DWARFS
Date: 1937
Stars: Happy, Doc, Grumpy, Sneezy, Sleepy, Dave Dee, Dozy, Beaky, Mick and Tich
Problem: The title is racist, dwarfist and has unpleasant overtones of cocaine.

Solution: The film is remade by Steven Spielberg, starring Whitney Houston and a bunch of animated puppets. The new title is *Coffee Cream and the Seven Cuddly Space Creatures*. Harrison Ford plays the Prince. Coffee Cream, who is in fact just seven years old (a remarkable make-up job allows Whitney to undertake the role), meets an adorable alien septet when her wicked step-mom and pop leave her alone in the house for the day. The story is so tooth-rottingly sentimental that no one is able to sit through to the end, hence our lack of information on the outcome. However, Spielberg makes so much money that sales of the souvenir T-shirt alone are worth more than the annual Gross National Product of Belgium.

Sly comes home to meet his loving Cher. Their famous "jacuzzi scene" is a wow with audiences all over the world.

GILDA
Date: 1946
Stars: Rita Hayworth and Glenn Ford
Problem: Rita Hayworth was one sexy lady, possibly two. But her selling point was her red hair and the film was in black and white. Plus she sang with a jazz band. Kids today can't deal with jazz. They want House and Acieeeed.

Solution: Bette Midler plays Hilda, a Beverly Hills housewife who is kidnapped by a bunch of kids who want to raise money to subsidise their careers as rappers and DJs. In an outrageous "caper" scene, Bette and the gang raid the old Columbia Pictures costume department where Bette discovers that she is totally unable to fit into Rita Hayworth's old costumes. Luckily Cher gives her the name of a great plastic surgeon and she is able to have her lower abdomen removed. This "splatter" element opens up the film to the massive horror movie audience, with the result that Hilda makes almost as much money as Steven Spielberg's T-shirts. ■

ASSAULT OF THE KILLER TABLOIDS

Sin news special

A SHOCK HORROR PUNCH PROBE INTO BRITAIN'S TRAGIC TABLOID TARGETS

By MITCHELL SYMONS

SEX-TALK SHOCK SHOCK

A shock report reveals today that the lurid sex-stories in Britain's tearaway tabloids are written in a language **totally unlike normal English.**

According to the so-called satirists at posh *Punch* magazine, the saucy, sizzling scandals you love to read are "a poetic combination of prurience and euphemism".

What those over-educated, limp-wristed lefties mean **in ordinary English** is that your favourite family papers wallow in smut, but don't use dirty words.

They're right. We don't want to be any more disgusting than we have to be. When we say "three-in-a-bed love triangle", **we think you know what we mean.**

But for the benefit of the namby-pamby know-it-alls who know about everything except real life, here is a tabloid lexicon of sex:

Love-making session = sex
Sex romps = more than one love-making session
Secret love-nest = friend's flat
Secret love tryst = what happens in a love-nest
Sun-soaked hideaway = a love-nest in Majorca
Vow = a promise made in the heat of the moment
Pledge = a vow made after the heat of the moment
Love child = illegitimate baby
Vice-girl = prostitute
My night of shame = sex-romp with a vice-girl
Rent-boy = male prostitute
My sordid night of shame = sex-romp with a rent-boy

It's beautiful. It's poetic. None of those Booker Prize posers could ever write half as well. That's why we say, if William Shakespeare were alive today, he'd be a sub-editor on your soaraway Sun. *Don't believe it? Turn to page 24…*

It's the talking-point that's caused more of a stink than a boxful of poisoned eggs.

That's what they're saying about invasion of privacy, the easy-to-learn foot-in-the-bedroom-door technique that's brought British journalism its most sordid scoops of the past ten years.

Now killjoy politicians like John Browne MP are trying to take away our fun. They say that the public is sick of lurid lies about the private lives of famous people.

One Bill has failed in Parliament. But more are on the way. And the chances are that the Government will lash out with tough curbs against the gutter press.

- **But how do newspapers get their dirty yarns?**
- **Why do sluts speak out for cash?**
- **And what makes readers cry, "Don't stop!", when their favourite papers are full of filthy fables?**

Intrepid Punchman MITCHELL SYMONS has spent weeks crawling through the slimy sewers of kiss'n'sell.

His findings are disgusting. They are controversial. They will change forever the way you look at sheep.

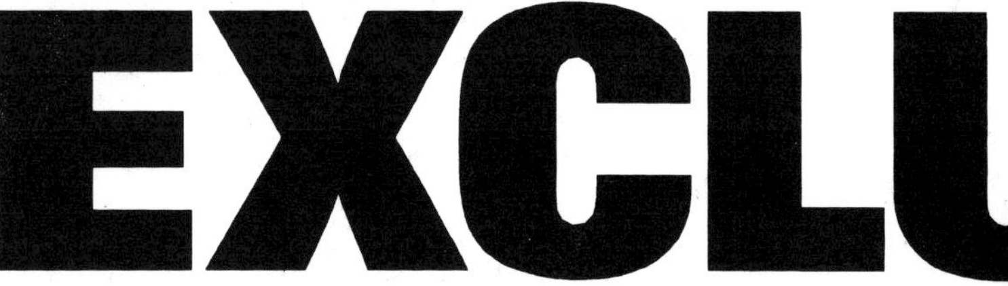

He was covered in sweat, but I kept my skirt on the whole time.

There is nothing new in men being caught with their trousers down. Men have been caught with their trousers down since before they wore trousers.

The difference is that, nowadays, newspapers will provide them with a complete record of their indiscretion. Fortunately for Messrs **MURDOCH** and **MAXWELL**, there is no shortage of chaps prepared to undergo "marathon sex romps" with the sort of girl who has adopted the **MAE WEST** quote "Keep a diary and some day it'll keep you" as a personal motto. Kiss and sell has replaced blackmail, the second oldest profession, as a source of income for the shirking classes.

However, before condemning kiss and sellers as modern blackmailers, we should ask ourselves if we would act any differently – given the chance. **SHARON RING, a *News of the World* feature writer** who has become a specialist in the world of kiss and sell, looks at the question from an interesting perspective. "A lot of people are very puritanical about kiss and sell. I think it's true to say an awful lot of women *would* sleep with a famous, handsome man they had just met and then, if they were offered a lot of money to speak about it, they'd do that too."

Sharon Ring puts the blame at the feet (or wherever) of the men: "These men are all successful in their own field but they seem to switch off their brains when they pull down their trousers. You can't expect loyalty from a one-night stand."

She dismisses the idea ►

SIVE!

Kelvin Mackenzie: evil genius behind those Sun sex shockers

"I really love Romeo. I just don't like his name, that's all."

WE MET IN THE GARDEN FOR SAUCY SEX-ROMPS

says Wildchild Heiress Juliet

"Honestly, I think he prefers poetry to nookie."

Our men in wait outside the Capulet £1 million mansion

By Punch Reporter Bill Shakespeare

Thirteen-year-old Juliet Capulet, the Lolita heiress at the centre of Verona's latest sex-scandal, yesterday admitted that she had enjoyed passionate midnight love-trysts with tearaway Romeo Montague.

Speaking from her family's hideaway mansion she confessed that randy Romeo, sword-stab killer of Tybalt Capulet, had climbed security walls to meet her.

As her stunning 36-24-36 figure quivered with emotion, scantily-clad Juliet (Jule to her friends and her nurse) continued, "He said I shouldn't worry about his past or his name. He said he'd still smell just as sweet if he was a rose. He was always going on like that. He's a bit of a poet, really."

Biting back tears, the teenage temptress denied that her relationship with Romeo was nothing more than a sordid bonk bonanza: "It was true love between Romeo and me. All he ever did was kiss me. To be honest, I think he prefers poetry to nookie."

As preparations went ahead for her forthcoming royal wedding to Prince's kinsman Paris, the schoolgirl seductress:

VOWED that she would rather die than marry superstud Paris, even though her mother Lady Capulet described him as "gallant, young and noble",

PLEDGED her love for Romeo Montague, and

REVEALED that she had in fact married Romeo in a secret ceremony conducted by controversial Franciscan friar Brother Lawrence.

"People have got Romeo all wrong," sobbed scantily-clad Juliet. "They say he's a murderer. And they talk about his love-pact with Rosaline. But he's always treated me like a queen."

Then she revealed, "I can't stand it at home any longer. My parents have always hated Romeo and they have sworn to make me marry Paris.

"But Romeo's in Mantua and my place is by his side. I've got a secret fake-death potion. If I can take that I can escape the wedding on Thursday and make a fly-away love-dash to Mantua.

"I really love Romeo. I just don't like his name, that's all."

▶ that it is wrong for newspapers to print such stories: "The bottom line on kiss and sell is that the *News of the World* sells more copies than our two main rivals put together." Let's face it, Sharon Ring is right: Sunday wouldn't be Sunday without the Sundays and the Sundays wouldn't be the Sundays without the scandals. We read the tabloids gleefully before turning to the weightier, worthier quality papers. Of course, there are people who profess themselves to be totally uninterested in the sleazy world of the tabloids: these are the people who cause the log-jam in the paper shop on a Sunday morning as they read what **Tracy Slut** has to say about her **"Torrid Nights of Shame with Top TV Soap Star"** before they pick up their copies of *The Sunday Telegraph*.

It is said of the puritan that he disapproved of bear-baiting not because it gave the bear pain, but because it gave the people pleasure. The puritan knew it gave people pleasure because he himself found it pleasurable. For similar reasons, his modern counterpart spends an awful lot of time in the "gutter" – just to check that it's still dirty.

And you don't have to spend too long in the gutter to know that it's getting even dirtier. Why we read the stories is clear: our repulsion/fascination with other people's sex lives neatly mirrors the British attitude to sex itself. Speaking strictly for yourself, the British really aren't very good at sex: all that writhing and squelching – it's so cumbersome, undignified and ... well ... unBritish. It really is best to leave that sort of thing to foreigners. Nevertheless, we are drawn to the subject in the same way that the vegan is obsessed by the abattoir.

Just as you don't have to be a psychiatrist to know why we read about sex scandals, so you don't have to be a sociologist to work out why the newspapers write about them. Circulation. **Circulation**. Everything – especially qualms – gets sacrificed to the Goddess Circulation. The pre-Maxwell *Daily Mirror* bought **VICKI HODGE'S** story about her romance with **PRINCE ANDREW** but then toned it down because they didn't want to offend the Palace. Through the *Mirror*, Miss Hodge assured the nation that no one had "touched the crown jewels". As we all know, this wasn't the case: Miss Hodge herself had partaken of the trinkets in question.

The reason we know this is because the bolder *News of the World* (in their first tabloid edition) printed the whole story and saw their circulation increase as a result. Newspapers have found that they can't afford to be coy. In wars, the first victim is truth; in circulation wars, where truth isn't even a combatant, the first victim is inhibition. Meanwhile, kiss and sell stories have become the most powerful weapons in the arsenal. To detonate these weapons, all newspapers have to do is sit back and open their cheque-books and the raddled ranks of bimbos, fading starlets, prostitutes and rent boys will do the rest.

BRITT EKLAND (who at least gave value for money with tales about the international set – Warren, Ryan, George, Rod, etc), **MARILYN COLE**, **MYNAH BIRD** and **VICKI HODGE** have passed on the torch to a new generation. **FIONA WRIGHT** and **SANDY GRIZZLE**, to name but two, name not only names but also numbers. Not very much is left to the imagination and, if it is, you can usually rely on a rival newspaper to fill in the missing words.

This franker tone is set not by the sellers but by the buyers (the newspapers). The sellers speak the same language they have always spoken: Mills & Boon. It is the newspapers, assisted and obstructed by a tawdry collection of agents, minders, "boyfriends" and other pimps, which decide this season's vocabulary.

A woman like Ms Grizzle may sometimes do her much-publicised lovers more good than harm. The right kind of privacy intrusion can actually enhance a "victim's" reputation. **TOM WATT**, formerly the wimpy **Lofty in *EastEnders***, suffered no harm after **"Beauty Queen" LEE SCOTT** told all about their ▶

THE MEN OF VICKI HODGE

Vicki Hodge is to kiss 'n' sell what Garfield Sobers is to cricket – the ultimate past-mistress.

Out of her own estimated tally of 100+ men, the following stand out:

1. Prince Andrew
2. Ringo Starr
3. John Bindon
4. Jamie Niven
5. Jimmy Mitchum (son of)
6. Gordon Waller (of Peter & Gordon)
7. Elliot Gould
8. David Bailey
9. Yul Brynner
10. George Lazenby

Quote from Miss Hodge: "I've only slept with people I've had affairs with, been in love with, or really, really super people." The interesting thing about Vicki Hodge is that none of her victims seems to resent her; she carries it all off with a certain élan*: perhaps being a baronet's daughter (family motto: "Glory Is The Reward For Virtue") helps. Compare her with Fiona Wright.*

WOMEN WHO HAVE BEEN THE VICTIMS OF KISS & SELL

1. NINA MYSKOW – the self-styled "Bitch of the Box" (and a former *News of the World* columnist) was sold by her toyboy lover as "a great naked white whale" with a figure that has "grown men reaching for their harpoon guns". (See Rules for Sold Stories.)

2. PATTI COLDWELL – TV PATTI SEDUCED MY BLACK STALLION "Our life's in ruins rages wife."

3. SAMANTHA FOX – victim of "Heartbroken Sharon Brough who got a divorce from her husband Chris because of his love for the Page 3 stunner". "She destroyed my marriage."

4. MANDY SMITH – interestingly, it wasn't Mandy who did the dirty on Bill Wyman but her boyfriend Keith Daley. Mandy restricted herself to wild pouts and tame quotes like "I am still a friend of Bill's and he is very supportive of my career."

5. KAREN STRINGFELLOW – daughter of ace kiss and sellee Peter had the whistle blown on her by kiss & seller Marc, a former fiancé. He revealed he had shared the favours of a waitress with prospective father-in-law Peter Stringfellow.

6. BRITT EKLAND – the queen of kiss and sell became the victim when singer Linda Lewis claimed that they "made frantic love" together. **"MY GAY NIGHT OF SHAME WITH BRITT."**

THE 10 "KISS & SELL" COMMANDMENTS

1. The more famous the sellee, the less salacious the story has to be.
2. The seller is always younger than the sellee.
3. The sellee is always more famous than the seller.
4. Any girl who hasn't been to bed with either Chris Quinten, Tony Knowles or – and this man is the benchmark for all Kiss & Sell victims – Peter Stringfellow – doesn't really qualify as a professional.
5. Women sellers don't believe in "one-night stands" and are not "easy": they just fall in love very quickly.
6. The word "TV" (as in "television" rather than "transvestite") must appear somewhere in the headline – unless the sellee is a Royal.
7. The wife of the sellee can always be guaranteed never to "believe it" and to "vow to stand by her man".
8. All the newspapers will trot out their agony aunts to proffer advice to the wives/husbands of sellees.
9. International "jet-set" names will be mentioned as often as possible in the newspaper story even though they are not personally implicated, e.g.: "after one marathon sex romp in our sun-soaked Barbados hideaway, we went out to eat in a restaurant where Mick Jagger and Jerry Hall had been only the previous week."
10. Those who live by the sword shall die by it: a seller can become a sellee in the time it takes an ex-lover to telephone the *News of the World*.

▶ frenetic encounters. According to Ms Scott, **"Tom had me stretched across his Saab 900 Turbo and we'd both reached the point of no return.** Unfortunately, just at the vital moment his elbow brushed against the lawnmower he's got hanging on the wall and that knocked a bicycle next to it. Before he could move, everything came crashing down on his head and practically knocked him out." Tom spotted Lee when he was judging a beauty contest which she won. The tabloids' answer to Paris and Helen clearly hit it off but, although she was wildly complimentary about his lovemaking technique, no relationship can survive disclosures like this: **"They (Tom's feet) were the most horrible things I've ever set eyes on – long, lumpy and covered with verrucas. Even his toenails were chipped."**

Tom Watt's adventures in the garage of love were richly comical. But many sex stories are run through with a streak of venom that causes even the most prurient reader to feel offended. When *The Sun* made a series of front-page stories out of a rent-boy's allegations about the life of **ELTON JOHN** they found that they had alienated their readers. People like Elton. He had, in any case, long since admitted his bisexuality and the stories turned out to be a pack of lies. Newspapers can go too far. And in this case, going too far cost *The Sun* a cool £1 million in out-of-court libel settlements.

If newspapers can be self-destructive, so can the men they write about. It's one thing to have an affair when you're married (e.g. Bernie Winters) or to choose girls who are indiscreet when you're single (e.g. David Essex with Sinitta); it's quite another when you choose to self-destruct by going with prostitutes. I mean, how polymorphously perverse can you get?

However, newspapers can't rely on chaps imploding and so they need a steady stream of regulars. Names such as Quinten, Knowles, and, of course, Stringfellow's are the staple diet of sellers and subs alike. After a while, these fellows earn your respect – if only for their stamina.

But Stringfellow and his friends are beyond harm. The phenomenon of kiss and sell can't damage people whose business is pleasure. It can, however, damage people whose business is business – or politics.

Thanks to kiss and sell, politicians can no longer afford to indulge in private vices whilst espousing public virtues. The Profumo scandal would probably not have happened in today's climate of indiscretion. **JOHN PROFUMO** would not have taken the risk that **CHRISTINE KEELER** might tell all to the newspapers.

Abroad is a different country: they do things **differently** there. When Cecil Parkinson resigned, **PRESIDENT MITTERRAND** was said to have remarked that if adultery were the criterion for resignations in France, he'd be without his entire cabinet. The same is true of other Catholic countries where the family is sacred and affairs are accepted as just "appetite": **PRESIDENT PAPANDREOU OF GREECE** enjoyed much sympathy – even admiration – when news of his affair broke. Although this sympathy evaporated as he neglected the affairs of state for the affairs of the heart, the fact that he could continue to see his young lady – even after the story broke – seems remarkably sophisticated to anyone born and raised in Perfidious Albion.

Of course, in predominantly Protestant countries it's different. In the United States, **GARY HART** was brought to his knees because **DONNA RICE** had gone down on hers. In South Africa, blacks can sleep easier now that the frightening demagogue, **EUGENE TERRE-BLANCHE**, has blown his dream of a Fourth Reich after an affair with a journalist. Meanwhile in Britain, as every Tom, Frank and Tarby knows, family values have always been considerably more important than families.

While this remains the case, kiss and sell stories will continue to dominate the front pages of the tabloids and chaps with any sense of self-preservation will keep their flies firmly buttoned. That is, of course, except for those chaps who don't and you will be reading about them shortly…

SIX

	FRANK BOUGH
Description of victim:	"Everybody's favourite uncle"
Description of assailant:	Bernice: "busty blonde vice-girl"
Was the victim married then?	Yes
Is the victim married now?	Yes
Headline:	THREE-IN-BED GAM WITH NAUGHTY FRANK
Antics (as reported):	"Sex-romps"
Alleged venue:	"His luxury London-flat
Specific allegations:	Hers: "He always seem so strait-laced and bor on the box, but I'm tell you… he was *wild.* He p by cheque … it was alm as if he wanted to get fo out."
Consequences:	For him – disastrous. lost his job as a BBC pres ter and is now to be fou on Sky TV, owned of cou by Rupert Murdoch, wh papers were larg responsible for Boug downfall in the first pl She disappeared back i obscurity.

OF THE BEST

R RALPH HALPERN	PRINCE ANDREW	IAN BOTHAM	TONY JACKLIN	TOM WATT
rton boss" ve-times-a-night tycoon"	"Randy Andy" "Romeo Prince"	"Troubled cricket star"	"The 44-year-old Mr Clean of the fairways"	"EastEnders wimp Lofty"
na Wright: "Britain's st famous bimbo"	Vicki Hodge: "Sexy ex-model" "Baronet's daughter"	Lindy Field: "Lovely Lindy, former Miss Barbados"	Donna Methven: "Pretty teenage waitress"	Lee Scott: "a former shop-assistant from Watford with a 35-23-34 figure and incredible 34-inch legs"
	No	Yes	No	No
	Yes	Yes	Yes	No
IBO BITES BACK AT KY TYCOON	ANDY'S SEXY SIZZLER!	BEAUTY QUEEN'S NIGHT OF PASSION WITH BOTHAM ... AND THEIR BED COLLAPSED!	NIGHT TONY MADE ME A WOMAN/GOLFER AND THE VIRGIN	LOFTY'S CAR-BONNET LUST WENT WITH A BANG!
ltiple sexual congress	"Love among the scented Caribbean roses" "Passion beneath the palm trees"	See headline	Sweaty goings-on	"He spreadeagled her on the bonnet of a car in his garage ... she really felt the earth move"
Ralph's flat	West Indian herbaceous borders	Botham's hotel	"In Jacklin's room at London's Churchill Hotel"	In the garage at his house
: "I met the girl about times for carnal reasons. s girl is a bitch. It's time earned a decent living the rest of us." s: "I did it for the reason woman has sex with a n – I loved him."	"He had strong, manly arms."	She said: "I fancied Botty from the moment I saw him. There was an immediate magnetism between us." He said: "I deny that I was ever in bed with Lindy Field. If only a quarter of the things that have ever been said and written about me were true, I ... would have sired half the children in the world."	She said: "He was covered in sweat but I kept my skirt on the whole time. I was prepared to give up my teenage years for him, but all he wanted was my virginity." He said: "This young lady came on the scene when I was at my lowest ebb. I'm no Roman Polanski, but it's been four months since Viv died. Life must go on."	She said: "I know Tom is football crazy and is apparently a right carthorse on the football field – but he's a stallion in bed. I think he reads the *Kama Sutra* more than the sports pages."
marriage broke up, but professional reputation ained unscathed. One ton shareholder called "the greatest English- n since Sir Winston urchill". She became the come of bimbosity.	He benefited – a young man sewing a few wild oats. She made a sum of money variously reported to have been between £40-100,000.	These allegations made little public difference to a man also faced with accusations about drink, drugs, fights, etc. Controversy is as much a part of his image as cricket.	Any distaste about these allegations was far outweighed by sympathy for a decent man who had recently lost a beloved wife. Methven's "nice girl" image was dented when she was pictured in *The Sun* wearing nothing but a Ryder Cup sweater and a pair of knickers.	His image was much enhanced. She has not been heard of since.

TE: All the quotations used in this chart come from genuine tabloid stories. The fact that they are genuine, however, does not necessarily mean that y bear any relation to anything that anyone, either living or dead, may actually have said or done.

HALDANE'S

BRIEF LIVES

"And Clive will always be remembered as the most hard-working member of the sales team."

"Not having had the benefit of a classical education, I just tend to call 'em huge slimy bastards."

"I don't know why you couldn't have bought an ordinary smoke-alarm like anyone else."

"You're too late. She chose a career in advertising."

SEND
Bears
Home
RETURN
BEARS
TO ARCTIC
HOME
POLICE
PINK
BRISTOL EXPRESS
ARCTIC POLLUTION
CRITICAL
OZONE
BREAK UP
ARCTIC ICE THAW
IMMINENT

The don't care bears

Misha the polar bear used to live in a circus cage. It drove him mad. He spent ten years recovering from the experience in Bristol Zoo. Then animal rights group Zoo Check discovered him. Now he's got two personal psychologists, hundreds of concerned "friends" and a Polar Bear Action Account at the Abbey National. It will probably send him bananas again. WILLIAM GREEN reports

Polar bears don't like zoos much. As a modern menagerie keeper would be the first to admit, they find life on a concrete iceberg pretty tame. Whether taken from the wild or zoo-bred, these splendid, savage beasts are prone in captivity to boredom and obsessive fretfulness, and there is a high mortality rate among their cubs. No European zoo has yet managed to design and build a successful "bear garden" – that is, an enclosure that fulfils the conflicting requirements of public exhibition and animal contentment.

Only nine of Britain's many zoos and wildlife parks still display polar bears (twenty animals in all) and nearly all of them have decided not to replace present specimens when they die. London Zoo itself recently abandoned its long-cherished plans to build an "Arctic Wilderness" on the old Mappin Terraces site in Regent's Park, and is currently designing something called a "Chinese Exhibit" instead.

This is an encouraging development for conservationists and animal lovers everywhere, and the nation's press showed a fair-minded appreciation of it in a recent flurry of headlines. TRAGIC POLAR BEARS. ZOO PAIR HAVE NOW GONE MAD. DOOMED TO DIE. MISHA SENTENCED TO LIFE OF MISERY. TURNED INTO A PSYCHOTIC WRECK. Thus was the public introduced to two new media stars, a couple of Bristol Zoo's sleepiest inhabitants, Nina (28) and Misha (age unknown).

There is nothing quite so nauseating as the use of ignorant, artificial moral outrage to boost the circulation of newspapers. But whence comes this sudden riptide of human sympathy for polar bears? And how long will it last?

The story started quietly a couple of months ago, when the Department of the Environment renewed Bristol Zoo's operating licence. It did so without ordering some recommended improvements to Nina's and Misha's enclosure, trusting no doubt to the zoo's own good sense ►

and discretion in the matter. This unremarkable bureaucratic act gave rise to strident complaints from animal rights pressure groups, and in no time at all Fleet Street picture editors were sending their teams down the Great Western Railway to enjoy a sunny day out and whip up a bit of a stink.

The synthetic nature of this stink is evident. There are nearly 400 zoos in this country, if you want to count every donkey sanctuary and municipal aquarium. Few, if any, are so well-kept, mild-mannered and downright respectable as the Gardens of the Bristol, Clifton and West of England Zoological Society. Its hard-working keepers and curators make the most unlikely of villains.

Wrong villains, and wrong victim. The difficulty is that Misha, "the bonkers bear", went animal crackers not last month but years ago, while in the possession of those well-known humanitarians, Chipperfield's Circus. He spent most of his career as a dancing bear living in a closed travelling cage. Bristol Zoo bought him in 1979, in a desperate state, since when his "mental health" has shown a steady improvement. Misha's mate Nina, although very old, is in good condition, and the two bears live together on friendly terms. When they peg out (lifespan is about 30 years), both animals will be replaced by some more docile species of mammal. Bristol's 1987 guidebook is categorical on the subject – "The Society recognises that urban zoos are not suitable for polar bears".

Unrepentant, *The Mail on Sunday* has stepped up its zoo-baiting crusade. The tabloid has teamed up with a pressure group called Zoo Check for a self-righteous Action Campaign "to help these pitiful creatures". The object of this is to whip up popular sentiment and raise money from any poor sucker who would want to be a "Friend of the Polar Bears". To date, amazingly, no polar bear has yet reciprocated the gesture to become a "Friend of the Humans". The loot from the fund is to be spent on the fees of "a top animal behaviourist" (TV psychologist Dr Roger Mugford), who has generously agreed to study the bears. His mission, it seems, is to try and break into tragic Misha's "lonely mental cell", by encouraging him to play with an indestructible rubber rugby-ball. It's not confirmed yet whether Gareth Chilcott will be brought in to act as a playmate.

The only outcome of this pointless rabble-rousing is that Bristol Zoo has felt obliged to appoint its own animal psychologist, Dr Maggie Redshaw, to the case. She is, as it happens, the wife of the zoo's scientific officer. This long-suffering woman must now spend 40 hours of her valuable time "observing" mad Misha and

nutty Nina. While Dr Mugford gives short-term consultations, she will watch for signs of "paranoid paresthesia" (bear scratches itself), "stereotypic tongue-clicking" (bear licks its nose) and other such indications of ursine schizophrenia. At the same time, Dr Redshaw has to reassure rumour-mongering hacks that Misha's melancholia is caused neither by toothache (too many glacier mints, perhaps) nor by tummy trouble (too many fish fingers).

And who, you may ask, are Zoo Check? Zoo Check are a bunch of animal lovers dedicated to the return of all captive creatures to their natural habitat. Set up and run by the theatrical happy family of Virginia McKenna and Bill Travers, they are a well-meaning crew, given to publishing dreadfully soppy poems in their monthly round-robin bulletin. But Zoo Check want to close all zoos (and donkey sanctuaries?). Never mind conservation. Never mind research. Never mind that some of the world's rarest animals, like the golden-lion tamarind, no longer have a habitat to return to. Zoos are horrid. Oh dear. They must go.

McKenna and Travers are best known as the human stars of *Born Free*, and other wildlife masterpieces. It was films like theirs that first encouraged the public to imagine that lions will lie down with lambs and children, and become great big cuddlesome kittens, if only those beastly evil poachers would leave them alone. Perhaps, if we tried appealing to their better natures and lent them copies of *Winnie the Pooh*, we could persuade polar bears to become vegetarians.

When I rang Zoo Check to ask if there were any animals – reptiles or hamsters perhaps – which adapted happily to captivity, director William Travers cautioned me against facile anthropomorphism. You can never tell when an animal is miserable, apparently. However unhappy he may be, no crocodile is going to shed tears and tell us his troubles. But Zoo Check want it both ways. Nothing delights them more than to compare polar bear Misha with Convict 99 in Broadmoor, "mentally deranged", pacing his cell in "a bleak, featureless world" and "waiting impatiently for death".

While on the subject of bleak, featureless worlds, we may as well look at how life is treating Misha's long-lost cousins up in the wide open spaces of the Arctic Circle. Freedom is certainly exciting enough for the bears at the moment. They've got 200-mile oil-slicks in Alaska, ozone holes over the North Pole, mutant seals with deadly toxic blubber, and drunken Eskimos on Skidoos. Further hazards include gelignite parties organised after dark by the mineral exploration companies, and tourists in low-flying helicopters who like to chase large white furry animals round and round the icebergs. To cap it all, there is a particularly painful threadworm epidemic doing the rounds at the moment.

> The object is to whip up popular sentiment and raise money from any poor sucker who wants to be a "Friend of the Polar Bears"

The realistic alternative for captive polar bears is not the Arctic Circle (recently described as "the world's septic tank") but the Big Chill and the Cold Slab. Taken all round, things could be a lot worse for Nina and Misha. They might be in Belfast, sponsored by a domestic appliance company and humiliatingly re-christened Wash and Tumble. They might be in Yorkshire's Flamingoland Leisure Complex, sharing an enclosure with a brown bear, only yards away from a rackety funfair roundabout. Bristol Zoo, after all, is up in Clifton, the city's most sought-after suburb. It is quiet and genteel. And there is an excellent fishmonger. ■

"Apparently, he didn't die in '77, he just wanted to drop out and live an anonymous life among ordinary people."

Called to the BAR

Cartoons by LOWRY

"This is the exact spot where I discovered the meaninglessness of life."

"Fortunately, the potency of cheap music has got nothing on the potency of cheap booze."

"I don't give a damn about the conversation flowing like good wine as long as the good wine flows like good wine."

"No thanks, Helen and I have given up enjoying ourselves."

TURNING

MIKE MARKLEW brings two great peoples together

Dear Mr Smith,

Our foundation has been created to assist families who have been relocated to this country from Japan, as part of the agreement forged between Prince Philip and the Japanese Prime Minister, Noboru Takeshita, during a booze-up held at the Tokyo British Club, following the funeral of the late Emperor Showa.

Your name was chosen from a list supplied by the Middlesex County Council, Dept of Cultural and Ethnic Affairs, to be host to a family of our Japanese friends.

The Ito family, pronounced Eat-oh, will be arriving at Heathrow airport at 3.30 am this Saturday on flight JL0069. Please be there to meet them.

The father's name is Ito-san and the mother's name is Ito-san and their two children (male, 14, and female, 13) are called Ito-chan and Ito-chan. Grandfather and grandmother, both in their late eighties, are named Ito-ojii-san and Ito-obaa-san, respectively.

None of the family is conversant in English, however all of them will answer "Yes" to any question. Being quite used to congestion, it will be possible for you to collect the whole family and bring them to your home in the back of your Toyota station wagon in one trip. They will be bringing with them most of their possessions in a six-piece, matching set of Louis Vuitton baggage. Their bedding arrives in a 20-ft sea container on the same day and will be delivered to your house before sunset.

A year's supply of wooden chopsticks and toothpicks are on their way to you from the Canadian sawmill which supplies Japan, and should reach you sometime early this week. The Itos' cooking utensils, a one-ring gas stove, six tatami *(rush mats), two* shoji *(paper and wood screens), a portable shrine and an object which appeared to this writer as a stuffed and bonsaied animal of dubious origin, have already been sent by air and are due to arrive on Friday morning.*

The six tatami *should be arranged in a square (attached diagram shows how) in a corner of your living room which has no windows and enclosed on the two open sides with the* shoji. *The space required is 9 square metres (the same as the house the Itos had in Japan) and will form the area which they will occupy during the five years they are going to stay with you.*

We have arranged with the Southend-on-Sea Fishing Club to provide a pair of fishing rods and a reasonable supply of bait so that you and your wife can nightly catch the 15 kgs of fresh fish required by the Itos for their daily food. The Japanese embassy will also send them, from time to time, portions of whale meat left over from research.

On Wednesday, members of HM Forestry Commission will arrive at your home to plant 120 Japanese tea bushes which have been flown in from Kyoto and fumigated. A fence will have to be constructed by you around the plot to prevent your pets or stray animals from urinating or defecating in the vicinity.

From 7 pm, Saturday, both directions of the M6 motorway will be re-routed either side of your house. It will be reduced to one direction later this year and discontinued at the end of next year, to allow the Itos gradually to become accustomed to the low level of traffic noise in your neighbourhood.

Thursday morning you will be visited by a mobile clinic from St Bartholomew's Hospital to give your whole family an examination. Please refrain from eating or drinking anything after 9 am, Wednesday. Any communicable diseases should be reported to the doctor-in-charge and the Itos will be suitably vaccinated before leaving Japan.

The family schedule is as follows. Ito-san will depart for the office at 7 am, and get back at midnight from Monday to Saturday. Sunday, when not playing golf, he will sleep all day. The Ito-chans go to school at 6.30 am, and come back at 4.30 pm. They will then leave for cram school at 6, return at 11 and do homework until 1 am. Ito-san's wife and parents will spend the day in fairly normal pursuits. They will watch television, prepare food, clean their room, wash clothes, drink tea and gossip.

Saturday nights, they like to bathe nude as a family and would welcome you, your family and friends to join them in the altogether. (Those shy about nude bathing indoors should wear a surgical face mask to hide their embarrassment.)

As a gesture of goodwill to your guests, we suggest you and your family spend the rest of this week practising some Japanese gestures, like keeping your eyes almost shut, bowing to each other and especially to the telephone after replacing the handset, putting your hand over your mouth whenever you giggle (no laughing out loud please) and starting every sentence with the words, "I'm sorry".'

Enclosed you will find the following handy booklets:

1. Converting your back garden into a paddy field.
2. Creating photo-chemical fog in your home.
3. Some tips on drying seaweed in a microwave oven.
4. 63,722 useful Japanese phrases.
5. The 155 most common meanings of "Ah-so".
6. How to answer negative questions.

Ito-san has insisted he pays you the same as he was paying in rent for his home in Tokyo and he will hand you this money in cash, in Japanese yen. (At current conversion rates this is £16,523.15 per month.) There is no need for a receipt.

We know you will be as excited about this project as we are and should you need any assistance, please feel free to call us at any time during normal office hours. (Please ask for the Banzai Division.)

Sincerely,
The Phil and Nobby Foundation for the
Enhancement of Britain-Japan Cross-Cultural Relations.

(Copyright 1989 Ye King's Head Co Ltd, Tokyo, Japan.)

'Saturday nights, they like to bathe nude as a family and would welcome you to join in'

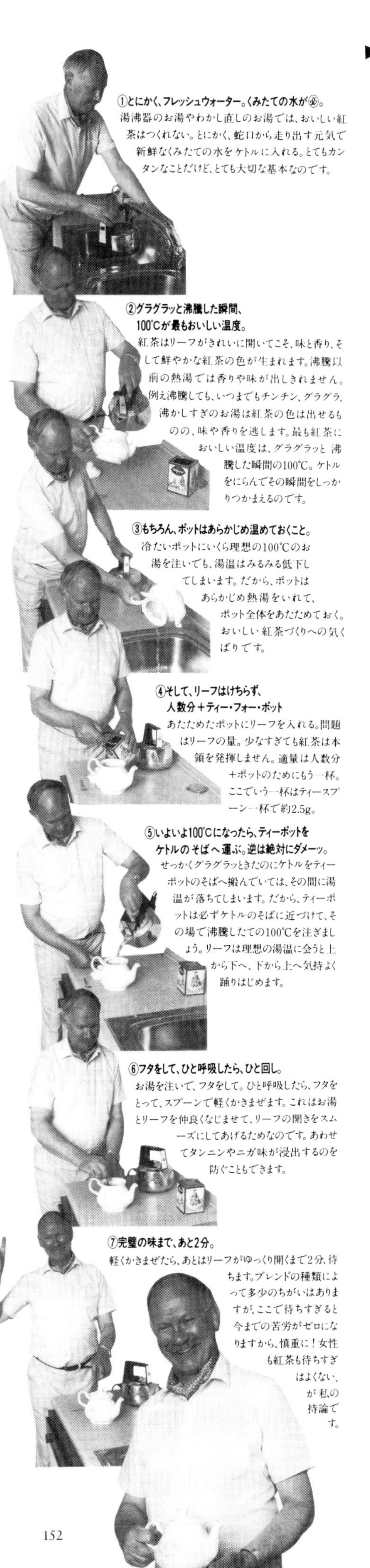

①とにかく、フレッシュウォーター。くみたての水が㊙。
湯沸器のお湯やわかし直しのお湯では、おいしい紅茶はつくれない。とにかく、蛇口から走り出す元気で新鮮なくみたての水をケトルに入れる。とてもカンタンなことだけど、とても大切な基本なのです。
②グラグラッと沸騰した瞬間、100℃が最もおいしい温度。
紅茶はリーフがきれいに開いてこそ、味と香り、そして鮮やかな紅茶の色が生まれます。沸騰以前の熱湯では香りや味が出しきれません。例え沸騰しても、いつまでもチンチン、グラグラ、沸かしすぎのお湯は紅茶の色は出せるものの、味や香りを逃します。最も紅茶においしい温度は、グラグラッと 沸騰した瞬間の100℃。ケトルをにらんでその瞬間をしっかりつかまえるのです。
③もちろん、ポットはあらかじめ温めておくこと。
冷たいポットにいくら理想の100℃のお湯を注いでも、湯温はみるみる低下してしまいます。だから、ポットはあらかじめ熱湯をいれて、ポット全体をあたためておく。おいしい紅茶づくりへの気くばりです。
④そして、リーフはけちらず、人数分＋ティー・フォー・ポット
あたためたポットにリーフを入れる。問題はリーフの量。少なすぎても紅茶は本領を発揮しません。適量は人数分＋ポットのためにもう一杯。ここでいう一杯はティースプーン一杯で約2.5g。
⑤いよいよ100℃になったら、ティーポットをケトルのそばへ運ぶ。逆は絶対にダメーッ。
せっかくグラグラッときたのにケトルをティーポットのそばへ搬んでいては、その間に湯温が落ちてしまいます。だから、ティーポットは必ずケトルのそばに近づけて、その場で沸騰したての100℃を注ぎましょう。リーフは理想の湯温に会うと上から下へ、下から上へ気持よく踊りはじめます。
⑥フタをして、ひと呼吸したら、ひと回し。
お湯を注いで、フタをして。ひと呼吸したら、フタをとって、スプーンで軽くかきまぜます。これはお湯とリーフを仲良くなじませて、リーフの開きをスムーズにしてあげるためなのです。あわせてタンニンやニガ味が浸出するのを防ぐこともできます。
⑦完璧の味まで、あと2分。
軽くかきまぜたら、あとはリーフがゆっくり開くまで2分、待ちます。ブレンドの種類によって多少のちがいはありますが、ここで待ちすぎると今までの苦労がゼロになりますから、慎重に！女性も紅茶も待ちすぎはよくない、が私の持論です。

▶ *Dear Mr Makoto Yamaguchi,*

Congratulations. You have the honour of being chosen to be host to a visiting British family as part of the agreement reached to promote understanding between our two countries.

The Special Branch has been observing you for the past several weeks and both it and we are completely satisfied your family unit is ideally suited for the purpose.

Mr and Mrs Sid Baker and their children will be arriving on flight AA69 at Narita on Saturday at 6.30 am. It will be necessary for you to hire two London black cabs to collect them.

Mrs Baker is called Ethel and the eldest son (18) is named Elvis. The two elder daughters (16 and 14) are Tracy and Jeanette, the two younger sons (12 and 10) are Ashley and Darren and the youngest daughter (8) is named Sharon. Their pit-bull is called Rover and their two cats are Fluffy and Ginger.

Their horse will be arriving next week and is called Perestroika. At the time of writing, their pet rock has not yet been given a name. The gerbils, fortunately, passed away last month.

Professor Wangjat Singh, from the Ministry of Education, will be visiting you on Tuesday to give your family elocution instruction on how to pronounce the letters "L" and "V".

A squad of SAS men will arrive on Wednesday to conduct a search. Golliwogs and other racially provocative items (ie coloured toothpaste etc.) should be handed to the officer-in-charge and will be taken to Okinawa, where they will be burned.

We have been provided with full details of the layout of your home by the Special Branch. Some minor modifications will have to be made, so that the five years the Bakers are going to spend with you will be less of a strain on them.

A working party from the Department of the Environment will arrive on Thursday to raze the houses either side of your own to create the space required for the Bakers' double garage, greenhouse, garden gnomes and reproduction post-box for Rover.

At the same time, they will install a Western-style toilet in your home. Your kitchen will be redesigned in an authentic Tudor-cottage style, with exposed beams and extractor fan unit over the whole hog rotisserie. Your roof space will be adopted as a museum of old mattresses, outgrown wellington boots, primary school swimming certificates and a vintage wooden-framed cot (collapsible).

On Friday the DoE wll be sending a team to widen the road outside your house to allow parking space for the Bakers' two cars, motorcycle and four bicycles.

This team will also replace the concrete surface of the children's park opposite you, with grass, for Perestroika.

'A mobile clinic will visit . . . to cap and straighten your family's teeth'

The Bakers' furniture will arrive on the same day in a 40-ft sea container and the Tokyo English Friendship Club plans to send some of their people to distribute the items correctly about the three rooms of your house.

Regarding the Bakers' diet, suitable arrangements have been made with Spud U Like, Pizza Hut, Wimpy, McDonald's, Happy Eater and your corner Tesco, for home deliveries.

A mobile clinic from the Tokyo General Hospital will visit you on Friday at 6 am, to cap and straighten your family's teeth. At the same time, you will all be given minor doses of some endemic British diseases to allow you to build up the necessary immuno-antibodies prior to the Bakers' arrival.

Commencing Sunday morning, the RAF will have a plane make a detour from its night landing practice to deliver daily editions of all major British tabloids, at 3 am, so that the Bakers can be kept up-to-date on world affairs, love affairs and the breasts of popular young English actresses. You will be sent a consignment of marker flares and one should be lit approximately ten minutes before the scheduled air-drop time, irrespective of the weather.

We suggest as a gesture of goodwill to your guests, your family practise some British customs during the few days before they arrive, like talking very loudly to each other, wearing your shoes in the house, shaking hands and slapping each other on the back with the words "Hello, matey! Can't wait for the electricity privatisation share issue, can you?"

Enclosed you will find the following helpful booklets:

1. All eleven common British phrases.
2. Some interesting uses for cigarette stubs.
3. A cast-list of "EastEnders" and "Neighbours".
4. The Department of Health's guide to avoiding Aids.
5. How to bonsai rubbish.

Mr Baker has generously agreed to pay you the same as the mortgage on the four-bedroom home he vacated in Epping and will be giving you his personal cheque. (At the current conversion rates this is Y2,321 per month.) Kindly issue him with a receipt.

We know you will be as excited about this visit as we are and should you need any further information or help, please do not hesitate to telephone this office at 0800-BAN-ZAII, during normal London office hours. (Tokyo time 11 pm to 6 am. Note, we are closed for lunch for two hours and Friday is a half day.) Please ask for Ms Lillian Longfellow.

Very truly yours, etc.

"I'm hungry."

"I'll go and get an Indian."

"That's an African."

Plus ça change, plus c'est le même

CHUNNEL

1888 **by George du Maurier**

OUR NATURAL ADVANTAGES.
M. le Comte (*who has come to London for the Season of 1888*).
"Ah bah! You are afraid of the Channel Tunnel! *Quelle bêtise!* Vy, it is not your 'silvare streak' zat protect you from ze invasion, *mes amis!* It is your sacred dog of a climate!"

1989 **by Steve Way**

The first-class ideas will be at the front of the presentation, next to the buffet; the second-class ideas at the rear...
SELLING THE HI-SPEED CHANNEL LINK
Saatchi & Saatchi

NO TO HI-SPEED TRAINS
Got the 19-30 trendy vicar, and the £40,000 retired chartered accountant...
Did you get the Maidstone Women's Institute?
NOT IN MY BACK TRAIN YARD
PROTESTERS ROUTE & TIMETABLE

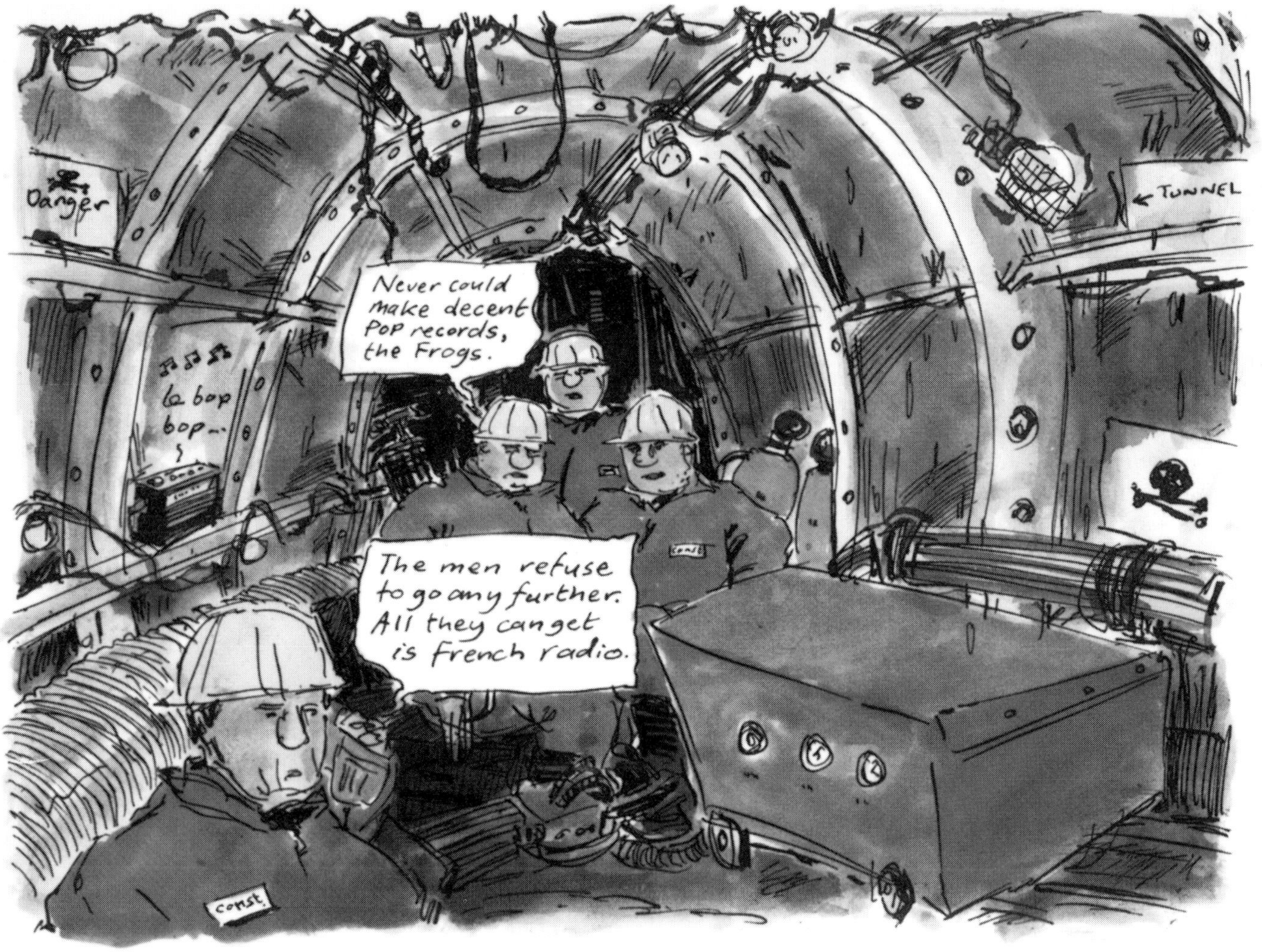

Never could make decent Pop records, the Frogs.

The men refuse to go any further. All they can get is French radio.

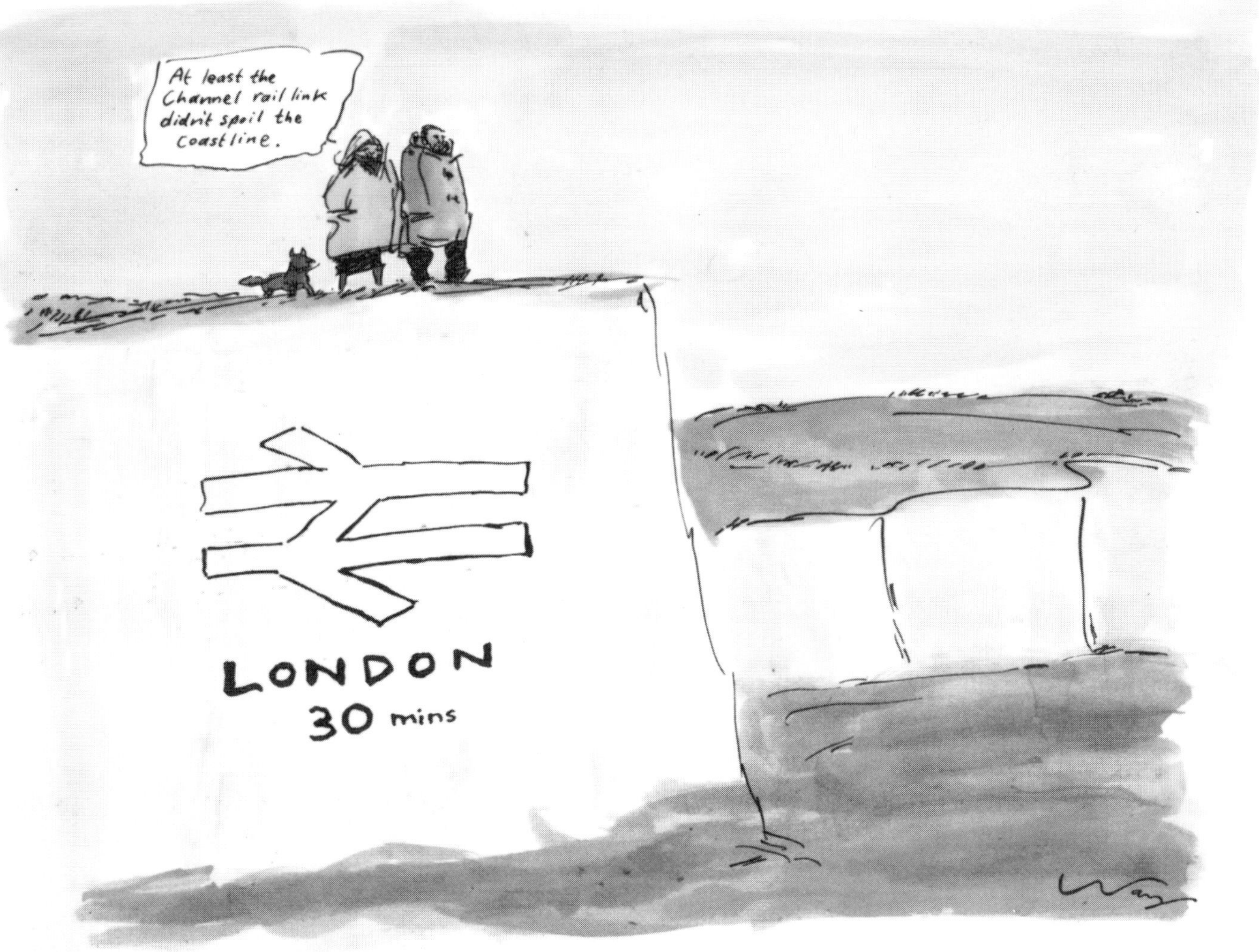

At least the Channel rail link didn't spoil the coastline.

LONDON
30 mins

Are you a Woman Who Loves Men Who Hat

Perhaps you're simply a Person Who'll Slee

there's bound to be something about you on th

JAN BURNEY meets the authors of the lates

from a male point-of-view

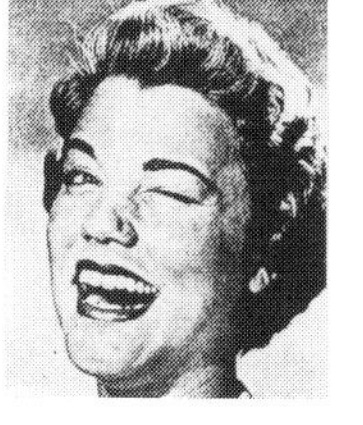

The number one Paraguayan best-seller

Men Who Eat Women, Women Men Spit Out: How to make yourself tasty and keep his juices flowing
Dr Raoul Peron and Dr Evita Torrid
Amazon Press, £16.95

Dr Peron and Dr Torrid, authors of the celebrated best-seller *Pathetic Women, Delectable Dishes* now reveal the secret recipes that fuel a man's lust and keep him drooling. Drs Peron and Torrid have been to 27 universities and are regularly heard on television phone-ins. Their innovative work, using sophisticated laundering techniques, has given them an unsurpassed insight into self-enrichment.

Having realised that by practising as individual therapists they could not hope to touch more than a few rich individuals, the authors have written this book in an attempt to relieve millions more of the surplus accruing from worldly success and help them reach fulfilment, liberated from inhibiting wealth. They begin by describing the kind of woman to whom they address their book and disarmingly emphasise how it is written from their point of view i.e. that of perfectly fulfilled, fabulously wealthy individuals who are utterly contemptuous of the kind of hopeless inadequates who would be driven to read this junk.

The first challenge thrown out by Peron and Torrid's book is how to purchase it. Those with more money than sense will have little difficulty in locating it on prominent display at the "pile 'em high, sell 'em at recommended retail price" type of bookshop, generally in the Women's Issues and DIY Therapy sections. You may at first have difficulty in distinguishing it from the myriad other volumes set in shiny silver and purple-blocked type and with similarly catchy titles, mostly some variation of *Women Who Love Men Who Can't Be Faithful Who Leave Women Who Love Foolish Choices Who Hate Smart Women*. Doctors Peron and Torrid probably wouldn't be too upset to hear this as they wrote most of the other books too and whilst they'd rather you bought them all, thus convincing yourself by reading them that you are an utterly hopeless and incapable human being and thereby ensuring that they have an audience for their *next* book, they would be distressed if you left the shop without leaving some contribution to their massive royalties.

So readers who are truly determined to discover just how lacking in self-assertion they are will find the actual purchasing process a useful little lesson in humiliation; particularly if they have a co-operative male bookshop assistant behind the counter, one who will loudly announce the details of their purchase to the other customers with exclamations of, "It's amazing how incredibly popular this book is, even with smart and successful-looking (i.e. not like you) women." (And don't tell him you're a journalist writing about the genre – he'll only laugh and tell you, "They all say that".)

When this man adds that, "Of course it doesn't seem to do them any good as they all come back for the follow-up," you know that he's only jealous of the authors' success and is almost certainly one of Peron and Torrid's "Pseudo-Liberated Males", otherwise known as Rats. The kind like Marvin, for example, a freelance carpenter and unpublished novelist, whose girlfriend, Marlena, wishes he would "just shut up and get on with the screwing instead of getting in touch with his feelings".

Peron and Torrid are experts on The Rat in all his disguises. This particular species of rodent is, however, irresistibly attractive to lower forms of life like Melinda, a gregarious powder-room executive who is pretty, talented, ambitious and *Cosmopolitan*-reading. Drawn to the thrills and danger of forbidden love, like most of her ridiculous sex, Melinda has fixated on handsome, athletic, tanned, wealthy yacht broker, Greg, whom she met when both were posing at a boat show. He seemed strong, unconventional, complex. She seemed easy to impress, disposable, an easy lay. Anyone but Melinda could see that this man was A Rat, but thanks to Doctors Peron and Torrid we know that he is also a Perpetual Adolescent and she is suffering from The Hunger for Love and possibly Hidden Dependency Needs.

This is all part of Being Foolish, but buying this book is the first step to Knowing When Love is One-Sided; the next is in Peron and Torrid's subsequent publication. Signs of this could be failure to acknowledge your presence, lack of response when you bombard him with calls and letters, and physical recoil if you attempt to engage him in a passionate embrace when you spy him in the supermarket, say. A particularly useful aspect of the book is the detailed case studies which so poignantly illustrate the disastrous effects of certain types of Being Foolish.

Nobody wants to be miserable, right? Wrong. Take Bonnie, for example. Married to charming, popular, clever Sheldon, she had adopted the role of The Martyr. Sheldon's clothes came from Calvin Klein and Armani, Bonnie's from the charity store. Bonnie cooked gourmet suppers for Sheldon but ate post-sell-by-date reductions herself. He slumbered between silk sheets, she had a bedroll in the garage. And when he tossed her the occasional trinket from his petrol coupon gifts, she immediately exchanged it for some more masculine gadget with which she crawled back to Sheldon. With their almost supernatural insight, Doctors Peron and Torrid are able to point out that there were certain subtle signs, albeit too arcane for the rest of us to perceive, that Bonnie's behaviour was less than irresistible to Sheldon. When he and his mistress finally banned Bonnie from even the garage, and poisoned her budgerigar, she had only herself to blame for not Letting Go of Self-Sacrifice.

Having accepted that you have spent most of your life Being Foolish, like all the women in this book, including the many dynamic, attractive, talented and ambitious attorneys, real estate brokers, IBM executives and orthopaedic surgeons who look to Peron and Torrid for personalised character assassination and ▶

Vomen? Or are you a Man Who Hates Women That Women Hate To Love? Vith The First Other Person That Asks. Whatever your description, elf-help shelves of your local bookshop. In a special *Punch* enquiry nplausible handbook, while STEPHEN GAMES observes the problem

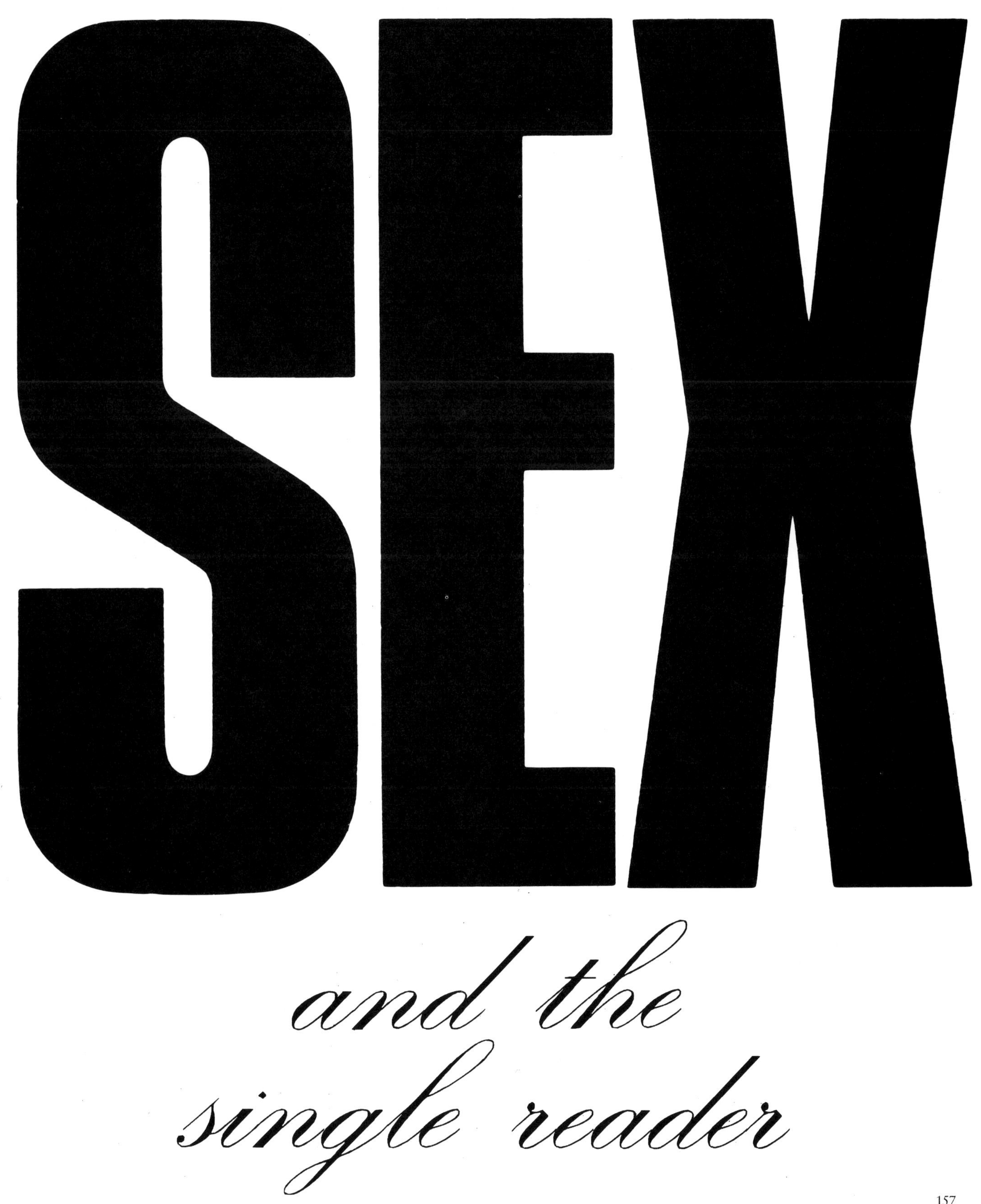

and the single reader

individual personality bashing, you are now ready to embark on Getting Smart. The second part of this exceptionally dispensable volume is full of wonderfully predictable tips on how to go about it, presented in simple formulae that anyone gullible enough to have got this far in the book could understand. Usually they take the form of a list of rules which, feather-brained little schoolgirls that most of us are, should be readily understandable.

Rules for Making Yourself Irresistibly Edible to The Right Man

Rule Number One
Nobody's perfect, least of all you.

Rule Number Two
Low expectations will avoid disappointments.

Rule Number Three
Don't talk, listen. That way you might make fewer mistakes.

Rule Number Four
Growing up means giving up. Forget anything you dreamt of achieving when you were a child – if you're reading this book it's too late.

Rule Number Five
Accept that there are good men around. They're just too good for you.

If you're still not convinced of the total impossibility of achieving edibility, you should continue to the very last section which takes the form of an exceptionally complicated quiz. For this you will need to supply your own paper as the book is printed on a particularly absorbent, greyish paper which disintegrates rapidly but, usefully, flushes away very easily.

Appetite Arousal Quiz
Write down the names of the last 49 (or most important 49) men you had relationships with. Using the list of adjectives below, write in the ones that best characterise the man, in two columns for each man.
In the first column, list the adjectives that describe how you saw him in the beginning.
In the second column, list the adjectives that describe him at the end of the relationship.

articulate • affluent • anxious • aggressive • apoplectic • benign • brutal • confident • catatonic • docile • domineering • extrovert • elusive • funny • furious • gleeful • glum • happy • horrified • intelligent • idiotic • jolly • jaded • keen • knackered • lively • lugubrious • merry • miserable • nice • neurotic • ordinary • onanistic • personable • prostrate • reasonable • raging • stable • screwy • tender • tetchy • unassuming • unavailable • virile • vapid • witty • wretched • zestful • zombie.

If you have marked four or more items beginning with the same letter of the alphabet, you have some of the warning signs of not Letting Go of Self-Delusion.
If you have put 50 or more words in the same column, you are definitely struggling with not Knowing When Love is One-Sided.
If you are dissatisfied with your test score, return to bookshop immediately for *Men Who Eat Women*, volume 23. ■

Riding Tall in the Saddle

STEPHEN GAMES on male assertiveness

In 1976, Anne Dickson visited America and enrolled in an assertiveness training class. On her return to England, she continued to be interested in the problem of female assertiveness and in 1982 she published *A Woman in Your Own Right*. This made several references to an earlier and very influential book called *The Assertive Woman* published in 1975. It recognised the difficulties some women have in handling criticism, saying "No" and expressing emotion, and offered exercises aimed at improving self-esteem for women to carry out alone or with friends. Dickson's book has subsequently been reprinted thirteen times.

Because it was stocked under Women's Interests in most bookshops, the book did not immediately come to the attention of male readers. However, in October 1987, it was discovered on the shelves of "Social Workers 'R' Us" by Timothy, a member of a men's consciousness-raising group in North London. Flicking through the introduction, he noticed that its author had noted that the techniques could be equally useful to men.

Over the course of four weekly sessions, the group discussed sections of the book and recognised that many of its own problems of neurotic lack of confidence and anxiety were similar to those of the archetypal characters in the book. They also observed that while the female archetypes, with whom its women readers were meant to identify, had names, the male characters, were anonymous.

In subsequent weeks, the group came to identify closely with that anonymity. They were struck by the clear delineation of faceless stereotypes and began to see these as positive role models for their own self-realisation. They discarded their own names – Andrew, Simon, Peter, Quentin – and adopted lapel badges instead. In this way, they felt freed from identities imposed on them at birth by domestic authority figures. Now, for the first time, they felt able to pursue rich new avenues based on character traits of their own choice. They became, in turn, The Thoughtless Employer, The Tedious Bore, or The Boyfriend With The Groaning Erection That Has To Be Relieved.

They began to comprehend that assertion is understood in contradistinction to aggression, which in turn is acknowledged as a masculine trait. They discovered that to be a man was to be competitive, over-riding and lacking in regard for others. They were astonished. Never had the principles of maleness been so starkly portrayed to them before. They began to meet more frequently. They held twice-weekly classes on selfishness, ending each meeting with a refresher session on crass insensitivity.

At first it was hard to get rid of their old habits of consideration and compassion, but encouragement and specific exercises helped them through this early critical stage. "Assertive men," said The Sexually Harassing Office Colleague, "I know some of us have a lot of trouble saying 'No' with clarity and conviction. Mocking Husband, would you tell us about how you say no?" "I think saying no can be callous, rude and even offensive," replied Mocking Husband.

"These are commonly held myths," The Sexually Harassing Office Colleague explained. "It sounds as if you try to soften the blow of negation with a winning smile. Small wonder that messages get muddled when you mask a rejection with a gracious apology. Mocking Husband, don't excuse yourself for saying no. Try this exercise: try saying 'I don't know, I need more information'."

Mocking Husband's first attempts at expressing uncertainty and confusion were guarded and ingratiating. But with the help of other members of his group, he was soon building up a rhetoric of frank and forceful expression: "I dunno, I haven't got a clue", and "Don't bloody ask me, you piss-head. Ask someone else". The group felt this a crucial and revealing oral transaction.

In subsequent weeks, the group moved on to Anger and the dangers of emotional suppression. "How to communicate that you are angry," said The Guest Who Wouldn't Leave, reading from page 78. "You can begin with a simple verbal statement such as "I am angry". If you say this assertively, this may be enough to get your message across. If not, you may need to add more force. Okay, Surly Waiter, would you like to start us off?"

"I'm angry," said Surly Waiter. "Is that all?" "I'm very angry?" "Okay, good. Perhaps you can develop that a little further." Surly Waiter looked anxious but said nothing. "Try," said The Guest Who Wouldn't Leave. "I'm trying but it isn't there. I'm sorry, I feel terrible." "Don't restrict yourself to the verbal. Use body language. Scowl. Shake your fist."

Surly Waiter raised a hand, then crumpled. "Reach that passion." "I can't." The Guest Who Wouldn't Leave turned to the rest of the group. "How do we react to Surly Waiter's passivity?" "We're angry," they roared back. "And do we suppress our anger or do we express it? Remember: EXpress, not SUPpress." "We EXpress," they shouted. "Right, then, let the bastard have it." And so, to consciousness-raising whelps, that is what they did. It was a culminating moment, they later agreed, in the realisation of their potential as assertive men.

They asked for, but did not get, Judge Pickles – "a real man" – at their trial and members of the group are now serving life sentences. But the group continues to keep in touch by mail. Its book, *The Assertive Long-Stay Offender*, will be published in May. ■

"Don't ruin my lovely clean floor – wipe your feet on me."

Wilson

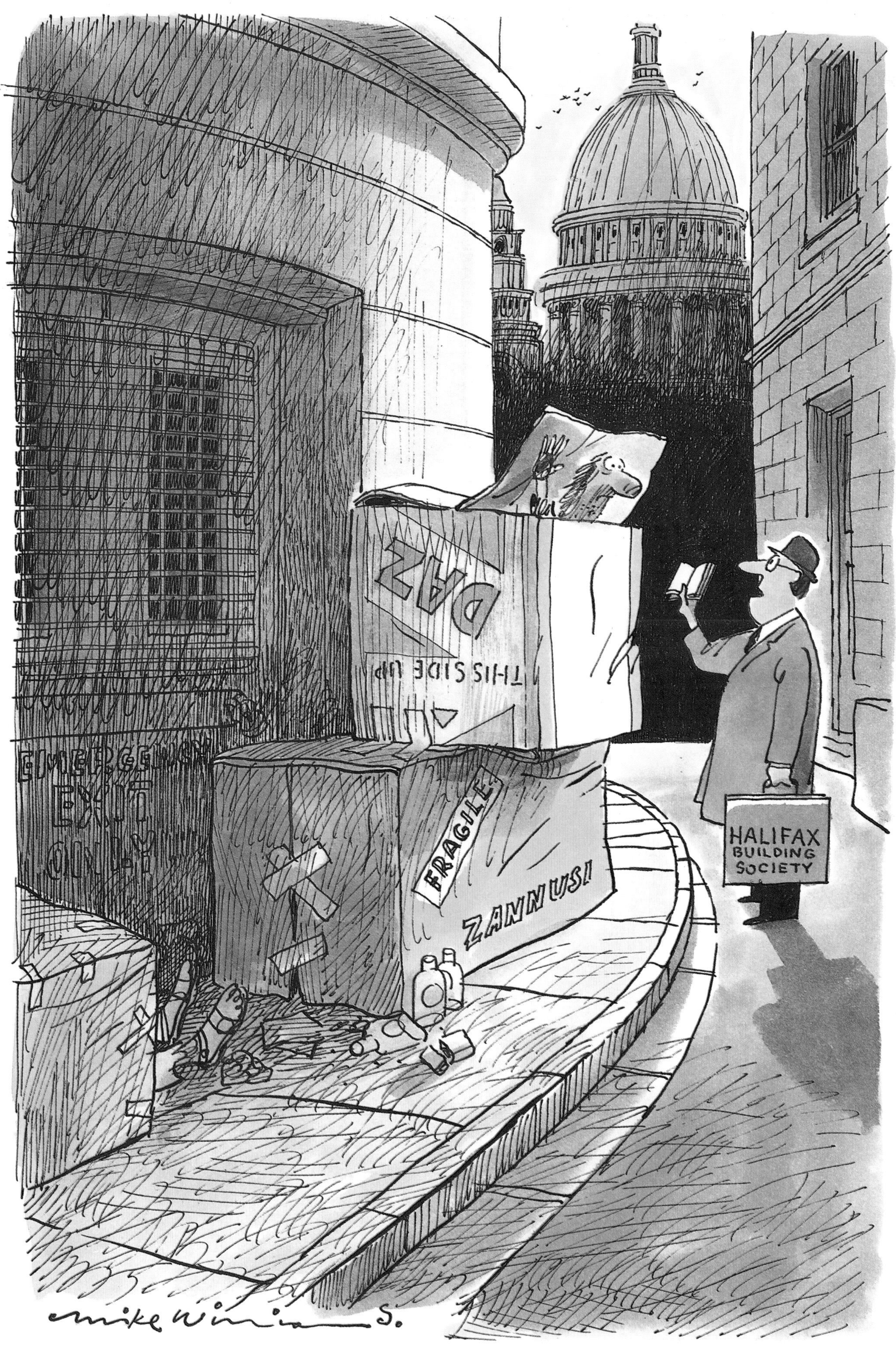

"Well, you should have considered mortgage interest rates before you built the extension."

LEVI ©

THE CAMPAIGN FOR

REAL ROCK STARS

by MARCUS BERKMAN. Illustration by ALAN MORRISON

If God had wanted rock stars to be caring He wouldn't have created Esther Rantzen.

If God had wanted rock stars to work for world peace He wouldn't have created Mikhail Gorbachev.

And if God had wanted rock stars to be sober He wouldn't have created Jack Daniels.

It's just that nobody's told the rock stars...

Something insidious is happening in pop music. And no, I speak not of Stock, Aitken and Waterman, nor of the forthcoming Bee Gees comeback, nor of the incomprehensible horrors of hip-hop. This development is more far-reaching, and unlike all the above, probably irreversible. Pop music has gone Serious. It's as though rock stars the world over have been replaced by simulacra-walking, talking, singing, songwriting *doppelgängers*, whose behaviour is entirely uncharacteristic of the drug-crazed, guitar-thrashing cretins of rock's glorious past. Hopeless excess is out; clean living and high seriousness are in.

Should we take these people seriously? In many ways it doesn't matter, for even if we tried we could never take some of them half as seriously as they take themselves. You can always tell when a musician is entering his Serious phase: (a) he stops smiling, (b) he starts wearing glasses. Suddenly, publicity photos of the star portray him not as a jolly, cheerful sort of character, with a bon mot on his lips and a luscious young lovely clamped to his arm. No, he becomes intense, moody, solitary and expensively four-eyed – in short, extremely Serious.

In this version of "Invasion Of The Bodysnatchers", though, the focus is not on a small town in mid-west America, but on Hampstead, Highgate and other centres of rock-star inactivity. These hubs of bohemianism manqué, where the weary popster puts his feet up after a hard year's touring, are the spiritual home of all things Serious. Does our Serious star drink far too much, inject himself with countless harmful chemicals, and trash hotel rooms in faraway places? Sadly not – he's too busy reading Schopenhauer and taking sensitive photos of rare wild orchids. Does he perform unimaginable acts of cruelty and violence to defenceless small furry animals on hundreds of stages a year? Not any more – for these days his quest is to promote global harmony, and make this the sort of world in which all small furry animals can live peacefully and happily, with cheeky little fluffy grins on their faces, without fear of carnal assault during the drum solo.

It was Live Aid that did it, of course. For years no one had taken the blindest bit of notice of what rock stars thought or said, but then Bob Geldof came along, saved the world and got a knighthood. This must have been galling to more successful rock stars, and also to their accountants, who noticed how well Geldof's autobiography sold. But the Irishman's saving grace is that, although a minor genius when it came to campaigning for funds, he isn't really much cop as a musician. His group, The Boomtown Rats, were notably hit-free in the years before Band Aid, and his later solo album has, with luck, wound up his pop career for good. This is a man who was clearly in the wrong job.

But for all Geldof's achievements, it is on him that we must blame the profusion of goody-goody rock stars pronouncing on any political or social issue that comes to mind. The Nelson Mandela beanfeast last summer was the natural culmination of all this wasted energy. Star after star paraded on to the stage over the event's twelve interminable hours to lecture us about the jailed African leader. The audience just wanted the acts to get on with it. During Whitney Houston's set, you could just make out, through the intense amplification, the chant of "Get yer tits out for the lads."

Outside on the concourse, the whole self-satisfied occasion was brought into perspective. "Get your Nelson Mandela T-shirts here! Four quid each!" "Free Africa Now sweatshirts! Only a few left!" "Last chance to buy sunglasses! Only £1.99!" In the stadium, it was remarkable how the press seats emptied and the bars filled as soon as there was any hint of Aborigine dancing, let alone tribal music from Zimbabwe.

If the audience was not much bothered about Mr Mandela (who in his South African jail must have felt rather bemused by the whole thing), at least the performers were – or so they told us, often enough. (My favourite was erstwhile film hunk Richard Gere, with his "Nelson Mandela! Whoooooooo! Nelson Mandela! Whoooooo!" – instantly proving to sceptics why so many actors find it hard to walk and talk at the same time.) But remember: just because they're being charitable doesn't mean that rock stars stop being their normal egomanic, narcissistic, publicity-crazed selves. The whole Mandela concert was beamed across the world to a TV audience of 400 million viewers. Is it any coincidence, then, that Whitney Houston and the Eurythmics, among others, played their brand-new singles (available now from your local

"SAYING SOMETHING STUPID LIKE..." A GRAPHIC HISTORY OF THE ROCK LYRIC

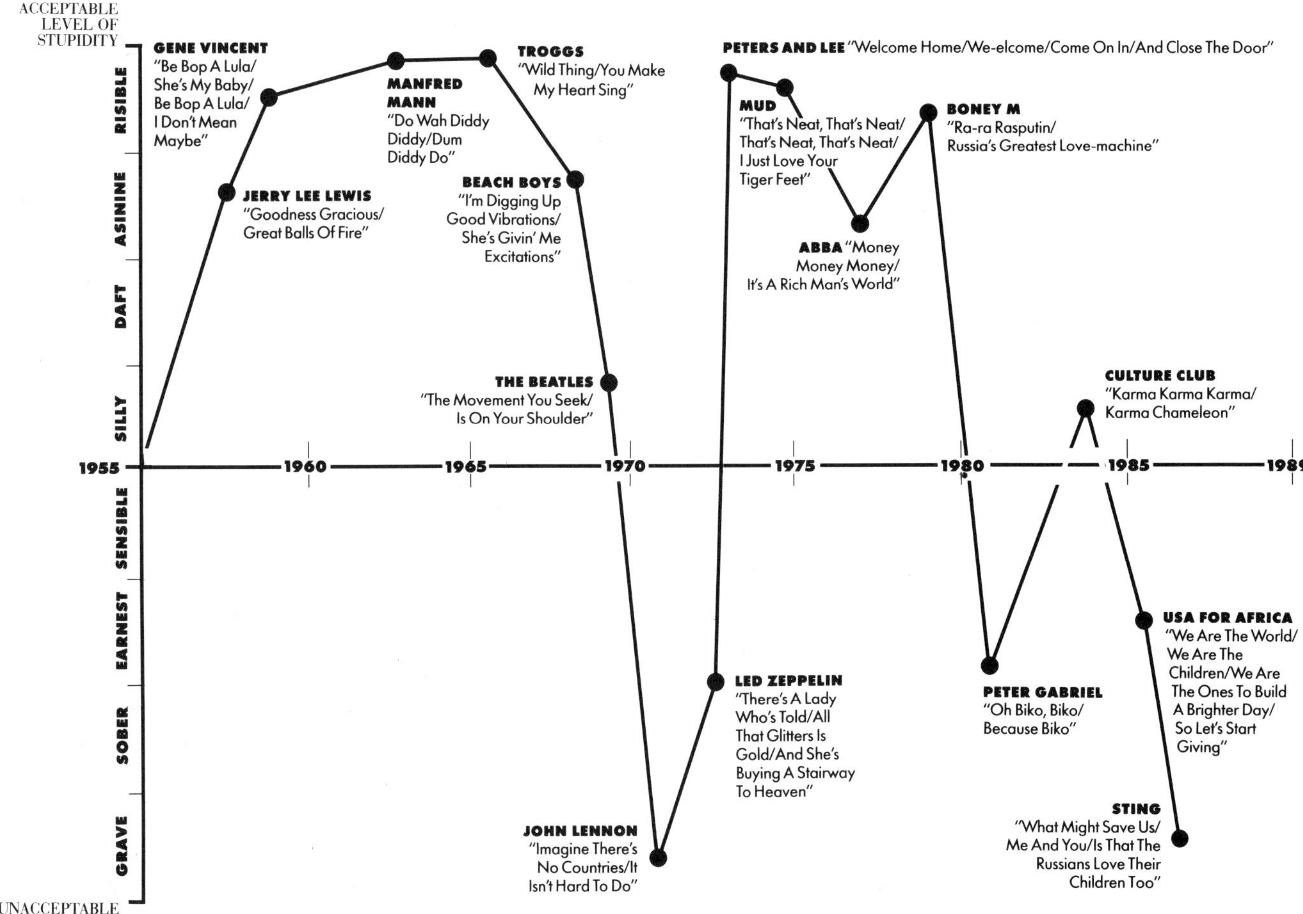

record stores)? And isn't it curious that the following weekend's Amnesty International benefit at Milton Keynes (television coverage, nil) was a flop because no big stars would play at it?

Amnesty did rather better later in the year when they persuaded a starry selection of acts to tour the world, promoting world peace and generally being nice. Of course, by coincidence, a TV link-up had been arranged on this one, which transmitted the final concert in Argentina across an expectant planet. Behind the scenes, Sting and Bruce Springsteen were allegedly scratching each other's eyes out for top billing, but on stage it was all cuddles.

The trouble with these concerts is that you really pay for your pleasure. Not financially – after all, it's up to you whether you go or not – but in the endless, self-righteous lectures about human rights, something about which, let's face it, pseudo-serious rock stars know so much more than we do. They would be the first to agree that theirs is, undoubtedly, the fuller, rounder experience, and that, since they are all so much more intelligent, creative and aware than we are, it's their inalienable right to tell us all where we're going wrong.

Knee-jerk reactions from adoring audiences do not help, of course. George Michael, last year at Earl's Court, told us that "The British Government's policy towards South Africa is a f***ing disgrace," one of the more reflective comments yet heard from one of pop's most fertile intellects. The crowd, mainly made up of thirteen-year-old girls who probably knew nothing of South Africa, let alone the British Government's policy towards it, yelled in thought-free approbation – most probably believed that a sanction was a new brand of detergent.

George Michael, of course, embraced Seriousness at an unusually early age. Since Wham! split he has rarely been seen to smile, and even appears to have had a wrinkle installed between his eyebrows just to confirm the appalling anguish he undergoes while earning $30 million a year.

Sting, too, is a convert to High Seriousness – so much so that even his girlfriend Trudie Styler now feels the need to wear glasses on public occasions. Interviews with him do not dwell on all the usual things rock stars talk about – tours, records, blonde models – but refer instead to Gödel's Incompleteness Theorem, or the validity of dialectical materialism in the post-industrial age.

Only Sting would counter an aggressive drunk on Hampstead Heath by quoting Shakespeare at him, and then tell everyone about it on the sleeve notes of his next album. Only Sting would greet interviewers whilst idly playing Satie's "Gymnopédie" on the piano, or announce that he likes to play Mozart on a spinet once owned by Samuel Pepys. References to Greek mythology and Jungian psychoanalytical theory are dropped willy-nilly into his songs, so that everyone will notice and say what a clever chap he is. If he could, he'd probably clone himself and invite himself round to dinner. Needless to say, he has the sense of humour of a breezeblock.

This is not how rock stars should behave. They should be in the Betty Ford Clinic, not the reading room of the British Museum. They should be living fast and dying young, not employing nannies for Sky (5) and Jake (3), having filmed both births on their video camcorders.

Few, of course, die young any more. Instead they do the nearest possible thing – join the Prince's Trust. Although on the surface a thriving charity led by the Prince Of Wales, this is in fact a social club for the middle-aged rockers' gentry. Members include Elton John, Eric Clapton, Mark Knopfler and Phil Collins, and they can usually be found playing on each other's tours, getting bit parts on *Miami Vice* and then turning up all together once a year to slaver at Princess Diana. It's all very cosy, and their records sell in billions.

It's the longevity of old bores like this that encourages the youthful rock stars of today to think of music as a career rather than a means to an early demise. Some bands take their families on the road; others ban all drink and drugs; while Rick Astley publicly admits that he looks forward to ending up in Las Vegas in a spangly tux. It's a corruption of youthful ideals on a scale unparalleled since the days of Tommy Steele.

Rock stars should be in the Betty Ford Clinic, not the reading room of the British Museum.

This is all in stark contrast to Keith Richards, who has courageously and selflessly spent the majority of his existence ingesting more harmful substances than a laboratory full of beagles. Whole decades can be no more than a passing memory. And yet he's still with us – looking a little like something out of Night Of The Living Dead, it's true, but surviving and flourishing.

Not surprisingly his 1988 solo album, *Talk Is Cheap*, was as good as anything else released in the year. To an extent it's still true to say that the best rock 'n' roll is made by people who are, well, not entirely all there. A few straws short of a bundle, you could say. Ten pence short of a phonebox. It could be because of whatever they have smoked, drunk, snorted, popped or injected over years of physical abuse, or it may be because, like Prince for instance, they're fairly bonkers to start with.

From the Serious Squad, though, everything is just a little ersatz. Some of them, like Sting, are even too Serious for rock at all, and play a sort of mushy jazz-cum-new-age thing, awash with synthesised nothings and concerned lyrics. You get the feeling that after all these years they have finally fallen for the con that the music is less important than the message – a fallacy on which all too many rock critics base their entire careers. Hence, we have Sting singing about Chile and the miners' strike; U2 moaning on about the American presence in Nicaragua; ▶

THE DECLINE OF THE WESTERN ROCK STAR: *THREE CASE HISTORIES*

1. JAGGER: *In recent times Mick Jagger has abandoned the Rolling Stones for a solo career. One possible reason for the less-than-Michael-Jackson-like sales of his LPs can be gleaned from a recent court case. A reggae singer called Patrick Alley claimed that Jagger's song "Just Another Night" bore a remarkable resemblance to a song of his called, by coincidence, "Just Another Night". Jagger's defence hinged on the fact that he couldn't have heard Alley's song on the radio. He listens only to classical music. Mick won. His career may never recover.*

2. BOWIE: *In late 1976 David Bowie, shattered by years of rampant cocaine-addiction and close to total physical and mental collapse, went to live in a flat in the Turkish district of Berlin.*

In the previous two years he had made a pair of classic albums – Young Americans *and* Station to Station, *toured the world with a brilliant stage show and given his finest acting performance* The Man Who Fell To Earth. *Over the following twelve months he would make two further albums, thereby keeping not just abreast, but ahead of the New Wave.*

Ten years on – rich, fit and entirely free of all noxious substances – Bowie set to work on an album and tour that would take him through 1987. The subsequent LP, Never Let Me Down, *was dismal and the Glass Spider Tour one of rock's most celebrated creative catastrophes. The conclusion? In rock music, health is bad for you.*

3. GABRIEL: *Peter Gabriel was always a little . . . odd. While still with Genesis he was wont to appear on stage dressed as a flower. But last year's Amnesty tour brought out a new side to his personality. At several stops on the tour, which prided itself on its wide-ranging itinerary, Gabriel read out a message to the local population written in their own tongue. This he did with a benevolent lack of fluency, reminiscent of a colonial administrator assuring the natives that the Great White Mother was still on their side.*

There were also strange overtones of the way in which the Pope speaks to his flock on his international pilgrimages. These were further enhanced by Gabriel's habit of standing on the edge of the stage in the crucifix position and then falling rigidly into the audience, there to be supported by his adoring flock.

Is this the action of a man who is selflessly dedicated to spreading the good news of the essential oneness of mankind? Or is it that of a raging ego-maniac with a 'roo loose in the top paddock?

Professor Norman Stone – a right Banana?

and Tracy Chapman talkin' about a revolution – which will no doubt be the nearest she ever comes to one.

Fortunately there is one rock-star trait that any amount of Seriousness cannot completely destroy. Here's a clue: "I should be so lucky. Lucky, lucky, lucky. I should be so lucky in love."

Yes, stupidity. For that is one of the rock star's greatest advantages over simpler life-forms – his, or her, remarkable lack of brainpower. Whatever their pretensions, most of them have the intellectual capacity of a jam doughnut. One would not expect Dave Hill of Slade to be a world authority on algebraic topology, just as one would be a little surprised if Norman Stone, Professor of Modern History at Oxford University, joined Bananarama.

Bananas aside, the banner of stupidity now lies in the hands of the wild men of Heavy Metal – one reason, perhaps, why the genre is enjoying such an astonishing, if cacophonous revival. This is a world in which a group called Megadeth can engage in bitter legal battle with another group called Megadeath for the right to use a tasteless and offensive band-name. And a world in which American bozo-rockers Motley Crue can be sued by a man who claims that he "was" their bassist Nikki Sixx for two years, while the real Mr Sixx was unavoidably detained in hospital.

Take Guns'n'Roses, a magnificently anti-social outfit from Los Angeles. They currently have two albums in the US Top Five. Why? Because teenagers do not want rock stars who care about the ozone layer. They want rock stars who make music loud enough to strip wallpaper and unpleasant enough to offend all parents within a five-mile radius.

Guns'n'Roses understand that the ideal rock song is like life – nasty, brutish and short. And it is they who give us hope as we launch our Campaign For Real Rock Stars. There's no guarantee that one of them won't throw a sofa out of a seventh-floor window sooner or later, or drive off a cliff in the drug-induced impression that he is being pursued by giant aubergines. But they certainly won't do it without our help. It's up to us, as responsible people, to make sure that rock stars go back to behaving appallingly whilst being ripped-off by their financial advisors. The world needs these people, if only as role models for future generations. And if none of the current stars is prepared to change, well, we'll just have to look further afield for people who want to die before they go bald.

Any volunteers? ■

GLASGOW

GLASGOW

GLASGOW

GLAS
GOW
McLACHLAN

TERMS & CONDITIONS

A graphic description of working life

"Quiet! I hear ten, no, fifteen corporate raiders approaching."

"Just remember, every last one of you is dispensable, except for Hodkins here, who makes the best cup of coffee."

"George Jonas of VideCom Tectronics? Imagine interfacing here with you!"

"Lunching with you is a real pleasure, Frank – you always eat as if you were paying for it yourself."

"I have an important business meeting right after this, Reverend, so if you don't mind, we'll just give you a blanket 'I will' on everything and move on to the next point."

"And, of course, with this position you'll be entitled to a company car."

"Er, well, yes, I suppose that could be constituted as a skill."

HERE BE DEAD

THE PUNCH POST-MORTEM MAP OF THE WORLD –
a unique guide to the present whereabouts of famous stiffs
by Roland White

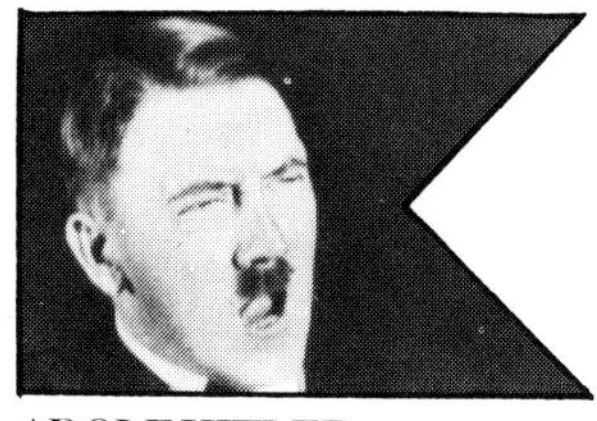

ADOLF HITLER:
died 30 April, 1945

- **STUTTGART: Working as a house painter under the name Robert Schneller (November 1988)**
- **ARGENTINA: Businessman Max Gregoric claims the Führer and Eva Braun lived quietly in the north of the country, with several adopted children. Hitler died, aged 97, in November 1986**

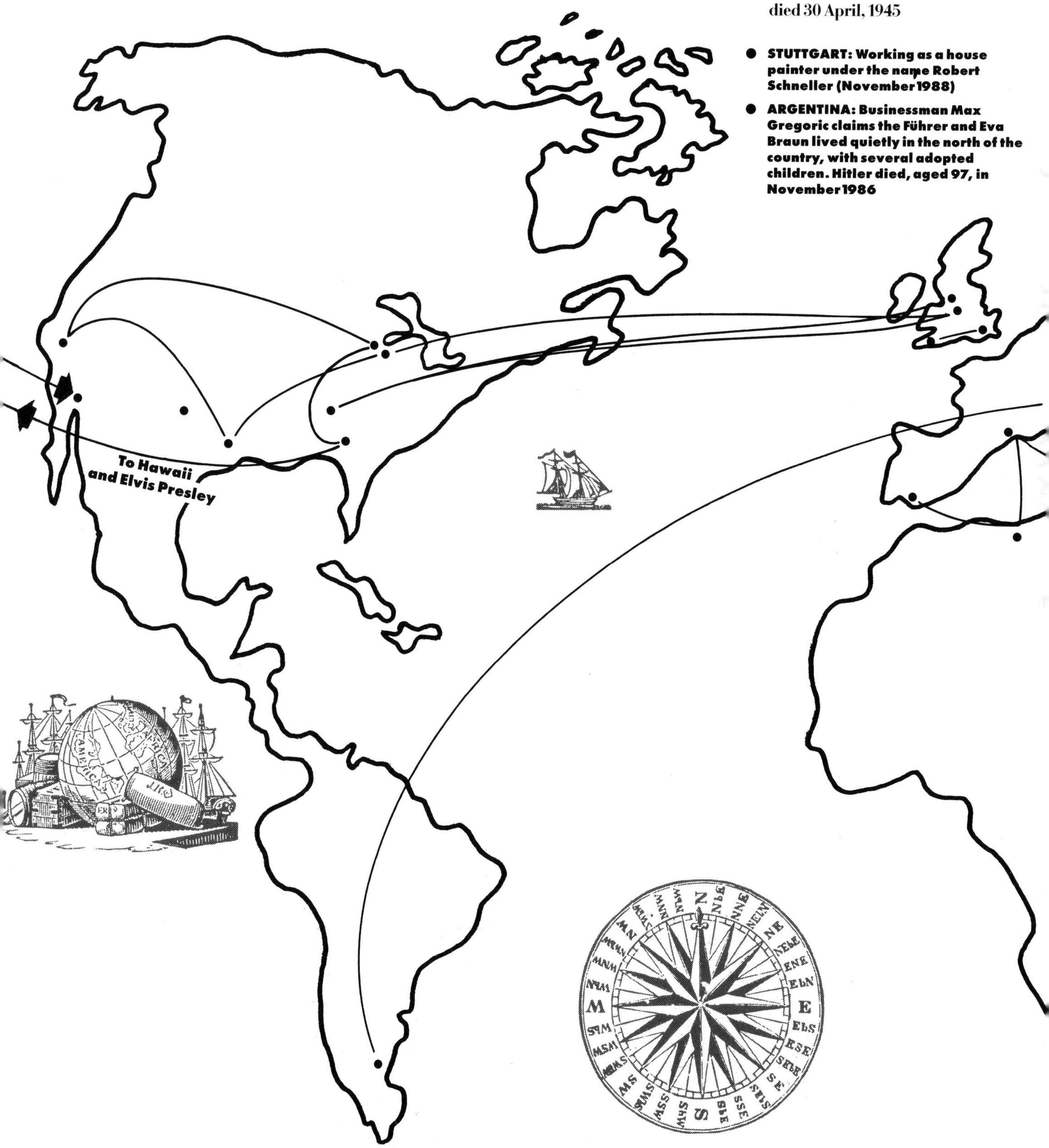

To Hawaii and Elvis Presley

CELEBRITIES

BUDDY HOLLY:
killed 3 February, 1959

- **LUBBOCK, TEXAS:** Walked into a bar wearing a pink frock and calling himself Peggy Sue (January 1988)

MARILYN MONROE:
died 4 August, 1962

- **SOHO, LONDON:** Seen working as a waitress in Bill Stickers restaurant (September 1988)
- **PLYMOUTH, DEVON:** Reported working as a nightclub stripper (December 1988)

LORD LUCAN:
missing 7 November, 1974

- **MELBOURNE:** Medium Peter Owen says Lucan is working as a rancher and wears a Paul Hogan bush hat (August 1987)
- **SOUTH OF FRANCE:** Medium Nella Jones says he is working in a vineyard (October 1987)
- **TUNISIA:** Model Shona McFarlane, 19, says she was seduced by Lucan while on holiday. Miss McFarlane reports: ''He was boring in bed.'' (June 88)
- **SPAIN:** Lucan telephones the *Sunday Sport* to say he is living on the Costa Del Sol (July 88)

Lucan has also been seen…

MOUNT ETNA: On a back-packing holiday

INVERNESS: Living in a mobile home

SAN FRANCISCO: Working as a waiter

CAPE TOWN: In a bar

SYDNEY: Lecturing at the city's university

CHESTER: Driving a BMW

RIMINI: On holiday

DEVON: Browsing in a gift shop

ELVIS PRESLEY:
died 16 August, 1977

- **BOLTON:** Psychic Michael Carrow claims Elvis has sent him three new songs from the spirit world (June 86)
- **MADISON, WISCONSIN:** Elvis hands in a cassette at record company CS Records, leaving an $85 tip for the receptionist (November 1988)
- **TWYFORD, DERBYSHIRE:** On the tenth anniversary of his death, a canteen till at Twyford toilet works sings ''Love Me Tender'' to staff
- **KALAMAZOO, MICHIGAN:** Louise Welling stands behind Elvis at a grocery store check-out, then sees him in the queue at a Burger King (October 1987)
- **WACO, TEXAS:** Waitress Candy La Falaire's Elvis Presley ceramic table-lamp sings ''Viva Las Vegas'' and ''Hound Dog'' (1987)
- **ENCICO, CALIFORNIA:** Window-cleaner John Carter sees Elvis at a Burger King. Elvis buys a hot-dog and sits on a park-bench to eat it (August 1983)
- **CHICAGO:** Elvis seen busking in a Subway station, singing ''Blue Suede Shoes'' and strumming a wooden guitar. He tells passers-by that he needs the cash for home-improvements at Gracelands (June 1980)
- **ATLANTA, GEORGIA:** A barmaid with a double-chin claims she has been having an affair with Elvis for three years (July 1981)
- **HAWAII:** Elvis records a taped interview to say how he was followed around a supermarket by a lovestruck fan. She recognises him even though he is balding and has dyed the remainder of his hair blond, and wears a brightly coloured women's robe known locally as a muu-muu
- **LAS VEGAS:** Photographed in a car-park chatting to his doctor (September 1988)

HERE BE DEAD CELEBRITIES

(THE STORY BEHIND THE MAP)

Keep your eyes peeled at the supermarket and you might catch him by surprise. He could be waiting at the check-out; he could be hovering by the frozens; he could be browsing in cereals. What you are looking for is a middle-aged man in a white satin suit that has probably seen better days. He will have a bit of a paunch, thick side-whiskers, and glasses. If he is also humming "Love Me Tender", wrestle him to the floor. It will be Elvis Presley for sure and if you can get him as far as *The Sun*, the editor will give you a million pounds.

Presley's family may be convinced that the King is dead, but his fans know different. According to them, he faked his death and burial, and for the past eleven years has been living a somewhat humble life, albeit rather an active one: serving petrol in New York, busking on the Chicago Subway, eating hamburgers in Michigan and California, strolling around Gracelands, visiting supermarkets in Hawaii, and having a three-year affair with a double-chinned waitress in Atlanta, Georgia.

It seems a surprise that Elvis has not bumped into Lord Lucan during all this time. The missing peer is also a widely travelled man. Since he disappeared fifteen years ago, he has been working in a vineyard in the south of France, while also holding down jobs as a rancher in Melbourne and a university lecturer in Sydney. He has been seen in Rimini, back-packing on Mount Etna, and sipping cocktails in Cape Town. He could, perhaps, invite Elvis to the mobile home at Inverness in which he stays from time to time, or to his favourite Devon teashop. Elvis probably just can't catch him up, since Lucan, wanted for murder, likes to keep on the move. He has been seen so many times and in so many places that it would save police time if all moustachioed men were rounded up and detained without trial, until they could account for their whereabouts on the night of 7 November, 1974.

Presley and Lucan are not the only people doing the social circuit of the afterlife. John Wayne has plucked drowning seamen to safety; Buddy Holly has walked into a bar in the Texas town of Lubbock wearing a pink frock (a perilous undertaking even for those who have not been dead for thirty years); Adolf Hitler has been painting houses in Stuttgart, while raising foster children with Eva Braun in the north of Argentina; and Marilyn Monroe has been working as a stripper in Plymouth, while waiting on tables in a Soho restaurant. I saw Aneurin Bevan – dead since 1960 – strolling through Pimlico last year, but I cannot see that gripping the popular imagination somehow.

Rupert Murdoch is not the only person hoping that nobody will actually take up *The Sun*'s offer and arrive at Wapping announcing, "I am Elvis Presley and I claim my one million pounds." There will also be some long faces and empty wallets at Ladbroke's and the like. Bookmakers must be wondering why otherwise sensible punters are staking their money on the reincarnation of an eleven-year corpse.

What accounts for our obsession with Presley and Monroe? And why on earth does somebody imagine that the 7th Earl of Lucan, a regular at the dining clubs and gambling tables of London, would choose to serve out the rest of his days in Rimini?

We are, in fact, rather fussy about the folk heroes who are granted life after death. Nobody, for example, has reported seeing Lassie in Acapulco or Mae West back-packing in the Dordogne. Nobody has seen Chaplin since

John Wayne has plucked drowning seamen to safety; Buddy Holly has walked into a bar in Texas wearing a pink frock; and Marilyn Monroe has been working as a stripper in Plymouth, while waiting on tables in a Soho restaurant.

"Ok, guys – next stop Buenos Aires."

his death, although the 100th anniversary this year of his birth makes a sighting more likely. There is nothing like an anniversary to jog the imagination. Exactly ten years after Elvis died, the canteen till at Twyford toilet works in Derbyshire sang "Love Me Tender" as staff gathered around.

The number of sightings and the intensity with which they are asserted to be real seems to bear a mathematical relationship to the number of suspicious circumstances surrounding the death. John Wayne, who died of cancer, has put in only one appearance since then. Buddy Holly, killed in a straightforward plane crash, has fared no better, and is now chiefly remembered for looking like Elvis Costello. Lassie died a perfectly natural death and has preferred to stay out of the public eye since then.

Hitler, supposed by historians to have committed suicide in his Berlin bunker in 1945, is widely rumoured to have fled to South America. But every Nazi who was not hanged or imprisoned is widely rumoured to have fled to South America, so it is merely good manners to include Hitler on this list. It is quite possible that the moustachioed men spotted in Stuttgart and Argentina were in fact Lord Lucan.

Only Marilyn and Elvis have retained their grip on the popular imagination, and in quite different ways. People may see Elvis in every hamburger queue and grocery store, but they actually believe themselves to be Marilyn. Thousands of teenage girls wanted to be like Madonna, but she fooled them by trying to be like Monroe. Caroline Taylor, a dancer who makes a living as a Monroe lookalike, has been so entranced by the role that she now claims she is a Monroe reincarnation.

These obsessions can be brushed away in terms of value for money. It seems a cruel waste that death should prevent our film and pop idols from reaching their full earning capacity. And for the fans, death leaves a gap in their lives which cannot be filled. The solution is clear – everybody can just carry on as normal.

If doctors can seriously consider a theory that an impostor sat twiddling his thumbs in Spandau prison for more than thirty years pretending to be Rudolf Hess, it does not take a tremendous leap of the imagination to suppose that Elvis Presley had a cancer-stricken double flown in from England to be smuggled into Gracelands to die without anybody noticing. While everybody else is at the funeral, Elvis then tiptoes back into the house, packs a small travelling bag, and heads for the open road and a new life.

Marilyn's case is more complex. She was, of course, killed because of her affairs with several of the Kennedys. It seems likely that she was behind the assassination of John Kennedy, a killing which she organised from the grave, and was behind the wheel of Teddy Kennedy's car at Chappaquiddick. The FBI are also following up information that could implicate her in the murders of both Abraham Lincoln and the little princes in the tower, one of which is widely believed to have been her lover.

None of this can be proved, of course – that's the magic of it. But take some advice: next time you go to the supermarket, take handcuffs – it could be your route to riches. ■

"Typical, you wait ages for one and then three come together."

Halo Goodbye

“My God, George, something’s happened, hasn’t it?”

GOD ...

This will be mysterious, even by my standards..

PLANS

ZASK!

*Isn't she . . . ?
Yes, she's
cover-girl
Emma Freud*

Emma is . . . Almost Famous

As a sub-species in the cultural underworld, celebutantes like Emma need a few words of introduction. That's how you can spot someone who's Almost Famous. The name isn't enough. You've got to have a description. So let's try "TV personality". TV personality Emma Freud . . . yowser, that's right – the girl who put on her pyjamas whenever she saw a camera.

FAME, FAME, FAME, FAME, WHAT'S YOUR NAME?

CARIS DAVIS observes the semi-celebrated lives of the not-quite-rich and Almost Famous

WOULD YOU KNOW THESE PEOPLE...

Prince Richard
Bob Holdness
Catherine Walker
Gary Pearce
Emma Sergeant
Emma Ridley
Conrad Black
Chris Lowe
Michaela Strachan
Bob Anderson
Piers Gough
Ed Mirvish
Emma Soames
Bryn Vaile
Richard Curtis
Sylvie Guillen
Levi Stubbs
Michael Ryan
Raymond Blanc
David Bryant
James Mackay
Martin Sorrell
Luke Rittner
Sue Carpenter
Jennifer d'Abo

Looking at media-mad image-driven Britain 1989, Andy Warhol might have revised his hackneyed dictum to include the word "almost": in a culture that strives many are shown but few are recognised. The specious society of celebrity is as selective as ever in its admissions policy; the litmus of acceptance remains recognition by those already established in the pantheon. Jonathan Ross says he realised he'd arrived when a track-suited Una Stubbs tapped him on the back in a London park and cheerily introduced herself.

If that's fame include me out.

Yet we all nurture our individual fantasies of fame. We all believe we can imagine what life would be like as a superstar, because its larger-than-life accoutrements and accessories are hourly blatted into our consciousness by a fat-glut of movies, soap operas and commercials. The reality is that for everyone who makes it, there remain a hundred others with a pushy press agent, an ever-ready smile and a desperate toehold on the greasy pole. Fame! They want to hype for ever. To the Almost Famous, immortality is just a pic away.

You can find them on *Loose Ends*. The Almost Famous are always panellists on *Loose Ends*. Radio 4 in general is a haven of the Almost Famous. Libby Purves and Derek Cooper seem quite happy with their lot in life and gollygosh, wouldn't you be? Foreign travel, the next-best seats in restaurants and glamour one millimetre thin.

But how many of these people would be recognised in a school classroom? A provincial office? Amongst random shoppers walking along Oxford Street? Compared to, say, Matt Goss or Mrs Thatcher?

Like time, fame is always relative. The equation here is: E equals MC^2, where E equals exposure, M is marketability and C credibility – notice that talent is not a factor in the volatile universe of celebrity.

Notice, too, that the difference between Almost Fame and the real thing can sometimes be a matter of social class. One man's star can be another man's... "Who?"

Among the chattering classes, for instance, John Mortimer is famous. Really famous – as in Famous Famous. But I can't see him being lampooned by Freddie Starr. For those of you at dinner recently with John Mortimer perhaps I should amend that to "Hamster-eating impressionist" Freddie Starr.

Many Almost Famous people secretly evince a fascination with the real block-busting thing. If only they could break out of their media-created barrier, that tell-tale tag attached before their name in the cuttings books... the fantasies of the Almost Famous beg the question – what is fame like?

Fame is like a virus. One person catches it by virtue of genuine achievement and spouses, family and friends pick it up from them in the form of Almost Fame. The carrier? The media – specifically that Typhoid Mary of the celebrity syndrome, the cuttings library.

Take Prince Andrew. He dallies with Katie Rabett and she becomes Almost Famous as "not quite Prince Andrew's girlfriend". She doesn't have to do anything – the process is automatic. So much so that Katie, who would much rather be known as "successful young actress Catherine Rabett", had to sue a newspaper that suggested she had exploited her supposed relationship with the Prince.

Nowadays she's a regular fixture in the colour supplements as one half of a marriage that is a paradigm case of Almost Fame. Her husband is Kit Harvey, who has already got ten Almost Famous bullets under his belt because he's part of Kit and the Widow, one of those cabaret acts that everybody vaguely remembers seeing – or at least feels they ought to have. If their liaison were ever to be rent asunder (hypothetically one hopes) both Katie and Kit's new flames would be inducted into the annals of neo-fame. With, of course, that explanatory tag "Cohort of Cabaret artist and Rabett-bagger Kit Harvey" or "Now ensconced with Prince Andrew's quondam girlfriend Katie Rabett."

A good yardstick is how the Almost Famous celebutante reacts to a photo opportunity. Celebrities suffer them. Celebutantes grab them.

The current crop of politicians, a "profession" who by definition not only want but need the oxygen of publicity to justify their existence, are interesting. Of the current cabinet Mrs Thatcher, Nigel Lawson, and possibly (just) Geoffrey Howe are Famous Famous. Coming up on the rails are Edwina "Egg on my face" Currie and Colin Moynihan, but the rest? Almost Famous – if they're lucky. The classic example is fatboy and prize booby David 'Fisherman' Mellor. And if he's lucky, I'm running in the next Grand National.

The transient nature of recognition in Britain today is well illustrated in the field of sports. Twenty years ago any schoolboy could reel off the entire Man Utd team who trounced Benfica: Stepney, Charlton, Best, Styles et al. Today only Robson stands out. Twenty years ago "nice one Cyril" meant Cyril Knowles, footballer. Today, it would more likely be Tony Knowles, the snooker player. TV's constant close-ups ensure Snooker players are Famous Famous – footballers are Almost Famous.

But making the transition from Almost Fame to Famous Fame is no guarantee of quality. At roughly the moment Zandra Rhodes began crossing over from former to latter, her credibility amongst fashion critics plummeted to an all-time low. This year's hot fashion star, sensitive young Turk Rifat Ozbek (there's that tell-tale handle again) is Almost Famous in upper case.

Journalism is the last refuge of the Almost Famous. When the writ comes down, today's inky climbers see not ignominy but a career opportunity. Nina Myskow had more epigrammatic sound bytes after the Charlotte Cornwell bottom court case than the Roman Road has muggers. Within months she had a slot on a drecky TV talent show where she slagged off hapless hopefuls with a whiplash tongue. Shoot that typewriter, roll those cue cards! A hack is dead – a star is born! TV supplies those who appear on it regularly with that crucial component of Famous Fame – pub credibility.

The ability to be talked about in boozers is something clearly missing among a whole group of Almost Famous thesps. They may have appeared in movies but their true calling is that home of the micro-talent, the mini-series. Ask Victoria Tennant (who always plays the English girl in NBC "blockbusters"). Or Julian Sands, Hughie Grant and Rupert Everett who are also doomed to the spectral netherworld of perpetual neo-fame.

When it comes to the Almost Famous, Time is a great dealer. William Allingham was the Jeffrey Archer of the Pre-Raphaelite poetry world. In its day, his massively sappy six volume oeuvre of Collected Poems drove critics to frenzies of sycophantic excess. A century later this ex-customs officer is consigned to footnotes in wilfully obscure theses on Yeats. Such is the lot of the Almost Famous.

Neil Webb of Notts Forest (above), and Emma Soames (left).

Who are the Almost Famous?

Anyone who says "Don't you know who I am?" in a loud voice in a public place.
Dancers on Saturday night prime time variety shows.
The babes in *James Bond* flicks.
Members of pop groups that had one hit that made it on to a K-Tel compilation and then broke up acrimoniously.
People who've appeared in the *News of the World* and collected £500 for denying that they've ever had an affair with Wincey Willis.
Wincey Willis.
World authorities on some esoteric area of obscuranta (eg: Larry Adler's barbed wire collection).
Larry Adler.
Most MPs.
Second division snooker players.
Third generation aristocrats.
Fourth wives of movie stars.

Who, specifically, are the Almost Famous?

THE *LOOSE ENDS* REGULARS, viz:
Lovely-pyjama-clad-recumbent-interviewer and celebrity-psycho-analysis-family-member ... EMMA FREUD
Lovable-Cockney-trend-spotter ... ROBERT ELMS
Wacky-Liverpudlian-poet-and-actor ... CRAIG CHARLES
Amusing-upper-class-critic'n'crumpet ... VICTORIA MATHER
Hunky-Scots-actor-male-model and TV-presenter ... RICHARD JOBSON
Crazy-down-the-line-from-York-comedian ... VICTOR LOUIS-SMITH

MEMBERS OF THE ENGLAND FOOTBALL TEAM WHO PLAY FOR NOTTINGHAM FOREST, ie
Central defender ... DES WALKER
Left back ... STUART PEARCE
Midfield ... NEIL WEBB

JAZZY BUSINESSWOMEN WHO ARE NOT ANITA RODDICK, including:
Sock Shop founder ... SOPHIE MIRMAN
Mini-skirted Pineapple queen ... DEBBIE MOORE
Media mogulette ... CAREY LABOVITCH
Aristocratic welly-maker ... LADY NORTHAMPTON

MEMBERS OF BROS WHO ARE NOT GOSS TWINS, eg
That other one who couldn't take the pressure

INDIVIDUAL MEMBERS OF BANANARAMA
Go on, just try to name them ...

WITHOUT THESE DESCRIPTIONS?

The Duke of Gloucester ...
***Countdown* game-show host ...**
Princess of Wales's dress designer ...
England's most-capped prop forward ...
Beautiful portrait painter ...
Wildchild ...
***The Daily Telegraph* proprietor ...**
Pet Shop Boy ...
Children's TV hostess ...
Champion darts player ...
Bespectacled architect ...
Old Vic owner ...
***Tatler* magazine editor ...**
Olympic gold medal-winning yachtsman ...
Comedy script-writer ...
French-born Royal Ballet star ...
Four Tops lead singer ...
Hungerford mass murderer ...
Manoir Aux Quat' Saisons chef ...
World No. 1 darts player ...
Presbyterian Lord Chancellor ...
Advertising entrepreneur ...
Arts Council supremo ...
Weekend news reader ...
Former Ryman's boss ...

MEMBERS OF THE SEVEN DWARFS
Ditto

OXBRIDGE COLLEGES THAT NEED TO BE FOLLOWED BY THE NAME OF THEIR UNIVERSITY viz:
All of them – *except* ...
Balliol
New College
Christ Church
Magdalen (but not Magdalene, Cambridge)
Trinity (but only Cambridge, not Oxford)
King's

COLONIAL WINNERS OF THE BOOKER PRIZE, to wit:
Nazi faction specialist ... THOMAS KENEALLY
Tedious Maori chronicler ... KERI HULME
Conqueror of *The Satanic Verses* ... PETER CAREY
South African one-hit wonder ... J. M. COETZEE

Use our chart to feel bad about yourself **NEXT MONTH** We make you feel even worse

ALCOHOL

WHY ARE YOU ALWAYS DRUNK?

There has never been such a deluge of tedious nagging. The police, the Government, *The Sunday Times Magazine* – even old bores in pubs. They all say the same thing . . . you're pissed. You're drunk, sozzled, smashed, blotto, half-cut. In short, you drink too much.

But what is "too much"? And how can you tell whether you've had it? Over the next few weeks, lots of magazines like this one will be sticking their noses into your business and making insulting remarks about your personal habits. If you drink more than 6½ "units" of booze a week, they'll imply that you're an alcoholic.

This is how you count the units:

0 units for any bottle of alcohol-free, coloured water-style beer
3 units for any can of Schickelgruber, Pils or a bottle of *Sunday Times* Special Offer Wine of the Week
18 units for a typical half-litre bottle of methylated spirits
79 units for four gallons of unleaded four-star petrol

Next month we'll let you know whether you have any prospect of survival, or whether you stand condemned to impotent, gut-rotted incontinence and serve you right.

YOUR DRINKING WEEK

Units	Sunday	Monday	Tuesday	Wednesday	Thursday	Friday	Saturday	Total
A quick half								
All right then, just the one								
Mine's a VAT								
Let's open another bottle								
Why is the ceiling spinning?								
								Total

"How's business?"

"It's not the same since the Mafia's gone computerised."

"I think the indoor pool was a mistake."

"It's not your day mate. I'm a real bastard of a Samaritan."

"Halt! Who's been there?"

Problems, Problems...

By HALDANE

"It's all right for you. You don't have to dust them!"

PARISH FASHIONS

Dishy deacons and pretty priests ruled the roost on the Synod catwalk.
JANE MULVAGH reports

Faux by day and fab by night was the message from Westminster this season as the ecclesiastical élite met at the annual synod. By day minimalist tailoring is offset with witty "false" accessories; be it a burgundy leatherette attaché case, toupee or teeth. The two-piece suit reigns supreme, popularly cut in shiny grey rayon, narrow through the shoulders and wide through the midriff. Culinary messages along the lapels are ubiquitous.

Clearly J. Wippell and Moubray, the clerical outfitters on the rue de la Tuffton, SW1, offered the most fetching expression of this mode in a charcoal grey, retailing at £70. For those who really want to integrate secularly, Wippell's have a three-piece, black, "John Travolta" tailleur – a snip at £100. Yes, you're the one that I want.

Few have adopted radical chic in this Thatcherite age. Even the mild weather failed to bring out the Jesus sandals worn with washing-machine discoloured nylons. That look was dismissed as "*trop, trop* Holy Roman, darling," as were Monsignor Quixote splashes of purple at the ankles.

The run-of-the-mill clerics dressed in the minimal monochrome look, with a black shirt and wide dog-collar. But their canine efforts suggested bulldog rather than saluki. Surely they should take the sartorial tip from their secular brethren that wide dog-collar hints at kipper tie?

The upper ranks still favour a much narrower collar, teamed with brightly coloured breasts; and the dog-walk was resplendent with multi-coloured bishops in fuschia – or bold cyclamen in the case of John Taylor, Bishop of St Albans – powder blue, azure blue and dove grey. These dashes of colour range from £17.50 to £19 at any leading clerical outfitters.

The sartorial lead at the breast was definitely given by the Palais Lambeth. Their muse and top model, Runcie, delighted us all with a new shade, "marron russell". For those seeking to emulate his gracefulness, here's a tip: we found a small swatch of said shade at Wimpell's, catalogue number 9875. His coiffeur, one hears, is by Phil of St James's and looked far more *à la mode* than the Jimmy Tarbuck mop and heavy gaucho moustache favoured by the younger ranks.

Gasps of delight filled the grand salon with the arrival of Dr George Carey, Bishop of Bath and Wells. His Creative Salvage/Neo-Punk collection was inspired by a mishap. Travelling to the synod on the Intercity express he discovered that he had left his dog-collar behind. Divine creativity came to the rescue. With a snip-snip of a fellow-passenger's travelling scissors, he cut the top off the British Rail plastic tea-cup and popped it round his neck, setting a new tone – Plastic Peculiar Bishop. Eat your heart out, Polly Styrene!

Accessories, be they faux or fab, uplift drab grey. Remember, boys, that's your base coat, you now have to embellish it. Think little-black-dress and then ACCESSORISE! A seasonal novelty was the casual way to wear the Madonna cross; slung round the neck on a heavy metal chain and then slipped into the breast pocket of your sports shirt. The asymmetric feel and the air of mystery, "Is it Celtic? Is it Coptic? Is it Maltese?", thrilled spectators. The large, Cockney-style finger ring, worn on ▶

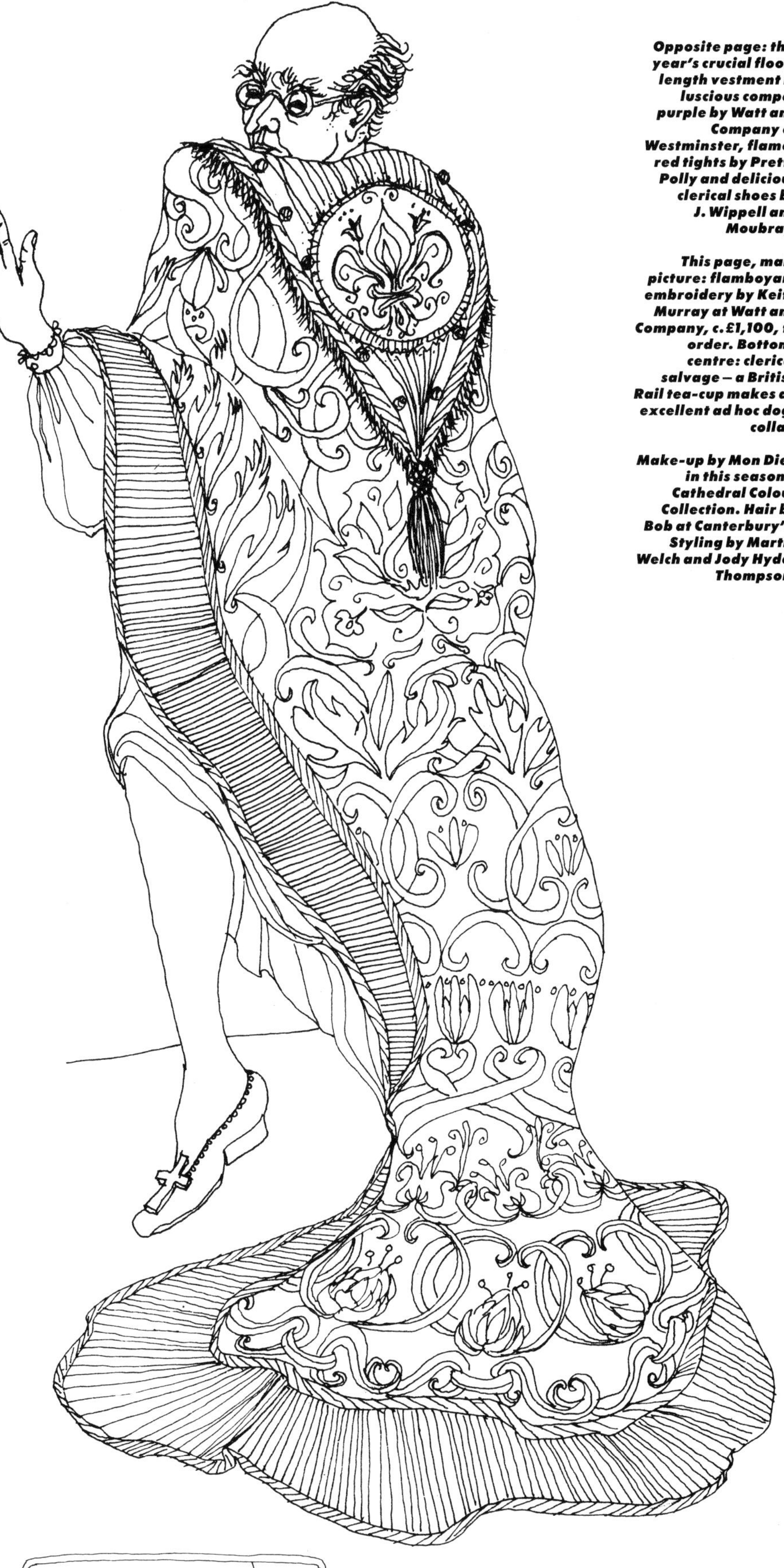

Opposite page: this year's crucial floor-length vestment in luscious comper purple by Watt and Company of Westminster, flame-red tights by Pretty Polly and delicious clerical shoes by J. Wippell and Moubray.

This page, main picture: flamboyant embroidery by Keith Murray at Watt and Company, c.£1,100, to order. Bottom, centre: clerical salvage – a British Rail tea-cup makes an excellent ad hoc dog-collar.

Make-up by Mon Dieu in this season's Cathedral Colour Collection. Hair by Bob at Canterbury's. Styling by Martin Welch and Jody Hyde-Thompson.

the fourth rather than the more gentlemanly little finger was favoured by senior bishops, who were obviously making witty references to the aggressive, rugged "hip-hop" trend seen in Brixton and Hackney of late. I feel that next season we might see the flowering of this allusion with the fashionable *poitrine* swung not only with crosses but also VW medallions.

Foppishness is very outré by day, with the exception of the polka-dot droop, created by floppily placing a red-and-white spotted handkerchief in the breast pocket of the jacket. Note that pockets are *patched*, not inserted, this season, to give a more common touch.

The fashion-conscious are still baffled by the great bag controversy, but I can report that three modes seem to hold sway – so take your pick. The Doctor Finlay-Gladstone bag is one option, worn battered and heavy, *à la* Runcie. The leather attaché case is bedecked with gilt, Chanel-esque fittings to give a "kept-cleric" look and goes down very well in the richer parishes of the outer suburbs, notably Weybridge and Hemel Hempstead. It is swung enthusiastically from a very long right arm or is tucked up cheekily under the armpit. For the *nouvelle vague*, the plastic shopping-bag teamed nicely with the tea-cup collar, and is self-consciously ripped at the corner – Bros fashion – to reveal a first folio edition of the Book of Common Prayer. The juxtaposition of *faux pauvre* and exclusive was deemed very witty.

Evening wear emphasised the long-held fashion adage that the hem is mightier than the cord...uroy shoes, so keep those cassocks down to the lower calf, boys. Messrs Watt and Company of Westminster showed the most dazzling collection, embellished by their star embroiderer, Keith Murray. His finger-deep embroideries out-glitz anything that Lesage and Lacroix have presented in Paris this season. Phoenixes rise up from flames to meet Pentecostal doves and together they ascend towards a sunburst.

For the more Fellini-minded think *Roma*-catwalk, with a swag of Maltese crosses across the shoulders of your cape, plus matching stole, burse and veil. Comper purple is all the rage or, for the pschyedelically unconscious, try a multi-coloured damask cape edged in red velvet and a Spanish-style fringed border at £1,154.68p. The

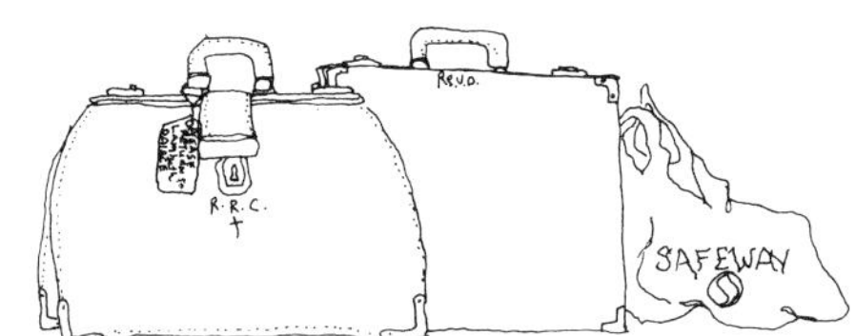

Poiret tassel has been ousted in favour of the YSL toggle as a fastening, and pie-crust frills are *de rigueur* for christenings. Byzantine stoles in liturgical colours retail at between £63.25p and £103.50p. We noted that minimalism is out by night – a plain white mitre had been slashed in the sale to £69. The *pièce de résistance* of the collections for a very grand evening must surely be the Gothic-inspired set of vestments by Watt's in oyster Bellini with an old embroidered sunburst and medallions worked in Japanese gold thread.

Between shows the congregation were seen stampeding to Vitello D'Oro, the Tour d'Argent of Westminster, for vitals. The in-crowd were to be admired upstairs, the liggers in the lower restaurant. But the true vestment-victims were to be found minding their figures and instead fingering the latest damasks and brocades along the rue de la Tuffton.

Talk at the shows was the God-slot issue on television. All feared that the imminent deregulation would reduce their media exposure. Was it worth investing in a new TV ensemble, they wondered? ■

"That's all we need – Jehovah's Ninjas."

TORVILL AND MUJAHEDIN

CREATURE *Feature*

Punch cartoonists' Wildlife Special

"White hunter? No, he drove the road roller when they re-surfaced the wildlife park."

"Oh, for God's sake Daddy! So what if people do talk –

"It's a worm – don't get taken in by the disguise."

"Excuse me asking but where did you study dentistry?"

Strange but genuine PROVERBS

"YOUNG MEN THINK OLD MEN FOOLS, OLD MEN KNOW YOUNG MEN TO BE SO"

I had to drive a thousand miles non-stop the other day and had plenty of time to think about my plight. Rain everywhere, fat men in dirty lorries and, damn it, alone again. Women. "I have known for a year that it would end in this misery." Oh yes? I personally knew nothing of the sort. I always expected that something nice would happen, there would be a knock on the door of my smelly hovel and it would be God, with presents: a nice house in Rutland, a Porsche Carrera, irrestible sexual charisma. Overnight I would become a Man; masterful, sun-tanned, Lichtenstein bank account, credit cards, greed, being horrible to people and not caring. Then, of course, women would love me.

But they don't. I'm too nice, that's the trouble, too ready to please, too. I don't know, spiritual, probably. This is the age of the complete shit but then it probably always has been, don't you think? That's what women want and that's what men want too, come to think of it, so there is little point in becoming a homosexual, even if one could. It isn't possible, of course. All hair and testicles. Won't do. No wonder women have to be beaten into submission and then compensated with wads of fresh money every day. No wonder homosexuals make such a fuss about how nice it is and how everyone should be one. It's like a blue man in freezing water saying, "Come on in! It's fine!"

Everyone wants to be pushed around and I wish I could get the hang of it. Assertiveness Training used to be popular but everyone has gone off that now. I used to think it was because it was so obviously silly and horrible, being locked in a room in a hotel – probably a room with a name like "The Marquis Suite" with folding doors and a smelly carpet – being shouted at by an American in a Dralon shirt and aviator spectacles and made to stand up and describe what a creep you are. I went to one once, in Seattle, having nothing better to do, and I was picked on. The American gave a nasty little lecture all about the importance of saying "No". How stupid. I have no need to learn how to say no. What I want to know is how to get people to make propositions to which I can answer "Yes! Yes! I'm your man! Wait a minute while I slip out of my things!"

After the little lecture I was told to stand up and describe everything that was wrong with my approach to life. I said "No", sort of hoping to suck up and show how much I had learnt, but the American was cross and disobliging. "You're a schmuck," he said. "You must stand up and share with us everything that you are doing wrong in your miserable life. Tell us exactly why you are a creep, guy." Well, I couldn't. Wasn't man enough. Instead, I told him why *he* was a creep, and said that the main thing wrong with my life was that I was sitting there listening to him.

Afterwards I felt incredibly assertive but it wore off after a few minutes and I went back to being a species of worm, crawling the earth with tears in my red-rimmed eyes, and whenever women said. "You know what's the matter with you?" I'd say, "Yo, I'm a creep!" and tell them what I was meant to tell the American, when what I *really* should have done was say, "Nothing! Shut up, woman!" and hit them. That's the only language they understand. Hanging's too good for them. I've never had one in the back of the cab but almost everywhere else, and the end result is always the same.

I don't know. I used to love Mozart. I used to understand exactly why Monteverdi was good. Now I can only listen to the blues, music designed by earth worms *for* earth worms.

I think I shall have to leave. It is time for a new life. The trouble is that for years I have been saying, "I think I shall have to leave. It is time for a new life," but there has always been someone to say it to: "I would leave the country and start again, repudiating my debts and abandoning my responsibilities, *were it not for you*." That made them cross but it prevented me from having to do anything about it. Now there really *is* nothing to stop me slipping my Johnny Copeland tapes into my Gaultier jacket, lacing up my Timberlands and buggering off, and it is worrying me. Where would one go? Anywhere is better than where I am, but where in particular? Somewhere with no traffic wardens and no tax men and no accountants, obviously; somewhere where the climate is fine but there are no tourists and certainly no "heritage" industry, no property developers or bores with briefcases and company cars; somewhere you can order a vodka, fresh lime and soda without some dribbling, bum-faced barman saying, "Oh, right, like what that Jeffrey Bernard drinks, right, yeah?" Somewhere where people live in houses, not properties. Somewhere where there is corruption. Corruption is fine. Nobody could possibly complain about bribing government officials. The ones we should violate then string up are the ones in grubby suits, the sanctimonious ones with the ruined faces and pursed lips, with wives with bad feet and BO, and nasty houses, and friends called "Basil-at-the-club" and a general air of going through life with a pubic hair trapped between their teeth *and no idea of how it got there*.

I don't know whether there is anywhere like that. I am told that there is an island in the mouth of the Amazon which is larger than Britain, and that seems hopeful, but the Amazon does go on a bit, wouldn't you say? There's Madagascar, too, but I have a nasty feeling that Madagascar is going to become a terribly smart tourist resort and I would end up bumping into my lost love, looking tanned and fit and marvellous on the arm of some despicable, pushy, dominating computer millionaire, and where would I be? Blackened and parched, no doubt, in a sweat-stained linen suit, shaking with malaria, debased and disfigured, with sprue, yaws and swamp fever, reaking of paw-paw homebrew and envy.

Perhaps the best thing would be to buy a guitar and move to Droitwich and learn to sing my own blues. I could be one of those awful people who live in Droitwich with a guitar and sing the blues, if you see what I mean, probably ouside the Kentucky Fried Chicken. I could get beaten up a lot and go home on the bus in my anorak, and grow bald with long greasy strands hanging down, and maybe after a while I could get myself a girlfriend, a fourteen-stone jukebox queen from Woolworths who smells of chips and Outdoor girl blusher, and then the whole thing would start again. It's the same thing: nothing ever changes. Hey! There's a blues in there! Hand me my guitar and the instruction book! Take it away! (But the mood passes quickly and once more there is silence broken only by the slow dripping of bile.) ■

Strange but genuine
PROVERBS
"WOLVES LOSE THEIR TEETH BUT NOT THEIR MEMORY"
"I won't forget this"
mike Williams.

There's no fool like a mad bastard but never mind: the retributions a well-trained lunatic can wreak are substantial, and I am working on it.

Madness is not as easy as you might think, though. There was a period when my hold on reality was tenuous and I would do strange things which people would talk about behind my back, the best place, of course, to talk about anyone. But events kept getting me, in one way or another, and I calmed down. At least, I think I did. It's hard to tell. I saw a friend of mine yesterday who went properly mad once. He thought he was being filmed by Mike Leigh from an upper window in Soho Square, and he rushed round and round being mad. Then a police car pulled up and the back door was opened from within. My friend got in, closed the door behind him, and said to one of the policemen: "Is that it? I mean, is it a wrap? Because if he wants me to do any more, I won't. I'm knackered."

This seems useful and convincing, and I have been trying very hard to believe that Mike Leigh is in the flat opposite me, but it is difficult. The real inhabitants are rather too noticeable: three jolly Lebanese who cannot work things. Anything. They come home at night and everyone is woken up by the bravura performance, complete with shouting, bangs, and sudden inexplicable cries of sexual excitement, as they try to switch off their Citroën and get out of it and shut the doors and lock them. Then they try to get into their flat but it never works out: the door falls off its hinges, or a window breaks, or one of them falls over and yells in pain and one of the others then trips over his fallen companion and the third then steps backwards and crashes down the stairs.

They had a lunch party last Sunday. I saw them coming in with huge carrier bags full of Australian Chardonnay and sausages and things. Halfway across the courtyard one of the carrier bags broke and within five seconds there was a *mêlée*. I went over to see if I could help and within another five seconds I was embroiled too. They apologised and I said, no trouble, the features editor of a magazine I wrote for was Lebanese too so I knew what it was like, and we got talking, and I said I knew a flautist who was back home in Beirut at the moment, playing music for World Peace and dodging shrapnel, and they said, oh, well, seeing as I was on first name terms with two Lebanese men I had better come to lunch too, because I was obviously all right.

Their party started early because the one-eyed Hungarian watch-repairer across the hall from them had another row with his huge wife and was crying on the staircase, so they gave him some Australian Chardonnay and he settled down to reminisce about his ancestors, who he said were genuine Magyars; his great-aunt had sung a song to Bartók once which he subsequently used in a string quartet, although he had got it wrong and anyway it wasn't much good without the words. The words were about a man who is telling his wife that if she doesn't unfreeze towards him he will start having if off with goats, and then we'll see how she likes bringing up the little kids; apparently (he insisted) the pun is similar in Hungarian, or whatever the Magyars speak. Then one of the Lebanese men said that his sister married a Muslim and say what you like about Muslims, they didn't boff goats, and the watchmaker said, huh, there speaks someone who has never been to Saudi Arabia, and his antagonist said, no, but he had been to the Hutovo Blato in Yugoslavia and that was quite enough for him.

I got the first wave of this through the open windows and scuttled downstairs and across the courtyard to see what happened next, but I was only halfway up the stairs when their flat blew up because one of the brothers had put some bottles of vodka in the oven and another one had subsequently put a pudding in it to cook, without looking. You can see why it is difficult to mentally erase these people and convince myself that Mike Leigh is living there instead, with a camera trained on me.

Perhaps they think that I am Mike Leigh. It would explain the running farce of what they doubtless regard as their "lives" but it doesn't help me. I remain polite and non-violent, though I think it may be cracking a bit. I had to come home on the tube yesterday and, to help the tube strike along, the staff at Piccadilly Circus had switched off all the silly automatic machines, so there was not only a huge queue for the few trains, but an even bigger one at the solitary ticket window. There cannot be a more appallingly-run organisation anywhere else in the world, except, of course, in England, where you could undoubtedly find many equally appallingly-run organisations. I was polite to the man behind the window because it wasn't his fault. What I really wanted to do was track down the awful man in a suit who runs the outfit, and torture him and make him scream for his mother, the drooling, engorged, smug, sclerotic git, and then finally snap his thumbs off, put mayonnaise on his suit and jam him in one of his automatic barriers.

So far, this is reasonable. The London Underground is a complete disgrace, starved of money by idiotic joke politicians who probably don't even know what it is, and run by an unending series of time-serving incompetents and ambitious dolts who have turned it into a sewer fit only for a sort of piggish, proletarian underclass which, having no Vodafones, Gold AmEx cards or BMWs, deserves no better. What is not so good, or possibly rather promising, is that all the way home I was fantasising about tying Mr Peter Bottomley to an organpipe cactus and breaking his glasses and reading the whole of *The Satanic Verses* to him in a monotone and employing a squad of camouflage-jacketed ALF activists to stand around telling lies about their carnal relations with his wife. Since Mr Peter Bottomley is nothing whatever to do with London's Undergound (although, it is true, he does richly deserve the treatment I outline) perhaps I am experiencing the beginnings of a paranoid obsession.

This could be useful. If I can really contrive to go mad, I will not have to content myself with frothing here, but can go out and do people in. There will be a rash of mysterious deaths and the nights will be disturbed by screams and wet squelches and the world will be improved. I shall cultivate Mr Bottomley. One day I will look out of my window and see his silly, grinning face peering at me from the flat opposite, then you can all watch out because I shall be round with my petrol-tin and secateurs. ■